Understanding
UWE JOHNSON

Understanding Modern
European and Latin American
Literature

James Hardin, *Series Editor*

*volumes on*

Ingeborg Bachmann
Samuel Beckett
Thomas Bernhard
Johannes Bobrowski
Heinrich Böll
Italo Calvino
Albert Camus
Elias Canetti
Camilo José Cela
Céline
José Donoso
Friedrich Dürrenmatt
Rainer Werner Fassbinder
Max Frisch
Federico García Lorca
Gabriel García Márquez
Juan Goytisolo
Günter Grass

Gerhart Hauptmann
Christoph Hein
Hermann Hesse
Uwe Johnson
Eugène Ionesco
Milan Kundera
Primo Levi
Boris Pasternak
Luigi Pirandello
Graciliano Ramos
Erich Maria Remarque
Jean-Paul Sartre
Claude Simon
Mario Vargas Llosa
Peter Weiss
Franz Werfel
Christa Wolf

# UNDERSTANDING

## UWE

# JOHNSON

### GARY L. BAKER

UNIVERSITY OF SOUTH CAROLINA PRESS

© 1999 University of South Carolina

Published in Columbia, South Carolina, by the
University of South Carolina Press

Manufactured in the United States of America

03  02  01  00  99   5  4  3  2  1

**Library of Congress Cataloging-in-Publication Data**

Baker, Gary Lee.
  Understanding Uwe Johnson / Gary L. Baker.
    p.   cm.   (Understanding modern European and Latin American
  literature)
  Includes bibliographical references (p. ) and index.

  ISBN 1-57003-282-3
  1. Johnson, Uwe, 1934-Criticism and interpretation.   I. Title.   II. Series.
PT2670.O36 Z56   1999

  833'.914dc21                                                    98-40217

*For Suzanne and Kyle*

# Contents

# Editor's Preface

*Understanding Modern European and Latin American Literature* has been planned as a series of guides for undergraduate and graduate students and nonacademic readers. Like the volumes in its companion series, *Understanding Contemporary American Literature,* these books provide introductions to the lives and writings of prominent modern authors and explicate their most important works.

Modern literature makes special demands, particularly foreign literature, in which the reader must contend not only with unfamiliar, often arcane artistic conventions and philosophical concepts but also with the handicap of reading the literature in translation. It is a truism that the nuances of one language can be rendered in another only imperfectly (and this problem is especially acute in fiction), but the fact that the works of European and Latin American writers are situated in a historical and cultural setting quite different from our own can be as great a hindrance to the understanding of these works as the linguistic barrier. For this reason the UMELL series emphasizes the sociological and historical background of the writers treated. The philosophical and cultural traditions peculiar to a given culture may be particularly important for an understanding of certain authors, and these subjects are taken up in the introductory chapter and also in the discussion of those works to which this information is relevant. Beyond this beginning, the books treat the specifically literary aspects of the author under discussion and attempt to explain lucidly the complexities of contemporary literature. The books are conceived as introductions to the authors covered, not as comprehensive analyses. They do not provide detailed summaries of plot because they are meant to be used in conjunction with the books they treat, not as a substitute for study of the original works. The purpose of the books is to provide information and judicious literary assessment of the major works in the most compact, readable form. We hope that the UMELL series will help increase knowledge and understanding of European and Latin American cultures and will serve to make the literature of those cultures more accessible.

J. H.

# Acknowledgments

Uwe Johnson once intimated that you do not forget people simply because the covers of a book close behind them. Such is the case with this work. I began writing this volume ten years after my first encounter with Johnson and his novels. Many people and institutions deserve recognition for helping me to bring this volume to completion.

Eberhard Fahlke, Jeremy Gaines, and especially Monika Gerhardt deserve a special expression of appreciation for helping me to find my way in the Uwe Johnson Archive.

Funding for an extended research trip to Frankfurt was provided by the German Academic Exchange Service. Both the Denison University Summer Development Program and the Denison University Research Foundation have been quite generous in helping to fund shorter sojourns in Frankfurt to further my research.

My colleague, Professor William H. Clamurro, and my spouse, Suzanne Simons Baker, provided invaluable suggestions on style and clarity. I thank them for their patience and kind support.

Finally, I thank Suzanne and my son, Kyle Simons Baker, for being unwavering sources of support and encouragement to me throughout the writing of this book.

# A Note on Translations

Unless otherwise indicated, all translations from the German are my own. Any other special circumstances involving the translation of Johnson's texts are explained in the notes.

# Chronology

| | |
|---|---|
| **1934** | Born to Erich and Erna Johnson on 20 July in Cammin, Pomerania, which is today in northwestern Poland. |
| **1934–44** | Lives in Anklam. |
| **1944** | Sent to a "Deutsche Heimatschule," an elite school for German children in the Nazi period. |
| **1945** | Family forced to flee to Recknitz in Mecklenburg. |
| **1946–48** | Lives in Recknitz with family. Father interned by the Soviets and never heard from again. |
| **1948–52** | Moves to Güstrow. Attends John-Brinckmann-Oberschule, joins Free German Youth, and receives *Abitur,* enabling study at an East German university. |
| **1952–54** | Chooses to study German language and literature at the University of Rostock. Becomes involved in conflict between the Free German Youth and the Young Congregation that ultimately leads to expulsion from the university. |
| **1954–56** | Attends Karl-Marx-University in Leipzig, finishing degree with Hans Mayer. Also studies with philosopher Ernst Bloch. Writes *Ingrid Babendererde.* |
| **1956–59** | Denied opportunity to continue for Ph.D. Works for publishing houses in the East as an independent translator (English to German) and appraises proposed literary projects. *Babendererde* manuscript turned down by publishers in the East and the West. Begins work on *Mutmaßungen.* |
| **1959** | *Mutmaßungen über Jakob* published. Moves to West Berlin in July. |
| **1960** | Awarded Fontane Prize in West Berlin. |
| **1961** | *Das dritte Buch über Achim* appears. Makes first trip to United States as guest of several universities. Hermann Kesten affair takes place. |
| **1962** | Lives in Rome with the support of a Villa Massimo Stipend. Receives International Publisher's Prize. Elisabeth Schmidt comes to the West, marries Johnson, and gives birth to their daughter, Katharina. |
| **1964** | *Karsch, und andere Prosa* published. Works steadily reviewing East German television programming for West Berlin newspaper. |

| | |
|---|---|
| **1965** | *Zwei Ansichten* published. Second trip to United States. |
| **1966–68** | Longer sojourn in New York City. Works for Harcourt, Brace, and World editing a reader for high school German students. Collects material for and begins writing *Jahrestage*. |
| **1969** | Becomes member of PEN-Zentrum of West Germany as well as of prestigious Academy of Arts in West Berlin. |
| **1970** | First volume of *Jahrestage* appears. |
| **1971** | Second volume of *Jahrestage* appears. Receives Georg-Büchner Prize. |
| **1973** | Third volume of *Jahrestage* appears. |
| **1974** | *Eine Reise nach Klagenfurt* published. Moves with family to Sheerness-on-Sea on the island of Sheppey in Kent, England. |
| **1975** | *Berliner Sachen* appears. Suffers heart attack. Marital difficulties cause debilitating writer's block and prevent continuation of *Jahrestage*. Receives Wilhelm Raabe Prize from the city of Braunschweig. |
| **1977** | Becomes member of the German Academy for Language and Literature in Darmstadt. |
| **1978** | Awarded Thomas Mann Prize in Lübeck. |
| **1979–80** | Lectures on poetics at Goethe University in Frankfurt am Main. Lectures published as *Begleitumstände.* |
| **1981** | *Skizze eines Verunglückten* appears in a festschrift in celebration of Max Frisch's seventieth birthday. |
| **1983** | Fourth and final volume of *Jahrestage* appears. Receives literary prize from the city of Cologne. |
| **1984** | Dies of heart failure sometime on 23–24 February in his house in Sheerness. Body discovered 12 March. |

# CHAPTER 1

# Misunderstanding Uwe Johnson

Uwe Johnson's life and career as an author delineate themselves in his experience of the vagaries of German history and the myriad of issues that confronted the Germans after the Second World War. He was born on 20 July 1934 in Cammin, a small town in what is today northwestern Poland; soon after his birth the family moved to Anklam. Uwe Johnson was only ten years old when the war ended on 8 May 1945. Despite the fact that, late in the war, his parents enrolled him in an elementary school for intensive training in Nazi ideology, he described his sense of the end of the war more as an "experience than a shock."[1] And yet, Johnson's postwar experiences became central to his work as an author. His family left Anklam in the face of the Soviet Union's advancing Red Army and moved further west into Mecklenburg to the town of Güstrow. Due to his association with the Nazi regime as a low-level administrator, Johnson's father, Erich, was arrested by the Soviets and died in a work camp some time in 1946 or 1947; after his arrest the family neither saw nor heard from him again. It is therefore not surprising that all of Johnson's novels contain single parents; in his fiction the politics and violence of war have always already taken one parent before the story begins. A genuine postwar shock, thus, came later when Johnson realized—through his missing father, through witnessing the war dead who were transported through his new home in Güstrow, and through his education in the East German school system—to what degree the Nazis inflicted suffering on their victims and the degree of guilt and devastation that the Germans had brought on themselves. The worst war in the history of humankind and the subsequent division of Germany between two world ideologies would remain Johnson's main thematic preoccupations throughout his career. Since German history was such a significant element of his life, it became a permanent and consequential aspect of the lives of his characters. He explained the significance of history for his work as follows: "Since history can demolish one's house, can shatter one's family, can change one's school curriculum, can teach one languages and forbid the learning of other languages; since history can earn one's own country a bad name in the whole world for which one is then liable in person; since history can displace one from a homeland to a foreignness and from there into an even greater foreignness: that's why history is substantially represented."[2] In this quotation, Johnson spoke of his own life as much as of the depicted lives of his characters.

Johnson, it seems, invested a lot of energy in disputing the labels placed on him by critics, politicians, and government functionaries.[3] He was called the "poet of the two Germanys," "difficult," a "refugee" from the East, and "procommunist." He was said, because of his apparently ambivalent political convictions, to exist on neither side of the Berlin Wall but on top of it; one critic accused him of writing fascistic literature because of the prevalence of nature in his books, and yet another called him a "Trojan Horse" since his books do not seem particularly to criticize East Germany. He often explained the policies of the East German government to westerners from the East German perspective, in the historical context of East-West relations. In other words, he discussed these issues in a manner that seemed to acquiesce to the existence of the authoritarian regime in the East. A critic once referred to him as a specialist in the difficulties of communication and understanding, the only label he did not dispute.[4] Johnson's public altercations with other West and East German artists, critics, and politicians lent substance to his remark that an author does not need resistance to pursue the profession: "It's enough, I feel, that the world around us is there."[5] All in all, Johnson often found himself unhappy about how he was perceived by critics, colleagues, and the entire nation, both East and West Germany, which, in the end, led to grave consequences for his emotional stability.

His first dispute with political authority came in 1953, when he was nineteen years old and serving as a representative of the communist youth organization. He disobeyed the directives of a higher communist party functionary when ordered to give a speech assailing the Christian youth organization known as the Young Congregation. He was supposed to make statements that he knew were false and that contradicted the right of religious freedom set down in the constitution of the German Democratic Republic. Instead of delivering the message in the expected form, he publicly told the truth of the matter, thus straying from a strictly maintained communist party line. Because of this incident he was expelled from the University of Rostock, although he was later readmitted to the Karl Marx University in Leipzig, where he studied with literary critic Hans Mayer (born 1907) and philosopher Ernst Bloch (1885–77). When Johnson finished his studies he was denied the opportunity to continue to the doctoral level. He hoped to use his knowledge of German linguistics and literature to work either in education or in a publishing house. Essentially, however, Johnson was released into unemployment, an absurd situation, indeed, considering the fact that one of the GDR's greatest social achievements was that all had "the right and the duty" (according to the country's constitution) to work. No publisher or educational institution was willing to hire Johnson, a situation that he endured until 1959. With little or no employment, Johnson used his free time to write fiction for publication.

Thus he commenced with the third possibility for a person trained in literature to earn a living. The political dispute concerning the Young Congregation was unsettled business in Johnson's mind, so he worked it through by using it as material for his first novel: "Thus somebody received his very own cause, his personal affair with the Republic, his fight with the world concerning when something is a truth and to what point a truth deserves punishment" (BU 69). But Johnson's career as a writer had a rather flat beginning. The novel, *Ingrid Babendererde,* eventually necessitated three rewritings, was turned down by East and West German publishers, and was never published in his lifetime. If anything, taken under consideration by four East German publishers, the manuscript probably insured that he would never find work in the East because of the novel's suspicious political contents. After this initial failed attempt, Johnson continued to have plenty of time to write and began work on his second novel, *Mutmaßungen über Jakob (Speculations about Jakob)* (1959). Johnson found a publisher in the Suhrkamp publishing house in Frankfurt am Main. Thus he was compelled to cross the border from East to West Berlin when *Speculations* appeared. He had considered publishing *Speculations* under a pseudonym so that he could remain in the East, but his friends urged him to reconsider. Johnson was concerned that the East German regime would misunderstand as an attack or criticism what he meant merely as "a story, an explanation."[6] Fearing criminal prosecution from the East German regime, he went to the West, a move he insisted time and again was not political but professional. He decided to live where he could find work. When *Speculations about Jakob* appeared, Johnson, heretofore unknown in the literary world, became an instant success at the age of twenty-five. Together with West German writers Günter Grass (born 1926) and Heinrich Böll (1917–85), he announced the arrival of a new generation of authors who wrote about their experiences in Germany during World War II, the reconstruction period after the war, and the evolution of the cold war.

In November 1961 Johnson experienced his first public confrontation in the West. The first serious denunciation of his political convictions came from an older writer, Hermann Kesten, and the foreign minister of the West German government, Heinrich von Brentano. Anticommunist sentiment, though always rather intense under chancellor Konrad Adenauer's conservative Christian Democratic regime, was especially acute in the aftermath of the Berlin Wall, which had just been erected on 13 August 1961. *Speculations about Jakob* was to appear in Italian translation and, to mark the occasion, Johnson's publisher in Milan, Giangiacomo Feltrinelli, invited him to speak before a panel of journalists and critics. Having come from East Germany only two years earlier, Johnson was expected to offer some remarks on the wall. He explained the wall in commonsensical terms, saying that the East German regime acted according to its own conventions of what was right. Coercing its people into accepting its brand of socialism was its method of persuasion; for the East German government, then, the wall fit into a logical course of action. Furthermore, the GDR was losing thousands of qualified workers every week, which greatly undermined the development of that already economically disadvantaged state. Kesten, who was on the program to offer introductory remarks, published an open letter in *Die Welt,* one of the most widely read newspapers in West Germany, in which he badly misconstrued Johnson's remarks. According to Kesten, Johnson referred to the wall as "good, reasonable, and decent" (BU 210). On the basis of Kesten's version of the incident, Brentano publicly urged the West German parliament to recall Johnson's government-funded stipend to pursue his work in Italy. Fortunately, unknown to Johnson and Kesten, one of the journalists in the audience recorded the session at which the authors spoke. The transcript of the tape was published in West German newspapers, revealing the gross misrepresentation of which Kesten was guilty. Although Johnson vindicated himself, the controversy further affected his career. In 1977 Johnson was inducted into the prestigious German Academy for Language and Literature in Darmstadt, whose published catalogue later implied that he had not defended himself convincingly against Kesten's accusations. Due to the implication, Johnson resigned from the academy in 1979.

Johnson's misconstrued comments on the wall and the building of the wall accentuated the divisive relationship that he maintained with Western popular opinion. The first recourse that the citizens of West Berlin took when the wall went up was to boycott the Berlin S-Bahn, the city's elevated train system. An Allied agreement from before the war's end stipulated that the Soviet sector of Berlin would operate the train system for the entire city. People in West Berlin paid train fare in hard currency that the East German regime badly needed to purchase products from nations with capitalist economies. Thus, by withholding train fare, the citizens of West Berlin made a political statement and hindered the GDR from realizing its desired economic stability. In 1964 Johnson published an essay persuasively outlining how the boycott hurt the citizens of West Berlin more than it did Walter Ulbricht's government. Again, Johnson attempted to point out issues of common sense and reasonableness, only to suffer phone calls in the night from people who called him offensive names and threatened him with bodily harm.

However, one cannot accuse Johnson of being flippant about an emotionally charged and tragic situation that separated families and violently divided a nation. Johnson initially lost access to his close friends in the East, especially those living in Leipzig and Mecklenburg. Moreover, Johnson's future wife, Elisabeth Schmidt, was still in the East when the wall was erected. While Kesten was accusing Johnson of supporting the building of the wall, Johnson was frantically arranging for Schmidt to cross the dangerous border, which she did in early 1962. The activities of a student group that smuggled GDR citizens across the border at cost, and Schmidt's own escape in this manner, became material for his third book, *Zwei Ansichten* (*Two Views*), published in 1965. Unlike the lovers in *Two Views,* however, when Schmidt came to the West, she and Johnson were married; their daughter, Katharina, was born later in 1962.

Residing in West Berlin had its advantages for Johnson. He lived in close proximity to his friend Grass and others who supported him in his writing and in his public altercations. West Berlin was not officially part of the Federal Republic of Germany, and so by residing there he avoided military service and distanced himself from West Germany, which he never felt was a viable alternative to the communist East. As a small but telling example of his attitude toward West Germany, he corrected his copy of the *New York Times* with a picture of the Berlin Wall captioned, "at berlin wall: West German children play alongside wall that the communists began erecting five years ago this week." Johnson crossed out the word *German* in black ink and wrote *Berlin* over it. In a way West Berlin was the best of both worlds for Johnson because it was an island of Western freedoms and Western living surrounded by the territory of his still cherished German Democratic Republic. After travel from the West to the East became more common—one-day visas from West Berlin to East Berlin became an important source of hard currency for the East German regime— Johnson reestablished contact with his friends in the East, created new relationships with other East German colleagues, and frequently visited the Bertolt Brecht archive, where he worked on an edition of Brecht's papers published by Suhrkamp in 1965 as the *Me-ti Buch der Wendungen* (*Me-ti Book of Expressions*). In West Berlin Johnson could also watch East German television, whose special programming, Johnson believed, deserved a place in West German and West Berlin public life. The Axel-Springer publishing house, which controlled many popular German publications, refused to publish the East German television schedule as long as the East German papers refused to publish the West German television guide. Some smaller independent publications made East German programming part of their television supplements to create a market niche for themselves in the face of Axel-Springer's high circulation. Here again, Johnson's actions ran against the majority of public opinion in the West: he agreed to review the contents of the "Ulbricht glimmer" ("fifth channel")[7] for the newspaper *Der Tagesspiegel,* one of the few West Berlin publications that printed the East German television schedule. Johnson performed this task throughout the second half of 1964. It was his first encounter with an externally imposed deadline, a situation under which he did not work happily, but the steady work put food on the table and paid the rent.

Johnson refused to champion either Germany's ideological position, recognizing instead the deeply disturbing aspects of both German regimes. The Stalinist tactics of Ulbricht's government were as repugnant to Johnson as the appointment and election of ex-Nazis to the West German government and their unproblematic acceptance in society. Fascists and Stalinists represented, for Johnson, the true enemies of humanity.[8] From 1959 to 1965, if he was not concerned about the activities of the East German State Security (the Stasi), which had been known to kidnap former citizens that it deemed damaging to the image of the GDR, then he was deflecting derisive public opinion about his sentiments for the East German way of life.[9] If his atelier apartment was not being broken into, objects moved about by Stasi agents, then he received anonymous phone calls from irate West Berlin citizens questioning his political integrity. Even with this level of discomfort and insecurity about his living situation in West Berlin, he resided there from 1959 to 1965 and again from 1969 to 1974. The Johnsons cherished their network of friends, their emotional and collegial support group, and West Berlin's diverse lifestyle. However, a change of pace was important for Johnson's literary production, which had come to a halt. In May 1965 Johnson traveled to the United States on professional business; the trip would shape the rest of his writing career.

Having received an introduction to the United States on a short trip in 1961, Johnson decided to return, this time for a longer, more exploratory sojourn. He had difficulties with the usual way that writers support themselves in the United States—that is, by becoming a writer in residence at a university. He refused to spend his time in the United States in a "golden cage" (BU 335), separated from more varied experiences. Johnson's American publisher, Helen Wolff, procured work for him at Harcourt, Brace, and World (today Harcourt, Brace, and Jovanovich), which commissioned him to edit selected German short stories for a high school reader. He worked on the reader from 1966 to 1967 and in doing so lived the life of a New York office employee residing on the Upper West Side of Manhattan. These experiences in the city and surrounding areas formed the beginnings of his novel about his "invented person," Gesine Cresspahl. The idea of describing Cresspahl's life in Germany and New York lent urgency to his desire to remain in New York for another year. Through personal savings and support from Harcourt, Brace, and World as well as a grant from the Rockefeller Foundation, Johnson managed a longer stay to commence work on *Jahrestage* (*Anniversaries*).

About his time in New York, Johnson would later say, "From visits to Germany I came back to New York like coming home."[10] His remarks on New York City accentuate his notion of homeland, which for Johnson, was a private realm comprised of friends and a landscape "to which one can declare one-self."[11] From an apartment on Riverside Drive the Johnson family overlooked the Hudson River and the green landscape of the local park. Johnson had before his door the basics of community living: the serenity of a country landscape, not unlike that of Mecklenburg's; fulfilling employment; and a culturally diverse and, at least on the surface, harmonious neighborhood. He enjoyed certain rituals that structured the day, such as buying the *New York Times,* visiting his favorite diner, and seeing the same faces on the subway every day. The two years in New York provided him with enough experiences literally to write for the rest of his life. His time in New York, the globally volatile news year 1968, the continuing exploration of the persons who inhabited his fictitious corner of Mecklenburg, and an in-depth study of the Mecklenburg cultural character became the elements of *Anniversaries,* which is today one of the most important novels in German literature.

Living in New York, Johnson had created distance between himself and West Germany. However, he informed himself through *Der Spiegel* and the *New York Times* about events in Germany, where student unrest mounted, Chancellor Georg Kiesinger's Nazi past became public, and the population increasingly turned to an extreme right-wing party, the National Democratic Party, for law and order. The Emergency Laws were passed, whereby the government could take absolute power over its citizens in the event of a national crisis. The West German government, in these years, acted in absence of any significant opposition because the country's two largest political parties, the Social Democratic Party and Christian Democratic Union, had joined in a coalition to form national policy, itself a point of protest for many young people. Johnson never expressed any desire to be among the dissenting voices in either West Germany or the United States. In fact, in 1967 he published a piece entitled "Concerning an Attitude of Protesting" in which he derided "good people" for protesting actual evils while ignoring the potential for evil: "The good people want a good world; they do nothing about it." "Good people" should never have allowed the human condition to become so bad in the first place.[12] Johnson's view of societal transformation lay on a broader foundation than opposition to concrete issues such as the Vietnam War or the Emergency Laws. His response to tumultuous times was to think about and to begin writing a novel that would describe the anatomy of a century in a permanent state of crisis, a century whose salvation could lie in a fledgling democratic socialism in a small nation in Eastern Europe.

In earlier works Johnson depicted people from Mecklenburg but did not really take issue with the region's distinct character or communal elements that constituted its special circumstances as a province. Mecklenburg continued to exist under an almost feudal social system well into the twentieth century. It is an agricultural region with a Low German dialect whose people are taciturn and not eager for outside contact. The region is so conservative that Bismarck supposedly commented that should the world come to an end, he would go to Mecklenburg because everything happens one hundred years later there. And yet, in their uniqueness, Mecklenburg's denizens represent people all over the world. In *Anniversaries* Johnson constructs a fictitious communal model valid for all of humanity with his in-depth exploration of Mecklenburg's character and history. Possibly due to his new life in New York, *Anniversaries* shows, then, a refocusing in Johnson's thematic point of emphasis toward a sense of home and community that must persist in the wake of sweeping historical forces—that is, a clash between the steadfast and destabilizing aspects of human existence.

In 1969 the Johnsons moved back to West Berlin, and the first three volumes of *Anniversaries* appeared in relatively quick succession in 1970, 1971, and 1973. But the fourth volume was, for various reasons, long in coming. Berlin was no longer a location for collecting new experiences from which Johnson could draw for his creation of fiction. In 1974 the Johnsons moved to Sheerness, England, on the isle of Sheppey. The top floor of the house at 26 Marine Parade extended over the imposing breakwater to offer a view of the mouth of the Thames River where it flowed into the English Channel. The motivation for the strange move from a metropolis, where the Johnsons were surrounded by their native language, to a small town in England is open to speculation. The ostensible reasons for the move, according to critic Bernd Neumann, were concerns for Katharina's acquisition of proper English and the safer schools in Sheerness. The Johnsons had always wanted a house that overlooked a vast body of water, but real estate on the Baltic Sea in Germany was too expensive. Johnson's former professor and friend, Mayer, claimed that the move was for professional reasons; at this point in his writing career Johnson needed the tranquillity of a small town and hoped to find new story material in Sheerness. Neumann adds that, in actuality, Johnson hoped to refresh the material for *Anniversaries* and keep the narrative alive through inspiration from the sea and contact with the simple life of a small unpretentious community.[13] Moreover, Johnson could ensure his figurative and literal insular existence in Sheerness. But the question remains open to what extent Johnson tired of living on German soil, where his works and utterances on national issues often brought criticism from the East as well as the West. The move to Sheerness could have been an act of self-imposed exile, a move to create distance between himself and the troubling affairs of the two Germanys. Most likely a combination of all these factors compelled Johnson's relocation. Nonetheless, Neumann points out the curious fact that in Johnson's lectures dedicated to the "exterior circumstances" of his poetic production, he elaborated extensively on the importance of his two-year sojourn in New York, but Sheerness, where he had lived for close to five years when he gave the lectures, was hardly mentioned.[14] Yet, in a direct, negative way, what Johnson learned in Sheerness about his life had a major impact on his personal and professional existence.

If the first crisis in Johnson's life, his altercation with the East German regime at age nineteen, launched him into a career of fiction writing, the last one almost eliminated him from the profession. In 1975 Johnson suffered a heart attack and a crisis in his marriage, two setbacks that led to a debilitating writer's block. Johnson was able slowly to get his writing program back in order, but the physical and marital troubles revealed how vulnerable his writing conditions and methods were to disturbance. Johnson resolutely wrote only publishable sentences, which meant nothing went down on paper until it had been carefully formulated in his mind. Using a procedure that he had developed while in the GDR, where good typing paper was difficult to obtain, Johnson used the right side of a sheet for the text and retained the left side for comments and corrections. After the four versions of the novel *Ingrid Babendererde,* he only wrote one version of the works that followed. Johnson demonstrated a great mental capacity for detail as he outlined entire novels in his mind before putting any words on paper: "Usually I think about a book for approximately a year, making plans. Then according to these plans I type the text on the right side of the paper and leave the left open for corrections."[15] Moreover, due to his insistence on exactitude and factual correctness, Johnson's books were all meticulously researched before they were written, and Elisabeth and friends often helped him collect information. The content of *Anniversaries,* for example, was closely associated with Uwe, Elisabeth, and Katharina Johnson's life in New York. Elisabeth was also an invaluable contributor of information about life in

Mecklenburg. It is easy to see why the isolation of Sheerness and marriage difficulties could put a halt to progress on his final novel. Yet he continued to write. Between 1975 and 1981 he wrote a biographical sketch of his friend and colleague, Austrian writer Ingeborg Bachmann (1926–73), entitled *Eine Reise nach Klagenfurt* (*Trip to Klagenfurt*). He wrote the short stories "Versuch, einen Vater zu finden" ("In Search of a Father") and "Marthas Ferien" ("Martha's Vacations") (both published posthumously in 1988); he and Elisabeth edited the autobiography of the German wartime journalist Margret Boveri (1977); he published the Frankfurt lectures on poetics (1980); and he wrote what many believe to be a fictionalized version of his marriage troubles under the title *Skizze eines Verunglückten* (*Sketch of a Victim*) (1981). But none of these items were what the public and his publisher eagerly awaited, the concluding volume of *Anniversaries,* which did not appear until 1983, ten months before his death, after years of personal torment and struggle.

Johnson died sometime between 22 and 23 February 1984 in the upstairs part of his house that overlooked the mouth of the Thames. He was forty-nine years old. His insistence on privacy, his desire for isolation, the sometimes uncivil manner in which he treated his acquaintances in the local pub, and his frequent disappearances for weeks at a time caused locals to suspect nothing when Johnson was not seen for a while. He was not discovered until 12 March, when two neighbors finally broke into his house. Heart failure was the cause of death, probably the result of his frequent use of strong sleeping aids, heavy smoking, heavy drinking, and emotional stress. Even in death Johnson created controversy in the German press. A journalist named Tilman Jens, keen on doing a story on the strange man of Sheerness, broke into Johnson's house and illegally obtained documents for use in his report. The publicized marital difficulties and various disclosures about his personal life led to a pitched verbal battle in the West German press. Jens demonstrated little common courtesy in revealing Johnson's private affairs in his report in the 20 May issue of *Stern.* The consternation that arose among Johnson's friends and colleagues after the appearance of the report only three months after Johnson's death was loud and clear, and it filled the newspapers for weeks.

Johnson's unhappy existence resulted, to a great degree, from his close association with German history, whose course was cause for distress, grief, guilt, frustration, and debilitating losses. Johnson's complex fictions all possess disturbing subtexts that grapple with the division of Germany and the greater crises of German history. His *Begleitumstände* includes more than fifty pages of German history describing missed opportunities to unite the Germanys in the 1940s and 1950s; the policies of West German Chancellor Konrad Adenauer were, for Johnson, clearly at fault for Germany's division, then in its thirtieth year. The border was a vestige of the worst war ever to afflict humankind, part of the price that the German people paid for causing it. Every major work by Johnson addresses this fact of history that lasted from 1949 to 1990. Johnson's writing often proved to be a critical gesture against the propensity of the German population to forget the past, evade responsibility for crimes, and suppress the guilt of history. His fiction, which reconstructs the past such that it has become a permanent portion of Germany's literary tradition, remind all people of the duty to remember. This burdensome task of remembering, a duty he fulfills in every work, is a melancholy business indeed.

The second of his Frankfurt lectures on poetics opened with a warning to all who consider fiction writing as a possible profession (BU 57), a profession that he referred to as an "unfortunately fulfilled wish" (BU 442). In 1979, after years of a troubled life as an author, Johnson must have deeply sympathized with the words that Thomas Mann has Tonio Kröger say in the 1903 novella of the same name: "Literature is not a calling, it is a curse, believe me!"[16] In this novella, which Johnson quoted in his lecture, Mann thematizes the corrupt existence of the artist, on the one hand, and the bourgeois gentleman, on the other, where the artist is depicted as unfriendly to something Mann refers to as "life." For Kröger, life consists of all the normal pleasures of middle-class existence, or "a longing for the innocent, the simple, and the living, for a little friendship, devotion, familiar human happiness" or "the bliss of the commonplace."[17] Although Johnson differs from Mann in that he never really made the art-life dichotomy a central theme in his works—if he had, he would have juxtaposed the artist with tradespeople or the working class—Johnson lived the dichotomy. He continually compared his work as a writer to that of carpenters, waitpersons, blacksmiths, and other working people in what seemed like an attempt, on Johnson's part, to connect his profession to working-class life. But he was never quite successful at making such a connection for himself. Like Mann, a fellow north German, Johnson was an intellectual and humanist with a troubled relationship to his nation. This relationship alienated him, prompting his exile as well as compelling him to write, and that situation, in the end, caused him to turn his back on life.

# CHAPTER 2

# Approach to Narrative and Storytelling

## Essays and Interviews

Uwe Johnson's conception of poetic expression is not available in any cohesive, unifying treatise. He was never one to speak freely about literary production except when asked directly, and then he would speak only in the most fundamental terms. He supported no particular school, movement, or tradition in his utterances about literature, even though he knew about the literary theories of his day. Thus, secondary literature about Johnson's approach to narrative and storytelling is practically nonexistent, save for the instances where critics mention certain of his statements in the context of their own explications of his texts. It is possible, however, to think of his book *Begleitumstände,* his published essays of the Frankfurt lecture series on poetics, as a treatise about poetics in general. It offers insights into Johnson's poetic vision but only in conjunction with his published (and unpublished) work. However, in the lectures of *Begleitumstände,* given in 1979 and published one year later, Johnson holds himself up as a negative example in describing how he inadvertently entered the profession of writing. The book, therefore, evidences a heavy autobiographical focus from which to deduce his opinions on the author's role in society, the idea of literature as a process of truth-seeking, the value of stories for people in their everyday lives, the political function of literature, and other poetic issues that come to mind when thinking of Johnson's work. However, *Begleitumstände* does not offer any concise overview of Johnson's ideas on the issues of literary expression. Two short essays that can pass for Johnson's unsolicited views on poetics will do better for this purpose and are therefore the subject of this chapter.

The essay "Berliner Stadtbahn (*veraltet*)," literally "Berlin City Train (*outdated*)" but translated as "Berlin, Border of the Divided World," was derived from a lecture given in 1961 in Detroit. Another piece, "Vorschläge zur Prüfung eines Romans" ("Suggestions for the Analysis of a Novel"), published in 1975, is the shortened German title of an earlier unpublished essay in English entitled "Conversation on the novel, its use & dangers, recent degenerations, indignation of the audience & c."[1] Viewed comparatively, the distinct, discursive literary projects of the two essays affirm their corresponding ideas. The "Berliner

12

Stadtbahn" essay's descriptive purpose complements the critical and normative points that Johnson makes in the "Vorschläge" essay. "Berliner Stadtbahn" describes this author's difficulty in approaching material that will become part of the story that he wishes to write. The "Vorschläge" essay, conversely, discusses novel writing from the point of view of the reader, thus inversely describing, in Johnson's view, what a writer needs to consider when producing a genuine novel. These essays—together with copious published interviews and talks—give a comprehensive and serviceable view of Johnson's poetic vision.

## Truth-Seeking and the Moment of Narration

Johnson draws conclusions about writing that attempt to mediate the subjective and objective elements inherent to the activity of storytelling. One of the statements referred to most frequently by Johnson scholars when explicating his work is his opinion that authors of fiction are obliged to say that their work is invented. Writers can do so "by not passing off as pure art what is still a manner of truth-seeking" (BSv 21). In "Berliner Stadtbahn" Johnson makes a distinction between truth and truth-seeking to illustrate that the latter can be the only feasible goal of writing where truth is at all a concern of the writer. Genuine truth-seeking represents authors' only method of attaining or presenting anything close to the truth. In a paradoxical twist, Johnson utilizes objective markings—that is, an observable event with a specific time (1960), place (divided Berlin), and action (man riding train)—to demonstrate that a putatively objective description requires a representation of the events and therefore necessarily results in a subjective invention of them. Through the questions that he poses to himself about this event, Johnson illustrates an obvious but often forgotten fact: there is no knowable, objective truth. In an interview recorded late in his life he said, "I believe in individual truth, private truth."[2] This basic and ironically realistic presupposition, that there is no objective truth, guides Johnson's entire ideology-busting literary production.

The acknowledgment of the author and realization of the reader that no objective truth exists possesses tremendous implications for the narration of a story, fiction or nonfiction. Without the notion of an absolute truth, there can be no narrators who behave as though they know everything about a story or the persons involved in it. Johnson demonstrates to his readers time and time again the impossibility of the omniscient narrator. Johnson's misgivings about the all-knowing narrator possibly reveal the influence of an essay by literary critic and philosopher Theodor W. Adorno, who wrote that the novel requires narration and yet it is impossible to narrate.[3] Johnson deems "suspicious" (BSv 20) and only appropriate for nineteenth-century literature the total authority and God-like view that the omniscient narrator possesses. Balzac's nineteenth-century realism possesses far too much confidence in its narrative certainty about its literary material to be suitable for describing or relating to the complex issues of twentieth-century existence. Johnson's unassuming example of a man entering a train in the eastern part of Berlin, traveling to the western part, and getting off the train there brings with it all the complexities of the century, complexities that need to be reflected in a narrative about this particular passenger who has just crossed an infamous border. As Johnson intimates elsewhere, the simple crossing of the border in Germany can be extremely complicated: "Under such conditions as exist in Germany, one cannot actually say that the writer makes things difficult out of pure obstinacy."[4] Johnson believes that writers are obliged to pay attention to the complications of any story in the narrative and thereby not make it easy on themselves by playing the authority on the subject. For Johnson, then, the narration of stories grows out of the author's struggle with contradicting information, disorienting considerations, and philosophical skepticism that are markings of modernity and postmodern writing.

In "Berliner Stadtbahn" Johnson presents the problems that arise for a writer who wishes to recapitulate this simple event as part of a greater narrative project. In a city such as Berlin, which from 1945 to 1990 represented the geographic meeting point or point of confrontation between capitalist West and communist East, this everyday occurrence had far-reaching consequences. To cross the border between East and West Berlin was to change economic and political systems; the border was unnatural and apparently permanent, so crossing it meant the transcendence of the result of cold-war politics gone awry. Upon crossing, although German was spoken on either side, the codes and semantic contents of one's language altered and shifted in subtle and sometimes not so subtle ways: "Both cities of Berlin call themselves free, the other unfree; themselves democratic, the other undemocratic; themselves peaceful, the other hostile; and so forth" (BSv 19). In recognizing these external circumstances, observers must ask what possibly motivated such a crossing, why someone would choose one side of Berlin over the other. The complicated circumstances of the action grow exponentially as a function of how deeply one probes into the background of this individual's move. To ponder this event in its political, historical, and economic contexts already creates unanswerable questions in the observer's mind. The unknowable truth lies somewhere in a decision, which was made by weighing alternatives that, against other variables to consider, presented themselves as dilemmas. Researching and dissecting every aspect of the short but significant train ride and making the results explicit is what truth-seeking is all about for Johnson. Wrapped so tightly inside a knotted maze of external circumstances, personal desires, physical possibilities, societal constraints, purely coincidental happenings, and historical events, the truth gives meaning to Johnson's curious and often pondered equation, "Truth is pumice stone" (VPR 33). For Johnson, the author's task is to wear away at the outer crust of events to come closer to the unobtainable truth. The quest for the truth is paradoxically and simultaneously the invention of the story that is created by a path of infinite reduction as each new piece of disclosed information prompts the next query into the story behind the observed moment. The next plot point is created by each new question, as one inquires deeper into the motivation(s) for the border crossing. Johnson considers this quest for truthfulness an unwieldy but necessary task of the conscientious storyteller.

## Literary Category and History

In the "Berliner Stadtbahn" essay Johnson refers to the German-German border as a literary category (BSv 10) because of its essence as something that simultaneously separates and connects two adverse worldviews (BSv 12). When Johnson considers for literary treatment this lugubrious vestige of cold-war politics, the border's existence renders impossible any sense of homogeneity in understanding reality. The border undermines a totalizing sense of reality because its existence enforces the destabilizing actuality of fiercely differing views, contrasting ideas, and the inevitability of varying versions of events that transpire in its vicinity. This is where literature finds its fertile ground because stories evolve from disparity and antagonisms. The border marks a line of confrontation analogous to lines that can be drawn in any novel that creates dialectical relations between characters and their worlds, between reader and writer, and between fiction and reality. Many story types harbor such lines of differentiation where individual happiness clashes with uncontrollable external circumstances. For example, Johnson views the "aggrieved, deceived, hindered, not to be experienced love affair" (VPR 31) as one of the oldest story lines in human history. One could describe the former German-German border in a similar fashion and in place of "love affair" one might write in "unification." Both "literary categories" have a sense of separation and loss with a joining, a fusion or rapprochement, as the resolution to the conflict.

In Johnson's example of the man riding Berlin's city train, the descriptions of the train and the stations seem to flow freely. The speculation and narration of the occurrence begin when the decision has been made and executed by the figure in question, while another has observed or heard about the incident (BSv 17) and wishes to describe it. The observer of the action can be reasonably confident about what he sees, and he does not falter in his task of narrating the descriptive detail of the man's short trip. Despite the objective character that the description of surroundings can have, Johnson implies that these surroundings could say something about the motivation for the man's trip. With this implication, the description of objects reveals itself as part of a subjective representation. The inclusion or exclusion of putatively objective details in the narration is, after all, part of a selection process, thus implying criteria for making decisions on the part of the one narrating the event. The train station in the East presents a barren and rather shabby contrast to the restored station in the West, which offers to the traveler an abundance of consumer goods (BSv 16). Complications arise when the observer questions whether the difference in appearance of the two stations has something to do with the man's move. After all, between 1949 and 1961, three million people permanently moved from East Germany to West Germany, many of them across the border in Berlin. Although several observers could probably agree on the validity of the descriptions of the man's surroundings as he travels, the answering of more intangible questions brings up other complex issues. Is this person representative of the three million others who made the same trip? Does the man prefer the apparently better economic system of the West, and if so, is that a good reason to leave one's homeland, possibly to acclimate oneself elsewhere? Does the economic well-being of the other part of the city mean that it has a more just social structure (BSv 17)? The same man, by virtue of this single action, could be considered a refugee in the West and a traitor in the East, but who or what is he really? How does one explain the ruins he passes or the bullet holes in the signs that tell us the name of the city train stop? Posing such questions as to whether the figure under consideration prefers capitalism to socialism, bears some measure of guilt for the Second World War, is a spy, or is seeking refuge from some persecution as well as any other speculation invites the observer to take a careful look below superficialities. Attempts to find the reason(s) behind this man's journey move from questions specific to his motivation for his ride to issues of greater moral, political, and historical significance. Continuing in this vein, the writer treads on slippery ground where the certainty of conclusions is concerned.

Thus the border, as a "literary category" or story material, paradoxically becomes boundless. Johnson demonstrates in all his works the importance of meticulous research necessary to describe truthfully a simple event. In other words, for Johnson, the site where literature and historical narrative exist cheek by jowl, and where they both find their critical moments, is within the process of outspoken and unabashed truth-seeking. For Johnson, prose fiction and history are narratives that depict human choices, judgments, determinations, and decisions made in the face of circumstances in which individuals, their recourses limited, find themselves. Through research, documentation, memory, and deduction the writer reconstructs the moment of action and reassembles its factual and normative substance in the final product of a narrative. Thus, in his novels, Johnson offers his readers versions of how and why events developed as they did. This explicatory gesture of his narratives serves as a resistance to the human propensity to disremember the past, especially a past full of atrocities and shame, such as Germany's. Johnson does not permit readers to forget history; rather, he utilizes the novel as a form of preservation of the past in an effort to confront the continuous "fading away" and "expiration" of time.[5]

Unlike historians, Johnson portrays fictitious personalities in a setting of historical authenticity. This approach to narrative fiction motivates his comment that "it is hardly possible to live on the outskirts of history.[6] For Johnson, no life is commonplace because all individuals retain reference to the world through contacts with the society in which they live (VPR 32).[7] Every life possesses meaning for other lives and for history; for Johnson, literature presents history in the human dimension of the individual life, which focuses on the individual fate within a broader historical framework. Described within the destiny of an individual or group of individuals, history thus becomes more meaningful to readers in their real-life circumstances. For Johnson, literature is more believable in this respect than are historical documents written by "those who had the power." Instead, reliance should be placed on "those who tried to show the actual conditions" of the time, by which he means those people who, like himself, describe a time period without a vested interest in how that time period is described in narrative.[8] For example, when learning about what a soldier's life may have been like in the Second World War, Johnson suggests that Heinrich Böll's stories are better sources than books by generals that speak of the military exploits of the war without consideration for the individuals who actually experienced it: "Mr. Böll proceeds with individual people who are asked whether they want to" be involved in the war. Böll explores the desires and cares of individuals caught up in war. According to Johnson he does not toss away "a pile of people in a single sentence." Thus, another element of the process of truth-seeking is a reconstruction of human experience from the perspective of the people involved; storytelling occurs on the scale of individual fate(s), their "personal characteristics and illnesses and mental difficulties of adaptation and practical difficulties of adaptation."[9] Johnson intimates here that, with the real concerns of common individuals as the focus of stories, writers cannot represent dominant ideological interpretations or power-interested legitimations of injustices. The day-to-day experiences and common concerns of individuals do not fit neatly or directly into ideological packaging.

Because the work of historians and their research methods comprise an integral part of all of Johnson's texts, he actually produces his work in concert with historians. In an essay entitled "Wenn Sie mich fragen . . ." ("If You Ask Me . . ."), he cites Aristotle to elucidate the difference between the writing of history and fiction, the upshot of Aristotle's thoughts being that "the narration that invents is more useful than history writing, because fiction has the essence (of human life) in view and not merely the particulars."[10] Johnson does not belittle the necessity of historical particulars. His main concern, however, is how those characters conduct themselves in their specific settings of time and place. Historical circumstance, to a certain extent, sets and guides the actions of the individuals whom he depicts in narrative. Decisions made by leaders, "those with the power," manifest themselves in the repercussions felt by people and the effect exerted on individual decisions in the face of financial, political, and social circumstances, all in consideration of how best to survive the next turn of fate: "I am convinced that the 'simple people' deliver the more relevant example for living conditions in our time, not only because of their numerical superiority, also not only because they are disadvantaged in the distribution of national income beyond all just circumstances; especially because they must mercilessly pay for every change for the worse, must overcome their difficulties with the acutest risk without money reserves that cushion them and privileges that protect them."[11] When Johnson incorporates historical events into the lives of his characters, war manifests itself in everyday life, rebellions interfere with the workday, civil strife is at the front door, and the ideological conceptions that maintain the world in a constant state of strife and tension reveal themselves in school lessons. He views the grand trends of history, the centuries of tradition, from the perspective and on the scale of the individual or within the constitutive homeostasis of a farming village or small town. In essence he creates in his stories sociological thought experiments. He describes the macrocosm from within the confines of the microcosm in a persuasive, revealing, and ultimately assertive manner that not only strikes readers viscerally but causes them to reflect more profoundly about how they live.

## Characters or Invented Persons

Johnson referred to his characters as "invented persons" and often corrected critics and interviewers who spoke of the "characters" in his stories. This introduction to Johnson refers to "characters" because it is the accepted literary term for people depicted in fictional narratives, but Johnson would oppose this terminology in the context of his own creations. Johnson thought of the people in his books as "independent persons" or "'composites,'" even as "replicas of living people."[12] These persons possess a level of reality and independence that limits what he can do with them in fiction: "I must deal with all these people, since they are real for me, I must work together with them on the story. It goes without saying that we stand across from each other as equally entitled."[13] The high level of autonomy that Johnson accords his characters results in a situation in which he cannot abandon his persons once he has invented them. Even if they die in one novel, they continue to affect later narrative creations. Johnson's invented persons, then, recur and reveal interconnections that give readers the feeling of getting to know a community or extended family. In other words, Johnson recycles characters, a fact that helps him remain with what is comfortably familiar and also means that his characters continue to develop not exclusively within a given novel but across novels: "One doesn't simply give up on a person if a book cover has simply closed itself behind them. They remain alive for me."[14] This refusal to abandon the invented people of his stories means an accumulation of persons and places, both fictitious and real, that, by the end of his career, filled 299 pages of a so-called *Adressbuch* that accompanies all hardbound editions of *Jahrestage.* Although this "address book" accompanies *Jahrestage,* due to Johnson's propensity to recycle characters, it also contains many of the persons who appear in his earlier works.[15] Johnson does not view characters as functions, mouthpieces, or even alter egos; they are persons with an almost legal status, possessing the right to vote and veto where the writing of the narrative is concerned. The exceptional authenticity of his invented persons carries over to the places they occupy and the events that move them such that Johnson's stories come to occupy a curious site between fact and fiction. With these invented persons Johnson produces fictions within the rearranged actualities of history that constitute the unquestionable plausibility of his stories.

Novelists differentiate themselves from historians in the sense that fiction writing concerns itself more with the characters caught up in the events of the story than with the events themselves. Johnson stresses in "Vorschläge" that the persons and their relationships to each other constitute the essence of novels and that the greater the number of such relationships, the more novel there is. Johnson explains: "To count would be the relationships between the persons, the incidents, the settings, the units of time, motifs, techniques of the substructure and, once more, the persons" (VPR 30). The group of persons and their relationships comprise the fundamental fabric of the novel. Here Johnson exhibits the influence that Virginia Woolf's essay "Mr. Bennett and Mrs. Brown" exerted on his conception of the novel. In this essay, to which Johnson alludes in "Vorschläge," Woolf's central premise is that the depiction of character represents the essential element of novelistic creation: "But novelists differ from the rest of the world because they do not cease to be interested in character when they have learnt enough for practical purposes. . . . The study of character becomes to them an absorbing pursuit; to impart character an obsession."[16] The development of characters constitutes a significant distinction between the approach of novelists and historians to their material: "All these great novelists have brought us to see whatever they wish us to see through some character. Otherwise, they would not be novelists; but poets, historians or pamphleteers."[17] Johnson familiarizes his audience with life depicted in events because his characters or invented persons reflect back, in the dimension of history, the lives that readers live. They relate to Johnson's characters with their own life experiences and thereby identify with the characters in an empathetic way. Johnson's invented persons become the readers' window to the world of the novel by providing the vehicle through which readers fuse with the human situation—that is, with the events of the story and its specific historical context.

Johnson's characters are never larger than their creator and are thus on a par with readers' life dimensions. He seldom knows more about a character than what they already know about themselves. In his materialist approach to depicting life in fiction, Johnson's main characters are endowed with no special powers, they are not wealthy, they do not possess vast amounts of property. They hold no influential political office, they usually have modest levels of education, they have no greater insights into the ways of the world than do most people. Their concerns are those of the average person, whose family, friends, property, security, and income constitute everyday joys and worries. Johnson is adamant and consistent about depicting characters as working people whose jobs represent a daily activity and a part of what they are as persons. In fact, he believes that the depiction of work in the lives of persons in novels is a necessity that adds to the beauty and authenticity of the novel (VPR 32–33). As people with humble backgrounds, Johnson's main invented persons are not particularly philosophical about their existence, although they do possess convictions, persuasions, and principles that become guidelines for living and extend their consciousness of the world beyond self-interestedness. They act according to these principles even to the detriment of their own comfortable existences, which is often the action that makes their lives initially and primarily novelistic. Where societal and material constraints meet or collide with individual conviction is where the story is born, or as Johnson explains, it is "through persons, through what has happened and can happen to them and what society has given them for means to resist these events . . . that a story of the persons comes into being, and, so I hope, also a story of society."[18] It is exactly the "ordinariness" of his characters, their mistakes and their possibilities, that engages readers in their own life circumstances. Johnson views stories, in general, as a way for readers to extend their experience of the world beyond work and family (VPR 32). Thus evolves a pedagogical undertone in Johnson's work, as he writes his novels keeping readers' preoccupations with life circumstances in mind.

Although Johnson believes that novels have only limited possibilities for political engagement, they do possess the capacity to bring readers to question profoundly their surroundings. Through an authentic depiction of the world in the novel, authors will bring readers to a cognition "in which we recognize: that's how we live" (VPR 33). As mentioned above, only readers can attest to the verity of novels, where the novel contains a world to hold against the world (VPR 35) in contrasting likeness. Holding the world of a particular novel up to the world as readers know it will hopefully prompt the question "But do we want to live that way?" (VPR 33). If change or transformation is possible with novels, then it is so only in this limited but quite efficacious manner. Johnson believed that novels could increase the awareness of society's human condition only one individual at a time. He evidences here a holistic and guardedly optimistic view of social change, for if novels invoke a change in a single individual, they invoke, indeed, a modest but authentic transformation of society as a whole.

## The Author, the Story, the Reader

Johnson understands the role of authors in society in specific ways that point to a certain societal purposefulness. First, authors are obliged to write stories for the use and pleasure of their readers. At the end of his "Vorschläge" essay, he states, "Then there would be a division of labor to ascertain. While you are occupied in a different way, the novel writer supplies you entertainment and information" (VPR 36). This is where Johnson locates the legitimacy of the author in society. Johnson believes that the novelist "serves a basic human need, which [publisher] Peter Suhrkamp once defined as the curiosity of persons about their neighbors and about themselves."[19] The characters are central to literary production in Johnson's view because readers feel compelled to read stories to learn about other people's lives. According to Johnson, people have a need to know about what happens to their neighbors almost as much as they need to eat and drink.[20] Johnson thus also reflects a materialist view of writers in society: writers respond to and satisfy people's need to read stories about other people. Fiction writing, for Johnson, plays to the "nosy neighbor" in everyone.

Although Johnson claims elsewhere that novels have infinite narratological possibilities, those possibilities can only be realized in the sincere mediation of the stories.[21] Johnson places this limitation on the novel to shield it from misuse by those with blatant political agendas. He believes that a book in which the political message takes precedence over the characters and the story is no longer a novel but a "container with agitation material" (VPR 35). In such a case, an ulterior motive, a purpose, or political tendency that reaches beyond the story drives the narrative. Therefore, something else takes over and mars the appropriateness of the novel as entertainment, information, and edification for readers. Form and story serve something removed from themselves and not only impair the novel in its effect on readers but also belittle its function as material potentially instructive for real-life problems and situations. Johnson believes that a novel is an invitation to think about and discuss its story and persons.[22] A book aimed at persuasion, in contrast, allows no discussion but rather delivers declarations that readers must either accept or reject. In such books, although the political message may be honorable, there is no equal partnership between readers and the book. In Johnson's thinking, only a limited freedom is left to readers, whereas the writer should be encouraging readers' unique and singular "cooperation"[23] in the continued renewal of the book's interpretive possibilities. This is not to say that political topics, ideological beliefs, or religiously grounded morals have no place in novels. They should not, however, represent the overarching glue of the narrative and instead should be included as attributes of specific characters.

Even in a political strategy, the novel is not suitable as a "revolutionary weapon" (VPR 35). For Johnson, there is nothing spontaneous about a genre whose creation is so deliberate and necessarily delayed that the concrete cause about which an author might write is bound to be forgotten before the novel is finished and available to readers. Johnson recalls that novels are only read by one person at a time; it is difficult to move masses of people to engage in protest or undergo political action in any practical way by means of a novel.[24] Although he does not mention the novel by title, Johnson seems to offer the case of Erich Maria Remarque's (1898–1970) antiwar novel *All Quiet on the Western Front* (published in 1929) to illustrate his point. This book had been widely read but exerted no demonstrable effect on the millions who obeyed or acquiesced to the call of military service in 1935 to fight in a war that eventually cost more than 55 million people their lives (VPR 35).

Reading and readers hold special places in Johnson's conception of narrative because he views reading as the beginning of writing a story. In his own experience, he claims that an early indication of his future occupation as a writer was his voracious appetite for fiction as a youngster (BU 57). Johnson affirms readers by according them control over the life of the text once it enters the public realm. If the writer offers readers a "container with agitation material" or some moralistic exigency—in other words, if the author does not remain free of political purposes and explicit metatextual messages—then it is up to readers to recognize the intended appropriation or ideological steering as the writer's implicit goal. In this respect, the reader-writer relationship becomes a system of checks and balances because it is up to readers to reject such a narrative as a novel. Johnson displays a genuine concern for readers when he warns, "Defend your independence to the final page of the book. If you are expressly told what the novel tried to say, this is the last moment for removal of the book. You have obtained the right to a story. The delivery of a quintessence or moral is breech of contract. The story is promised with the novel" (VPR 35). Inversely, reader independence represents a counterpart to the independence of the writer. As Johnson says, "Beware of the dog" (VPR 35)—that is, beware of writers who serve masters beyond the story of the novel and the independent profession of fiction writing. Johnson privileges readers, then, on two accounts: recipients of the novel must remain sole possessors of the right to discuss and interpret the book, while judging the "truth" of the book remains readers' duty as well (VPR 35, 33). Again, the author provides the story, but readers possess the responsibility to determine the relevance of that story as a text. In other words, Johnson takes the authority from authors and places it with readers.

## Form and Content

In this unwritten contract between novelists and readers, writers mediate the story to potential readers in an appropriate form, one suitable to the story though not necessarily easily accessible to readers. Johnson believes that the form is not the author's completely free choice, nor should it be a contrived courtesy (or discourtesy) to readers. His utterances about form and content demonstrate that Johnson has reversed the accepted relationship between the two. Many theorists and writers have thought of form as the determining factor of content, but for Johnson the story exercises the determining function. In other words, if the writer has a story to tell, its contents will determine the form in which it is most suitably presentable: "It has been my experience that every story that I knew required its own completely specific form. This form cannot be transferred to other stories."[25] Although there is a singularly different form for every story worth telling, the author still confronts the chore of deciphering that form. This challenge confronts the author when writing a novel because form and story must fit perfectly in the final product: "The problem of form and content may no longer be visible. The story must have pulled the form onto its body. The form has exclusively the function of bringing the story undamaged into the world. It may no longer be separable from the content" (VPR 33–34). The novel fitted in form and content is the mediation of authentic human experience through the external package of its form. The story is brought into the world through the midwifery of the form. This attitude explains Johnson's skepticism about the cogency or appropriateness of the French *nouveau roman,* in which, he implies, there is so much attention to form that the story is compromised.[26] This is not to say that writers must limit themselves in the "artistic skills" or formal choices of the (post)modern age (VPR 34). As in any profession, writers of fiction require and create new approaches to narrative to perform their tasks of telling stories, more authentically, or more truthfully, in a way that naturalizes the form-content constitution of the narrative. Johnson claims that if readers have difficulty with new approaches to writing fiction, the problem is not with the new approaches but rather with the schools that educate young people, which represent nothing but an "ancillary industry to industry" (VPR 34). Better readers have less difficulty with new, less accessible forms.

Johnson describes literary material most suited for the novel as "newness," "just found," and "primal" (VPR 30). Thus, novelistic material possesses an element of always having been there, an element that contains the capacity to be timelessly significant for readers' lives: "It is an old story: but new again and again" (VPR 30). Thus, stories from long ago can also be "new" and important for the present. A story about neighbors in another country, in the apartment next door, or from two hundred years ago can indeed be new and instructive to modern readers.[27] Although this concept initially sounds contradictory, it makes sense in light of Johnson's examples. As discussed earlier, the theme of unfulfilled love has been treated in fiction time and again throughout the centuries, from Hero and Leander to Romeo and Juliet up to the lovers in Johnson's own *Two Views.* This primal story material, set in various circumstances, becomes new with each retelling of its basic plot because it shows in its new setting what "can come between lovers now or for the present" (VPR 31). Authors revive the primal story by setting it in distinctly different circumstances with persons of varying backgrounds. Thus, when Johnson speaks of "new," where certain story themes are concerned, he does not mean new as in the world of commodities or in the sense that something is extraordinary or unusual. The material should not be the result of a stroke of inspiration but rather something found, authentic in its actuality. A story should be already there and can come from any time period as long as it displays timeless attributes. If it says something about the current world, the story possesses a novelistic value: "New would be a novel that has something to do with the time in which the reader lives" (VPR 31). Thus, Johnson views novelists less as inspired inventors and more as attentive and circumspect observers of the times in which they live.

# CHAPTER 3

# *Ingrid Babendererde*

## Political Maturation

Even though *Ingrid Babendererde* was Uwe Johnson's first novel, it was published posthumously in 1985. Its publication one year after his death conflates, in a curious way, the fact of Johnson's life and death with a structural principle of many of his works. The story-laden moment as the point from which the story evolves reveals itself with the novel *Ingrid Babendererde* as a literary moment for Johnson's life as a writer. Thus, the germinating elements of his literary production revealed themselves to the reading public in this novel published after his death. Only in such books as this study of Johnson's life and work can *Ingrid Babendererde* sit at the beginning of Johnson's literary production, where it offers a sense of linearity in Johnson's development as an author, a linearity that Johnson never sanctioned in his stories. Many of the themes and experiences that lie at the root of Johnson's later stories are present in this text, initially conceived by a youth of nineteen years. In 1970, Wilhelm Schwarz said of Johnson's feelings about his first novel, "Today Johnson is glad that this work never appeared, because he considers it to be an immature product of a young man."[1] However, in 1956, the possible publication of this text meant a lot to Johnson, who wrote to Aufbau Verlag, one of the most well-known publishers in East Germany, "It is important to me that the pages that lie before you will become a book in the Democratic Republic."[2] After those years in which this novel was written, 1953–56, Johnson's writing style evolved dramatically to become one of the most fascinating—some would say perplexing—styles in German literature. Thematically, however, Johnson remained consistent from this first literary attempt up to his final opus, *Anniversaries.*

It is important to keep in mind that Johnson intended for *Ingrid Babendererde* to be published in the GDR and to be accessible to readers in that country. Johnson wrote about the party slogans written on bright red banners, the public newspaper displays, the Freie Deutsche Jugend (Free German Youth), the Junge Gemeinde (Young Congregation), and the dreaded Stasi, which together comprised the prevalent novelistic trappings familiar to an East

German reading public. Johnson hoped to join in a discussion about life in the first socialist republic on German soil with a sincere desire to improve it through the publication of a critical novel about life there. In *Ingrid Babendererde* the characters, although they enter into conflict with representatives of the state, do not question the principles on which GDR society was based. Although the mornings in school are "boring"[3] and the atmosphere of the newly established republic offers little excitement to these young people, the novel's earnest and constructive critical stance is built on an implicit belief that the socialist society of the GDR can be ameliorated. This novel generally concerns uprightness in government, a commitment to democratic socialism, the misuse of education as ideological conditioning, the importance of friendship in the face of adversity, and the unfortunate historical development of the GDR as a Stalinist-inspired dictatorship. Stagnating dogmatism faces off against youthful energy and hopeful anticipation while a Mecklenburg community comes to terms with or attempts to adapt to another authoritarian political leadership. Against this backdrop Johnson casts the story of a love triangle similar to those in his later novels, *Speculations about Jakob* and *The Third Book about Achim*. Thus, *Ingrid Babendererde* is also a love story about two young men vying for the same woman, but they do so in a strangely noncompetitive, undramatic manner typical of Johnson's stories. As in much of his work, the Mecklenburg landscape plays an important role in the description of homeland. In other words, readers come to understand that the mere topography of the land is a deeply significant element that somehow connects to the emotional makeup of his main characters. The novel ends with two young people crossing the border to the West, thus irretrievably losing the landscape, the dialect, and the people with which they grew up.

If this novel had appeared in 1957 in the GDR, as Johnson had intended, it would have, due to its candid depiction of life there, transformed the East German literary scene and probably would have brought international attention to East German literature much earlier. As it turned out, that transformation came after the Berlin Wall was erected in 1961 with the appearance of novels such as Christa Wolf's *Der Geteilte Himmel* (*Divided Heaven*) and Erwin Strittmatter's *Ole Bienkopp* (*Old Bienkopp*) in 1963 and Erik Neutsch's *Spur der Steine* (*Trace of Stones*) in 1964. All of these books, though legitimizing in the end, depicted life in the GDR from an undeniably critical posture. *Ingrid Babendererde* was, in light of these other novels, a manuscript that came before its time in East Germany as well as West Germany, where the Peter Suhrkamp publishing house turned it down.

Because it was rejected in both the East and the West, the publication history of *Ingrid Babendererde* elucidates, to a certain extent, the political and cultural nature of its contents. The novel was conceived, before its final published version, in three other versions. The first version of ninety pages, mentioned by Johnson in *Begleitumstände,* is lost (BU 73). The other manuscripts are stored in the Uwe Johnson Archive at the J. W. Goethe University in Frankfurt am Main. Johnson began writing in the spring of 1953 at the age of nineteen and reworked the manuscript to be less critical of East German political functionaries and altered the narrative structure before he finally submitted it for publication.[4] Soviet leader Nikita Khrushchev made a speech to his country's leadership denouncing the way Stalin dealt with national affairs. This speech was only intended for the rulers of the Soviet Union, but it was somehow leaked to the Western press. On hearing that the Soviet leadership had admitted to mistakes made in the past—in other words, due to a perceived thawing of relations between the Soviet government and the peoples it ruled—Johnson believed the time was right to publish his manuscript (BU 88). In July 1956 he submitted his novel to four different East German publishers in the cities of East Berlin, Leipzig, Rostock, and Halle. But the liberalizing tone of political discourse was not as extensive as Johnson believed. Although the editors recognized Johnson's talent as a writer, all of them rejected the manuscript because of the political potency of its critical contents. An internal memorandum from one East German publishing house dated 18 July 1956 and published in *Der Spiegel* in 1992 concluded about Johnson, "Author needs a brainwashing."[5] The unpublished manuscript drew attention to him as an unreliable citizen much more than it served to affirm (as he would have hoped) his sincere desire to contribute to a constructive conversation about improving life in the GDR. In the West, Suhrkamp turned the manuscript down at the behest of Siegfried Unseld, one of his chief editors and eventual successor. Unseld's main criticism was that the author demonstrated "too little worldliness."[6] (Johnson was, after all, only twenty-two years old and had never been out of the GDR when he submitted the final version to Suhrkamp.) Unseld's afterword to *Ingrid Babendererde* is one of those rare and enheartening instances in which a powerful and influential man admits that he was guilty of gross misjudgment years earlier. He reveals in his candid discussion of *Ingrid Babendererde* other possible reasons for having advised Suhrkamp against publishing the manuscript. Unseld intimates that he used metaliterary criteria to form a negative opinion about the text. Those criteria include the social context in which the story takes place: the socialist concerns of the author, the provincial north German town, the use of Mecklenburg dialect, and the pervasive naïveté of the school pupils. These reasons plus the party loyalty shown by the author to the East German communists all "cut off"

Unseld's "access" to the text.[7] Furthermore, Unseld was apparently uncomfortable with the ubiquitous descriptions of landscape and nature that placed the novel, in his mind, too close to the "blood and soil" novels of the fascist years.[8] Interestingly, in 1957's anticommunist atmosphere, Unseld perceived too much communist loyalty in the text, while the East German publishers found the novel too critical of GDR functionaries. This interesting set of circumstances brings Colin Riordan to conclude, "Johnson's self-censorship may thus have left him with a novel which confirmed neither side's image of the other sufficiently to allow publication."[9] As Johnson later discovered, like his manuscript and the truth, he was at home neither in the East nor the West.

## Historical Situation and Plot

As with most of Johnson's major novels, the story in *Ingrid Babendererde* was inspired by historical developments in the newly established GDR. Soon after the Second World War, the Communist Party in the Soviet occupation zone founded a youth organization called the Free German Youth (FDJ). When the GDR came into existence in 1949, the Socialist Unity Party, derived from the fusion of the Communist Party and the East German Social Democratic Party, became the state's leading political party. The party's youth group enjoyed special privileges from the government, because the government wanted to position the FDJ to exercise the greatest influence on the youth in East Germany. The FDJ was rivaled in popularity and influence only by the Christian youth organization known as the Young Congregation. As far as social issues are concerned, one can see how a Christian group and a communist group might share some common cause. Moreover, with the exception of Jews, Christian faithful and committed communists were the most persecuted people under Nazi rule and formed, in this way, a genuine antifascist alliance. But after the war their differing world views became cause for animosity, especially on the part of the Socialist Unity Party. The official atheism of the FDJ was a direct affront to the teachings of the Bible that formed the backbone of the Young Congregation. As the Socialist Unity Party positioned itself to establish its dominant role in the lives of the GDR's people, it tolerated no challenges to its power. It effectively negated all political opposition, took control of the media and industries, and attempted to curtail the church's influence. The government exercised coercive powers through its youth organization, its State Security Service (the Stasi or SSD), and its political apparatus to contain and eventually eliminate the Young Congregation's role in the lives of East German youth. The aggressive and overtly implemented negative campaign against the Young Congregation lasted from 1950 to 1953. In June 1953 there was a violent and spontaneous reaction to the pressures put on the population by policies of the Socialist Unity Party.

Although the uprising was mainly a protest against food shortages and higher production quotas, it was also a reaction to the attacks on the church and its youth group as well as offensive tactics exercised against the other political parties allowed by the GDR's constitution. The communist government then rescinded its aggressive campaign, but many people had already been arrested or fled.

The plot of *Ingrid Babendererde* describes an incident of coercion and thus serves as a small-scale example of how the East German state's campaign against the Young Congregation took shape. The novel also portrays the population's reaction to the Socialist Unity Party's aggression against its own citizens as two intelligent and promising young people reluctantly turn their backs on their homeland to live in the West. The plot centers around a confrontation similar to one that Johnson experienced as a young man. At the University of Rostock, where he was a leading FDJ functionary, Johnson was to give a speech accusing members of the Young Congregation of attacking a Red Army recruit with a knife. The incident was fabricated, which Johnson pointed out in his talk. He also drew attention to the fact that the GDR's government was contravening its own constitution in its attempt to eliminate the Young Congregation. Indeed, Article 41 of the East German constitution guaranteed religious freedom. Ironically, while Johnson had little to do with the Young Congregation, his defense of the organization ruined his future in the GDR. Johnson was expelled from the university for his candid speech breaking with the party line, and he was only allowed to return to university studies after the popular uprisings in June 1953 (BU 63–66).

The altered, autobiographical story in *Ingrid Babendererde* revolves around high school class 12A, whose members are preparing for the *Abitur,* a rigorous German high school graduation examination also referred to as a *Reifeprüfung,* or test of maturation, from which the subtitle of the book comes. The exams at the Gustav Adolf-Oberschule are scheduled for May 1953, one month before the country will erupt in rebellion. The narrative focuses on three friends, Klaus Niebuhr, Jürgen Petersen, and Ingrid Babendererde, who are preparing for these exams and enjoying the favorable spring weather to engage in all manner of water sports as a welcome diversion from studying. Klaus lives with his brother, Günter, and their Uncle Martin and Aunt Gertrud in a house by one of the many locks in Mecklenburg's waterways. Martin is a foreman for the *Wasserstraßenamt* (Department of Water Transportation) in that province. Klaus and Günter live with their aunt and uncle because their parents were murdered by the Nazis on 4 August 1944 (IB 169). Jürgen is a party loyalist and sincere believer in the socialist ideals that have been introduced into their lives. His father is absent from the scene as well, having been arrested and taken away after the war for his association with the Nazi party. Klaus and Jürgen's friendship is truly remarkable because they have two reasons to be antagonistic toward each other—not only were their parents on opposing sides during the war, but both young men are in love with Ingrid. She is an intelligent, beautiful young woman who is a popular and highly respected person in the school and community. The narrator describes how Klaus, Ingrid, and Jürgen nurture their friendship and interact with their families, their community, their classmates, and their teachers as well as cope with the school's negative political climate. This friendship becomes novelistic by virtue of the irreversible life choices that these young people are forced to make at the story's end.

Klaus, Ingrid, and Jürgen feel compelled to decide for or against the GDR because of another member of their class, Elisabeth Rehfelde, who belongs to both the Young Congregation and the Free German Youth. When pressured one day by the head of the FDJ to choose between the two supposedly irreconcilable organizations, Elisabeth, in a gesture of defiance, tosses her FDJ membership booklet at his feet. The school director and party loyalist, Pius Siebmann, politicizes the incident, which is merely an immediate emotional response to an unfairly imposed constraint. The party organization uses this incident as a pretext to intensify a demonization process aimed at the entire Young Congregation organization. Jürgen attempts diplomatically to defuse the situation by approaching Elisabeth to admit to her that a mistake had been made and to return her membership booklet. But the party line represented by Pius prevails. Eventually Ingrid is appointed to speak to the assembled pupils, denouncing the Young Congregation as a spy organization financed and controlled by the enemy in the West. As Ingrid takes the stand before a full auditorium, she changes the subject to the importance of individuality for the development of a socialist society. She also takes the opportunity to point out indirectly that the representatives of the GDR's ruling party should have more respect for the republic's written law. As a result of this courageous speech, Ingrid is expelled from school and ejected from the FDJ, Klaus withdraws voluntarily from school, and Jürgen is reprimanded by the party because he shares Ingrid's views and will not renounce his friendship with Klaus or Ingrid. While Jürgen decides to remain in the GDR, the closing scene of the novel describes a police motorboat speeding off to a larger town, where Ingrid and Klaus will catch a direct train to Berlin and then cross the border into the West.

## Narrative Structure

*Ingrid Babendererde* is by far the least prismatic of Johnson's novels—that is, the organization of the narrative is relatively straightforward compared to his subsequent works. Little is known about the first version of the novel, but one of the later versions possesses an identifiable witness named Dietrich Erichson who narrates the story (BU 77). (Erichson, or D. E., appears again as Gesine Cresspahl's friend and lover in *Anniversaries*.) Johnson abandoned the idea of the identifiable witness for an almost omniscient narrator in the final, published version. The narrator is only almost omniscient because there remain vestiges of the book's earlier conception as a narrative of a specific, this time unnamed, witness who speaks with the reader: "there you can see" (IB 109) and "but look there" (IB 208) serve to show that another person is telling the story.[10] The most obvious sign of a knowledgeable but not all-knowing narrating witness reveals itself when Klaus, Ingrid, and Jürgen are out for their last sailing tour together. Only the three friends are in the boat, so Johnson's "unnamed witness" can only offer the perspective from land: "But (as far as can be judged from land) they were doing well" (IB 239).[11] Otherwise the narrative approach is straightforward.

Still, the narrative does not begin in a conventional manner with the initiating event of the story. Instead, Johnson commences with the adverbial construction "on the other hand" (IB 9), thereby creating what Bernd Neumann refers to as an "ironic reversal of dialectical causal thinking."[12] In other words, Johnson shows the reader first the result of the combination of events that make up the story. Effect comes before cause as two pages later the words "on the one hand" (IB 11) introduce the story of how the flight of the youths presented on pages 9 and 10 comes to be. In no other book does Johnson make so explicit the story-laden moment around which he weaves his narrative. The four larger sections of the book each open with a two-page description of the progress of the youths' emigration: section 1 alludes to the train ride to Berlin; section 2 shows Klaus and Ingrid resting in West Berlin; section 3 alludes to a stopover in an acquaintance's apartment; and section 4 describes them boarding a plane to West Germany. At the end of section 4 the narrative catches up with itself where the final page (IB 248) describes the midnight boat ride that chronologically leads back into the first page, their train travel to Berlin. The descriptions of the emigration are not included as part of the numbered chapters and they are printed in italics; their separation from the main body of the text is augmented by the vagueness of the descriptions, which represent allusions to events more than being part of any concrete plot structure. This trenchant separation of the result from the cause focuses the reader's attention on the issue of why the emigration takes place. The story behind the flight, however, remains intact in its linearity and causality, clearly laid out in sixty-one short chapters.

The prime number sixty-one possesses its own significance as an indication of Johnson's resigned agreement with Walter Benjamin, one of his principal philosophical and literary inspirations. Benjamin claims in the last of his thirteen theses for the writer that in the end, "the work is the death mask of the conception."[13] The death mask is a metaphor for the form and printed words that become the work when it is finished. The primordial inspiration, the experience of the lived moment, the authenticity of the narrative instant, and the initial idea of the work all disappear when the work comes to stand on its own in textual form (BU 88). Its original conception has flowed from it, and the shell that is left is, from that point on, open to any conception that readers supply. The life that the work subsequently receives comes from readers as they read the text and, in doing so, once again bring it to meaning. As Johnson admits, "One cannot help a book that is offered to people and read by some people. Whatever effect occurs is completely withdrawn from the control and the supervision of the author."[14] In his discussion of thesis thirteen, Johnson is either recreating his youthful disappointment at discovering such a notion or demonstrating a measure of ambivalence about Benjamin's thought. Johnson refers to this thesis as the fatal one and yet advocates similar ideas in his essay "Vorschläge zur Prüfung eines Romans," where he says that readers can and should claim authority over published texts. Despite the "fatality" of thesis thirteen, ironically, it is the condition on which the text can gain new life in reading, for the text sheds its Benjaminian death mask momentarily with each new reading. In this manner, the total number of chapters equaling the prime number sixty-one represents a disheartened acknowledgment of Benjamin's thesis written after the prime number thirteen (BU 88). Johnson recognizes the reality of Benjamin's thesis thirteen, however, for all the rest of his work and as an underlying principle of all narrative production.

## The Individual and the State

In remaining with his dialectical treatment of the subject matter, Johnson sets up certain oppositions in *Ingrid Babendererde* that serve to elucidate the antagonisms of the plot. The dissonance between individual desires and the interests of the state take their place as the fundamental opposition of the entire novel. In fact, this basic opposition would later represent the thematic focus of much of East German literature. As such, Johnson's *Ingrid Babendererde* could have been the first work in an East German literary tradition that would make as its central theme the individual's problematic relationship to the collective. In practice, the state creates an atmosphere and social order in which individual desires must clash with the state's ideologically justified interests. Ingrid's speech to the school addresses this problem as she throws open for debate the state's intrusive appropriation of individuals who believe and think differently from the state. Those who do not comply are summarily rejected and/or harassed by the state's institutions and denied access to the fruits of society, such as an education or a meaningful profession. The crux of Ingrid's speech is that the contradiction perceived by the state between individual desires and state interests is unproductive and senseless. The simple example of a pair of pants worn one day by her classmate, Eva Mau, suffices to make a point of political and sociological gravity. Eva purchased the pants in West Berlin, the territory of the capitalist enemy. The school director, Pius Siebmann, orders Eva to never wear the pants to school again, and she complies. Ingrid too has been the target of such constraints. She owns and still wears a "scandalous dress" (IB 24)— scandalous because it comes from the capitalist West. Ingrid shows that the state's control has reached absurd levels that alienate individuals from the state's goal of a socialist society more than convince or persuade them of its moral superiority.

A figure for whom the invention of qualifiers such as "Ingridbeauty" (IB 40), "Ingridirony" (IB 53), and "Ingridcountenance" (IB 42) is warranted is most suitable for addressing the importance of the individual within the collective. Unseld found these constructions *unangenehm* [unpleasant] when he initially read the manuscript.[15] In actuality, these annoying or awkward creations constitute the author's attempt to make his champion of individuality in a society that set the interests of the state, in the guise of class interests, above the interests and constitutional rights of the individual. Even her last name possesses significance for Ingrid's role as the champion of individuality. In Low German, Babendererde means "on the earth" (BU 98); thus, Ingrid conducts herself in a concrete, grounded, and basic manner that shows that the individual must possess some autonomy to become an active agent for a socialist society. The individual separated into private and collective selves represents an analogy to the prevalent Marxist theory of society, which holds that the economic base has a cultural superstructure. In other words, party functionaries who curtail and scorn expressions of individuality are unquestionably familiar with a premise for thinking in terms of dichotomous positions (base and superstructure) that form and shape each other. However, the application of such dialectical thinking does not transfer in government representatives' minds to the distinction between the private self and the collective self. Ingrid's rhetorical speech questions whether it is more important that young people support the party doctrines in a genuine manner or that they stoically submit to the party's heavy-handed tactics. In this respect her speech is not confrontational but is a plea for understanding and prioritizing with the needs of individuality in mind yet on behalf of the state's goals to establish a socialist society.

Ingrid does not defend individual self-determination in direct defiance of the dogmatic and all-powerful school director. In fact, she attempts to remind the assembly of the words of the director himself, ostensibly by quoting him— "In this time all ways lead to communism" (IB 174)—and implicitly by expressing her opinion candidly, taking Pius at his word that they live in a truly democratic order with the freedom of expression as one of its social and political pillars: "Pius had spoken for some time about the right of democratic expression of opinion" (IB 173). Ingrid does not argue against the validity of Pius's "books" for their education, but she defends Eva's right to wear any pair of pants she wishes while expressing that Peter Beetz has the constitutionally guaranteed right to belong to and wear the badge of the Young Congregation. In her speech, Ingrid goes from the benign and insignificant to the lofty and ethereal elements of being an individual, from a decision of what to wear to school on a given day to a principled belief system by which to guide one's practices in life. She shifts the focus of the discussion from the putative incompatibility of the communist and Christian world views to the value of the individual in the collective, which for her is a more basic and immediately pressing issue. She implies that socialist society will only establish itself after individuals can know themselves, which requires a type of fundamental freedom that the state is apparently not willing to grant. Ingrid suggests that communism can evolve only from the basic starting point of the self-assured and free-thinking individual.

The discrepancy between the state's words and its actions exposes the fact that it does not take its own words seriously or demonstrate any trust in its people. If the state is really only interested in the blind submission of its people and superficial compliance with party doctrine, then the legacy of socialist ideals will never be passed down in any genuine manner to future generations. Jürgen intimates as much when he accuses an especially ambitious and militant fellow pupil and party loyalist of having "the wrong way of going about persuading" (IB 114). Just as the Marxist base determines the views and institutions of the superstructure, so the quality of an individual's private life will create the public person who is an agent for the good of the collective. Johnson's precocious young people quickly ascertain that the Socialist Unity Party does not believe in its own idealistic notions. Klaus, Ingrid, and Jürgen are constrained to create among themselves a sort of resistance movement in the face of this dogmatism.

However, modifiers such as *heroic, brave, intrepid,* and so on are too flamboyant and superficial to suit Johnson's manner of positioning his characters against the state's ideological imperatives. The ethos of resistance in *Ingrid Babendererde* is captured in two prevalent words that only occur in conjunction with characters in the community who either maintain a resistant association to the dominant power or come into open conflict with it. Thus these modifiers, *überlegsam* and *höflich,* apply only to characters who possess a decidedly distanced relationship to the state. *Überlegsam* is an especially curious neologism whose meaning is difficult to discern. However, taking the meanings of *überlegen* in its various forms together with the suffix -*sam* results in a working definition of "reflexive in a superior manner." *Höflich* means "polite"—that is, to be conscious of or recognize the relative position of and demonstrate respect for (an)other person(s). Politeness involves everything a community requires to be human and civil in its demeanor, a sense of the word that comes through in *Speculations about Jakob* and *Anniversaries* as well. Both adjectives describe a communal attitude that is set against the aggressive, self-promoting, and unreflective power represented by the school director. These modifiers take the segmenting and decentering competitiveness out of the community's political existence. They slow down the political tempo and confuse the antagonistic atmosphere that the party seeks to create, while the *überlegsame* and *höfliche* person exercises an annulling effect on confrontational action. Only an individual of true independence can be "superiorly reflective" because only an individual can think about self and other simultaneously. Klaus, Ingrid, and Jürgen see the many sides of the issue at hand. These adjectives or adverbs are badges of integrity that, no matter how superior in a moralistic way, still cannot win against the political power of the party. Of course, *höflich* and *überlegsam* are modifiers that signal to readers a character of solid inner spiritual and personal strength. Thus, as words that describe persons in a state of passive resistance, it is not possible to say with complete conviction that the Socialist Unity Party ever really wins, despite the fact that its policies and tactics force Klaus and Ingrid to leave the country. Many who opposed the regime in a similar fashion did not leave. Nonetheless, history shows that the Socialist Unity Party never truly established itself as a legitimate political authority: in 1990, East Germans voted for a rapid unification with West Germany, demonstrating that relatively few citizens had been convinced that the socialist system in the form familiar to the population was worth reforming.

Johnson employs a musical motif to further distinguish between stagnant party discourse and youthful exuberance—that is, he accentuates with music the difference between expected uniformity and the desire for self-expression. Nothing fluidizes the humors more readily than music; listening to jazz thus offers a refreshing respite to these pupils from the quiescent and oppressive atmosphere of school. Jazz, however, signifies something greater than just another venue of escape and self-determination for Klaus, Ingrid, and Jürgen. For Johnson the spirit of the individual does not live only in his characters but also exists authentically and suggestively in this music. The jazz motif comes through with consistency in the text and represents a musical discourse in line with these young people's struggle to claim and defend their individuality. Born out of the African American musical tradition, jazz has often served as a music of resistance, a function that it performs in Johnson's novel as well. Listening to jazz, something Johnson himself often did, is a political risk for Klaus, Ingrid, and Jürgen. It is a genre not officially sanctioned by the East German government and is available only via the American Forces Network, the enemy's radio station in West Berlin. For Johnson jazz codifies the dynamic relationship of the individual to the socialist society depicted in *Ingrid Babendererde*. Johnson places the students' love of jazz in sharp contrast to Pius Siebmann's speech patterns, which are "almost singing" (IB 87), "melodic" (IB 221), or like a "song" (IB 226). Thus, jazz music stands in marked contrast to the singsong fluency with which Pius expresses the party doctrine to his pupils. Often the words in Pius's oratorical barrages are spelled together to stress their monotonous flow and their total uniformity, something he expects of his pupils. Here the spontaneous and joyful improvisations of jazz explode the repressive and mindless submission to party doctrine expected by the state. In jazz, although there is one overriding harmonic structure to which the musicians adhere, individual players improvise their own variations and unique musical statements within that framework. Thus, in its resistance to rigidity, its structure of organized disorder, and its unifying harmonic framework, jazz entirely harmonizes with the attitude of the three friends (especially Klaus). Jazz codifies in the novel an ideal fusion of the private and the public, the individual and the collective, a social dynamic in which there is room for expression of the self within the broader collective. It is music that is part of a world of escape but also a metaphorical affirmation to how circumstances could be different, for jazz music creates an analogy to a society in which flight to the West would not be necessary.

The experiences of Klaus, Ingrid, and Jürgen in their water environment and in school represent yet another opposition that gives balance and proportion to the narrative as well as creates a revealing dichotomy in the text. Norbert Mecklenburg refers to the morning hours of school as wasted life, as opposed to the afternoon hours of the love story and a successful, fulfilling life.[16] The natural surroundings of Mecklenburg are the locales for the bonding of these young friends; their love, trust, and respect for each other resonate with the wind, the water, and the reeds of the familiar landscape. In school they are bored and forced to make a stand in their relationship to a regime that accepts nothing less than absolute loyalty and obedience to the party line. It is in their altercations with the state that the potential for weakness in their bonds of friendship become apparent. The results of the assembly to which Ingrid delivers her talk turn out to be nothing more or less than an ideological litmus test as Pius discovers who is for and who is against the party. The fustian charade of the assembly stands in marked contrast to the honest and open assessment of the political atmosphere outlined by Ingrid in the assembly and later by Jürgen in private consultation with Pius. Symbolic of their potential division in the face of political confrontation, the friends find themselves in three distinctly separate spaces as each person copes differently with the climactic event. Klaus, in a gesture of individualism, avoids the conflict completely and goes sailing by himself. Jürgen, seated in the auditorium, remains quiet throughout the meeting but is one of the seventeen dissenting votes against the 289 who vote to expel Ingrid from school and the FDJ. Ingrid—and this is the reason the novel carries her name as its title—counters the injustice done to her classmates honestly, unreservedly, directly, and with her integrity fully intact at the podium in front of those who will judge her. The last year of school forces the three characters through an unpleasant maturation process that they do not wish to face. In the natural environment of the Mecklenburg landscape there is no necessity to grow up, while the approaching final examinations and political expectations of school and society represent the vacuous, hypocritical world that awaits them as adults.

Since Jürgen has voted against Ingrid's shunning, he creates yet another opposition in his stance against Pius's dogmatic and ineffectual pedagogical style. If Ingrid champions the individual in a socialist society, then Jürgen is the champion of a humanistic, pluralistic, and democratic socialism: "He felt that the arguments used were pretexts that were supposed to justify the prohibition of another opinion instead of discussing it" (IB 226). Jürgen lists the articles of the constitution that were breached in Pius's action against the Young Congregation and those who refused to join the attack on the group. Pius and Jürgen obviously disagree on the fundamental issue of the function of the constitution. Jürgen views the document as a broadly based consensual agreement on the ultimate value and inalienability of certain human rights. For Pius and the party apparatus, it apparently has no function in politics save for its use to advance particularistic party goals. In other words, whenever the establishment of its unquestioned power is at stake, the party recognizes no mistakes or contradictions in its actions. This particular party stance underscores Pius's otherwise inexplicable name: "Nobody knew why Pius was called Pius. Popes were called such, and indeed Pius was at the head of the school and its party organization with such authority" (IB 86). The authority and infallibility of Pius, like those of the Pope, manifest themselves in his actions and reflect an expected ideological premise of the time expressed in a poem and popular song of the period in which a line reads "Die Partei hat immer recht" (the party is always right). Standing independently, Jürgen engages the dogmatism of the school director, admits that he voted against the party line, and suffers a reprimand, which he rejects on both moral and legal grounds. The blemish of a party admonition on his record, however, leaves little doubt that Jürgen will have difficulties advancing or obtaining meaningful work opportunities in that society. He has revealed himself to be "politically unreliable," a label used in the former GDR by the party to mark and stigmatize undesirable citizens. His personal traits of honesty, sincerity, and fairness as well as his dedication to a humanistic altruism where the constitution is concerned point more to tragic flaws than to useful values that are rewarded in the context of the GDR's existing socialist society.

## Test of Maturation

The novel does not dwell on the emigration of Klaus and Ingrid to the West or Jürgen's adversity with the Socialist Unity Party. The fact that their lives have been negatively affected by party politics is the result of a greater issue that involves the lack of a consensus concerning the ideals on which their society purportedly bases itself. Johnson creates in Klaus, Ingrid, and Jürgen three people who should feel quite at home in the new socialist order. Johnson provides each character a basis on which he or she could feel a sense of solidarity with the socialist regime. Klaus's parents perished at the hands of the same fascist government that sent many communists and Social Democrats to the concentration camps. On this account he should be a preferred child of the regime. Ingrid has wealthy relatives in the capitalist West, in Lübeck, but expresses personal difficulty in her relationship with them and their money. She could have chosen to live with them years ago but desires to remain with the community in which she feels comfortable. She possesses an innate sense of social fairness for the distribution of wealth, one that is in line with party doctrine. As Johnson intimates elsewhere, Klaus and Ingrid leave for the West, to a way of life that they consider wrong (BU 87). Jürgen, whose father was a Nazi, is especially drawn to the new ideals of the fledgling socialist society despite his origins in the propertied middle class (his mother owns a lawn and garden shop). He believes in socialism because of what Johnson has referred to as the "two moral roots" of GDR society: the antifascist stance and its social achievements.[17] Johnson wrote this novel with a presupposition about the psychological and emotional development of these seventeen-, eighteen-, and nineteen-year-olds. He claimed that like most people their age, they want to accept the social order in which they live: these young people "of course" try to live according to the socialist principles they learn in school.[18] Thus, any system caught in a falsehood or acting in contradiction to its stated values and guiding principles, "can get eighteen- and nineteen-year-olds riled up and cause them to doubt the wisdom of the State."[19] The tragedy of the story is that the government, as represented in this Mecklenburg community, is not able to prove to these young people that socialism represents a system morally superior to the previous regime or to the Western alternative, as the government continually states to be the case. The implementation of socialist ideals through arbitrary intimidation, coercion, falsehoods, and demonization of certain communal elements smacks of fascist strategies. The party obviously seeks to annihilate all opposition to consolidate its dominant role in the lives of the population. In an unpublished version of the novel, Johnson likened the Stasi of the Socialist Unity Party to the Gestapo of the Nazi party.[20] The manner in which the regime, represented by Pius Siebmann, treats the young people of the school as they attempt to defend the socialist and democratic ideals from abuse by the very regime that propounds them leads to Klaus and Ingrid's disillusionment and ultimate flight to the West. Only the optimist Jürgen is prepared to stay and see what will come of the principles in which he sincerely believes.

Johnson's novelistic conflict ostensibly revolves around a genuine political issue, the antagonism between the worldviews of the Young Congregation and the FDJ. However, as is often the case with Johnson's work, the circuitous poignancy of this text is located in revealing the corruption of greater values of trust, steadfastness, and consistency in upholding stated ideals. These are the deeper issues that resonate in the action of the story. After all, none of the main characters who forfeit their futures in the GDR by defending the right of the Young Congregation to undertake its activities freely is actually a member of that group. Viewed this way, the subtitle of the novel as a test of maturity takes on its full significance. Indeed, the young friends face dire circumstances in their coming of age, but the GDR government is also measured in its political maturity throughout the story.[21] The outcome of the many-leveled conflict of the novel proves that the state fails miserably to demonstrate the integrity of its goals, while the youngsters represent a level of mature and courageous conduct that reaches beyond any measure of development that the state can hope to achieve. Klaus, Jürgen, and Ingrid realize that they must stand by their convictions or commit themselves to an existence of falsehood or voicelessness. As Walter Schmitz explains, "The choice between the 'truthfulness' of a direct perception of reality and the 'realistic' adaptation to the power creation of the party signifies in Johnson's novel the actual 'test of maturity.'"[22] Even though the three friends are not involved in the particulars of the incident, none of them can stand by and allow principles in which they believe, emotionally invest themselves, and have adopted as their own to be marred by shortsighted, particularistic, political dogmatism. Their authentic sign of maturity is manifested in the fact that the pupils do not lose sight of their higher principles in the commotion of political altercation. They do not allow themselves to be forced to think opposi-tionally about their own self-interest as the state pursues its interests. Their attention remains fixed on the principles at issue while the party loses its vision for anything higher than the immediate, self-interested assertion of its power.

But Johnson's story concludes with some major questions unanswered and remains despairingly open-ended in this respect. Although maturity indicates a completion of a developmental process, the *Reifeprüfung* ("test of maturity") is unfinal and remains untreated in this novel. The perfection or completion in development that the term *maturity* implies is not attained because these young people make decisions for whose mastery they do not possess the emotional capacity. This is especially the case with Klaus and Ingrid, whose emigration implies that they believe they can live in the West in a less contradictory and more honest manner. In reality, new tests of maturity await them there, because the same premises that allowed them to relate to the East German state—the death of Klaus's parents at the hands of the Nazis and Ingrid's alienating rela-tionship to her wealthy relatives—will return to loom up at them as they live with the disproportionate distribution of wealth and witness the freedom of ex-Nazis to exist in peace in the West. Jürgen's decision to stay is equally naive since humanistic socialism is as impossible in the East as it would be in the West. Although humanistic socialism is potentially realizable, his party com-rades do not possess the courage or imagination to see their own errors and thereby to pursue socialism's grander possibilities. Thus, the reader can imagine a subsequent life for Jürgen that will offer him only frustration until he com-promises his beliefs, leaves the GDR, or is imprisoned.

## Politics and the Community

*Ingrid Babendererde* possesses an abundance of motifs and issues that speak to young people facing transitions in their lives and to the diversions that allow them to forget those anxiety-ridden changes. The friendship among Klaus, Ingrid, and Jürgen revolves around sun, water, boating, camping, swimming, studying, examinations, and social life. All three enjoy a harmonious life in the community before the party, in the person of Pius Siebmann, plays a more intru-sive role in their lives. Politics, in this respect, becomes an unnatural addition to the communal experience of the three main characters. What the party views as the evils of society are, in actuality, vital aspects of the harmony and homeostasis of the small community. Herr Wollenberg and Jürgen's mother are both, by definition, "capitalists" since each makes a living selling wares (jewelry and garden supplies, respectively) for profit. Since Jürgen is a member of the party, he maintains a rather difficult relationship to his mother, who feels threatened that the party that wants to dispossess her of her property is now, in a sense, living in her house. Herr Wollenberg is a kind old man who sells to Klaus (at a discount) a token of love to present to Ingrid. Neither Jürgen's mother nor Herr Wollenberg represents an enemy of the working class, although readers fear that they will end up like the farmer mentioned at the beginning (IB 13)—in the West with their property confiscated by the state. The Christian faithful in town are also viewed as enemies of a state that instructs its citizens to "purge vigilantly and inexorably our ranks of the enemies of our democratic order" (IB 140). Of course Herr Wollenberg and Frau Petersen are not industrialists who have millions in capital surplus at their disposal while they exploit thousands of workers; nor are the Christians, such as Elisabeth Rehfelde and Peter Beetz, Western agents working for the demise of the East German republic. Thus, the attacks on the putative enemies of the fledgling socialist republic immediately amount to attacks on friends and upstanding citizens.

The community in which the three main characters reside possesses a distinct common heritage and culture expressed in its common Low German language. The political aims pursued by Pius are interests of the Socialist Unity Party, putative class interests that are not shared by the members of the community. He expresses them only in High German, which has an alienating and distancing effect on the community. Johnson elucidates Pius's lack of compromise and a certain arrogance by never putting a Low German word in his mouth. But his lack of any Low German phrases is one more proof that his politicking is an unwanted external phenomenon lacking any real connection to the community. Jürgen is the only bona fide member of the community who has joined the party and adopted party doctrine as his own belief system. But even he does not see a "class struggle," as the party doctrine stipulates (IB 167). For Jürgen, politics comes from the foreign, unfamiliar outside as expressed in the time when discord reigns among the three friends; as Ingrid's mother explains, "It was nothing between you but something outside of you: something political" (IB 190). The local police, too, guard their fellow citizens against the intrusions of the state security apparatus as, one morning, one of its members trails Ingrid on her walk through town (IB 211). The police normally worked along with state security in pursuit of citizens it deemed suspicious, but here the policeman realizes that the political directive that motivates the hated Stasi is misguided. He knows this based on his familiarity with the person, with Ingrid. Thus, Heini Holtz's interference on behalf of Ingrid, ironically against the state that he is supposed to defend, only accentuates Ingrid's direct, natural, and unproblematic relationship to the community. It is an unfeigned, ingenuous relationship that neither Jürgen nor Pius can establish (IB 110). The schoolteachers themselves, supposed disseminators of ideological material in a dictatorship, cannot relate in any effective manner to the information that they must pass on to their students. Klaus realizes that his teacher cares as little as Klaus himself does about the material to be imparted: "Up there stood this well-bred and educated and thoroughly honorable gentleman . . . , he said things that were really unpleasant for him to say, because he certainly felt they were degrading and uncivil . . . things, moreover, that none of his listeners cared about (with one exception)" (IB 17–18). The political agenda of the Socialist Unity Party is unconvincing in its urgency and demonstrates itself to be, in its present form, an unnatural addition to the existence of this small Mecklenburg town whose houses stand with "discretion and reliability" and whose people speak "deliberately in an ironic friendly manner" (IB 36). The local imperviousness to ideological sway makes the 289 votes against Ingrid all the more a sign of necessitated and pragmatic collaboration rather than genuine conviction.

In their interaction with the dominant political doctrine, Klaus, Ingrid, and even Jürgen turn out to be distinct representatives of their community, Klaus and Ingrid because they reject outright the socialist society in its real form and Jürgen because he, in a true communal and democratic spirit, "seeks political discussion" within the newly established socialist order.[23] In a sense Johnson continues writing about Klaus, Ingrid, and Jürgen in his future works because their postures reflect those of many other characters. Ingrid and Klaus represent precursors of Gesine Cresspahl (*Speculations about Jakob* and *Anniversaries*), Karin F. (*The Third Book about Achim*), and Beate Dusenschön (*Two Views*), all of whom retreat or run away from the contradictions inherent in the socialist system. Jürgen possesses even more "epic twins"[24] such as Jonas Blach (*Speculations about Jakob*); Achim T. (*The Third Book about Achim*); and Dieter Lockenvitz, Pius Pagenkopf, and Gerd Schumann (*Anniversaries*)—figures who are, on some level, aware of the system's flaws and either placidly accept them or openly challenge the system in a bid to improve it. They all pay a high price for their close association with the state, either through imprisonment or societal alienation.

To distance themselves from the political arena in which Pius Siebmann has established his rule and his rules, if only superficially, the three go sailing together one final time. Here, while the other members of their class take their final exams, they lick the wounds dealt them in the assembly while silently reaffirming their friendship and loyalty to each other. Political confrontations are affairs that take place outside the comfort zone of their togetherness, which becomes most apparent when the three sailors encounter a storm. The shrillness of Pius's party rhetoric, the drone of the schoolteachers, and the complacency of fellow citizens toward the social order of the ruling party make the silent communication of these young people in the face of the storm all the more poignant: "It was important there that they could completely and quickly understand each other merely with glances" (IB 239). Despite the din of the wind and rain, each friend communicates with the other two; each knows his or her task; each understands what the other is doing; yet none speaks a word. In this highly symbolic scene the three of them operate the boat through the tempest in a silent team effort; like their friendship, their boat does not capsize (IB 240). Their relationship is based on such a high degree of trust and dedication that it prevails in the direst of circumstances. This scene establishes a metonymic connection with the community at large. It is one of Johnson's key images, one in which the quiet communication between members of a community or family creates a hermetic realm of seclusion to which the state possesses no access. The citizens of Jerichow in *Speculations about Jakob* and *Anniversaries* communicate constantly in this manner, merely with meaningful looks, glances, nods, and smiles. Beate Dusenschön in *Two Views* communicates in this manner with those who will help her across the border. Furthermore, Achim T. in *The Third Book about Achim* utilizes this type of communication with his team to win bicycle races for the state. The relationship of the three friends to each other and the school administration parallels, in effect, that of members of Johnson's invented communities to the superimposed political order of the Socialist Unity Party. Johnson offers literary examples of what later came to be known as the "niche society," described by the West German diplomat Günter Gaus as a private place in which East Germans found refuge from their overly politicized surroundings. It is a phenomenon that grew out of the necessity of GDR citizens to withdraw into "realms free from the ruling doctrine."[25] In this respect the water and the boat mean much more than mere recreation to this group of young people. Like the moat of a fortress, the water offers protection from the onslaught of the enemy trying to divide them.

## Political Education

When the students of the Gustav Adolf-Oberschule enter the school, they walk past quotations from Goethe and Marx. Above Goethe's name the pupils read, "May humans be noble, helpful, and good," while Marx reminds them, "Work is the source of all culture" (IB 24). These quotations represent a direct response to the terror regime that held Germany in its grip from 1933 to 1945. Goethe creates a connection to an earlier humanistic tradition in Germany whose national culture had been defiled by twelve years of fascist rule. The reconstruction of Germany necessitated a more positive cultural legacy, which ministers of culture and education found in classic German literature. Here Goethe sets a tone for a society that values and respects all individuals in the community and emphasizes the nobler character of which humankind is capable. Goethe writes in celebration of the innate, divine goodness in people. He addresses the entirety of humankind with his assumption that human beings are noble, helpful, and good, thus setting certain premises for societal norms. The quotation from Marx echoes his base-and-superstructure model of society. Work, as an aspect of the base, belongs to the economic structure in which women and men work and produce. According to Marx, culture and its institutions grow out of the economic base; thus, they appear according to and appropriate to the economic structure. The Marxist subtext here tells the pupils that their work in and for a morally superior socialism will lead to a morally superior culture. The socialist economic base, then, through the individual's work, will create suitable political, educational, and judicial institutions as well as shape philosophical, artistic, and cultural views in accordance with them. Furthermore, work promotes individual development while it creates a basis on which members of society can relate to each other. Thus, work helps to integrate the individual with the larger socialist community.

These short but meaningful utterances at the entrance to the school expose the students to an entire humanistic and socialist belief system that is meant to guide the school and the society in which they live. The conflict arises when the students see these noble beliefs on display every day as slogans but do not see them confirmed by the government that placed them there. Goethe and Marx are systematically ignored. The gap between the ideal and the real becomes too great to be tolerable for these idealistic young people, so they reject the falsehood that intimidates them.

In a school in which "Friendship!" has become an obligatory greeting, Friedrich Schiller's (1759–1805) poem "Die Bürgschaft" ("The Hostage") offers an obverse view on the story of Klaus, Ingrid, and Jürgen, and the friendship dictated by political authority that stresses the subversiveness of true friendship in the face of authoritarian rule. Schiller's poem is about a rebel who is caught in his attempt to assassinate a tyrannical king. The king arranges for an immediate execution, but the rebel asks for time to return home to marry off his sister. In other words, he must fulfill another obligation at home before paying his debt to the king. The king grants the request because the rebel's friend has agreed to remain in his stead and be executed should the rebel fail to return in three days. The rebel makes it safely home and marries off his sister but encounters floods, robbers, and extreme heat that hinder his speedy return. The rebel, however, perseveres and at the last moment bursts onto the scene to save his friend's life. The king is so touched by the loyalty of the two friends that he spares their lives and asks to be included in their exemplary friendship. By the sheer emotion of the moment and fine example of these two friends, he is converted from a tyrant to a friend.

In the subtly subversive stance he often displays, Klaus offers to read "Die Bürgschaft" for the German class conducted by an unpopular teacher whom the students refer to as the "Blond Poison." He does not read the original version by Schiller but a poetic study of Schiller's poem by Bertolt Brecht (IB 98–99).[26] Thus, Klaus presents the heritage of German classic literature with a Marxist twist. Brecht's version only alludes to the story of Schiller's poem and instead accentuates the themes of trust and loyalty as they pertain to contractual agreements and financial arrangements. Brecht implies that this example of trust maintains the capitalist system that counts on goods being delivered, contracted work being completed, and financial arrangements being honored. Brecht shows that noble principles such as trust, honor, and loyalty are, in actuality, based on self-interest. This reading ostensibly makes the poem acceptable in the Blond Poison's classroom, but the students evoke Schiller's subtext, in Brecht's version, about the power of goodness and steadfastness in the face of the tyrannical ruler. One student, in the many spontaneous reactions that erupt, shouts out, "What would the leader of all peoples say to that?" (IB 99). The "leader of all peoples" is the Soviet dictator, Joseph Stalin (1879–1953), who at the time of the novel has been dead for two months. He along with his miniature, Pius Siebmann, obviously represent, for Klaus and the entire 12A high school class, the tyrant in Brecht's and Schiller's poems. Klaus seeks to evoke that message with the poem, which in its own way touches on the major themes of the novel. He explains to his teacher that he possesses an "indirect" relationship to the classics. Thus reading Schiller through Brecht in the voice of a newscaster ironizes his use of eighteenth-century poetry to speak about twentieth-century life to such an extent that his innate criticism establishes a spiritual allegiance to his classmates while excluding the teacher. The immediate application of the poem's message for the students in their own grappling with political issues resonates more with Schiller's version. Klaus and his classmates understand the poem's subversive nature in the context of the antagonism between the FDJ and the Young Congregation as well as the value of real friendship in the face of the inappropriate and ungenuine friendship dictated by the party.

Thus Schiller's and Brecht's poems possess significance for *Ingrid Babendererde*'s plot on two levels. If trust, loyalty, love, and friendship are the qualities on which contracts and agreements can be made, then the ruling Socialist Unity Party proves that it contains none of these traits with regard to honoring the GDR's constitution. Its aggressive pursuit of the members of the Young Congregation is a blatant breach of its own contract with the people. Thus, the pupils involved with the conflict all understand that the constitution should be an objective document from which societal norms and rights are derived. It should stand as a promise above which no one can act. The integrity of the constitution is in jeopardy when political norms can be opened to the whim and arbitrary application of the ruling party. In a more private manner, the poem speaks to the possibility of transforming tyrants through an appeal to any humanistic feelings they may harbor. The poem foreshadows the negative outcome of the novel. The trust, loyalty, and love among Jürgen, Ingrid, and Klaus will remain strong, as in the poem, but the affirmation of their friendship in the face of the tyrant will have no affect on the miniature Stalin, Pius. Ingrid has a less idealistic reading of the poem as she realizes that tyrants do not possess the capacity to transform, which she acknowledges in a discussion of Schiller's version of the poem with the Blond Poison. Ingrid comes to this realization with a "start" (IB 101). As the thematic guide of the novel, Ingrid signals that readers should also know that tyrants are not predisposed to reform. This foreknowledge of the futility of their situation, the realization that they can neither reform nor conform, moves Ingrid and Klaus to leave their homeland. For these students Schiller's idealism does not become reality in their struggle with the tyrant.

# CHAPTER 4

# Deadly Choices

*Speculations about Jakob*

When *Mutmaßungen über Jakob* (*Speculations about Jakob*) appeared on the West German literary scene in 1959, it was an instantaneous success.[1] With the appearance of Uwe Johnson's first published novel and two other now classic novels, *Die Blechtrommel* (*The Tin Drum*) by Günter Grass and *Billard um halbzehn* (*Billiards at Half-Past Nine*) by Heinrich Böll, German literature again obtained world-class status for the first time since the 1920s and '30s. This new generation of authors announced the rejoining of Germany to the global community of literati. In its own way, each novel shows German cultural distinctiveness of the postwar period fused with timeless and culturally nonspecific human concerns. The narrative structures of these novels confirm the existence of mutually resonating literary influences that reached beyond the borders of contemporary Germany. Yet they demonstrate a continuity of narrative approaches that extends to authors such as Döblin, Thomas and Heinrich Mann, Sartre, Hemingway, Joyce, Faulkner, and other modern writers.

*Speculations* itself represents an especially interesting piece of work, for it reflects a diverse set of influences to which its young author (Johnson was twenty-five when it appeared) had been exposed as well as touches on certain themes that captured Johnson's interest and inspired him as a citizen of the German Democratic Republic. With *Speculations* Johnson introduced a new thematic element into the West German literary scene, accentuating thereby the uniqueness of his perspective. For the first time since 1945 a literary talent treated the issue of a divided Germany in fiction and did so in such a genuine and candid manner that dogmatic elements from both sides of the cold-war border treated the author and the novel with suspicion. Problems with West German officials came later, but in fact, Johnson was forced to leave his beloved GDR upon publication of the manuscript (BU 152–53), which meant for him a drastic and unwanted lifestyle change. Understandably the novel was never published in the eastern part of Germany until the GDR ceased to exist on 3 October 1990. Thus for the rest of his career Johnson would write about life in the GDR without his

East German compatriots ever reading his novels about their circumstances except for an occasional copy smuggled over the border.

Although generally well received, Johnson's first published novel came under criticism from the more conservative literary critics in the West. In *Speculations* Johnson utilizes a mixture of narrative strategies, including dialogue, inner monologue, and semiomniscient narrator to convey the story. In other words, Johnson employs first-, second-, and third-person perspectives to tell a story that, even with this much narrative innovation and perspective, completely eludes and frustrates readers' desire for a satisfying resolution. Inner monologues appear in italics (a device Johnson learned from his extensive reading of Faulkner), while dialogues are marked merely by a dash to designate another speaker. Otherwise Johnson provides no markers as to who is speaking, thinking, or telling the story. The translator of the novel, Ursule Molinaro, labeled the inner monologues with characters' names, but no such guidance is available in the original German version. There are five numbered chapters but no chapter headings that identify a particular point in the story line or a general thematic issue. Due to the difficulty of the book's narrative structure, the publisher urged Johnson to write a short synopsis for inclusion on the inside cover of paperback editions, which he did. However, Johnson crossed out the synopsis in at least one signed copy of *Speculations*, indicating that he did not intend any manner of help for readers, who must infer the speakers' identity from the contents and context of what is being said. Johnson's use of unorthodox orthography, Mecklenburger dialect, foreign languages (English and Russian), word order that mimics dialectal idiosyncrasies, and certain anglicisms adds to the strain on readers; these elements of the novel compelled one critic to call *Speculations* "unnecessarily complicated,"[2] while another critic maintained, "Seldom has a narrating book so stubbornly demanded so much goodwill from its readers."[3] But the complication level of the text is not insurmountable. Johnson reminded his public, "I wrote the book as though people would read it as slowly as I wrote it."[4] The novel is difficult, but there is much to gain by persisting in reading its 300 pages (German version) or 240 pages (translated) to appreciate the craftsmanship with which Johnson fused the content and form of the novel. Slow, attentive reading is the key to obtaining a fuller understanding of the narrative in its sensitivity to the personalities of its characters, the importance of the global issues it addresses, and the depth to which it goes to reveal the full complexity of people caught up in political and personal conflict.

*Speculations about Jakob,* like *Ingrid Babendererde,* was conceived and written in the former GDR: Johnson began writing *Speculations* in the spring of

1957. Although he never openly espoused any particular political party line, the theme of an ideal socialism is quite prevalent in this novel. Johnson moved to the West because he feared that the East German government would miscon-strue his text as a criticism of life in that country. In an interview he admitted his fear "that the East German authorities would misunderstand as attack or indictment what was a story or explanation. And this misunderstanding would have certainly had some manner of consequences."[5] It was not Johnson's inten-tion to criticize as much as it was his desire to portray, as authentically as pos-sible, the reality in which his characters went about their lives. Nonetheless, he was correct in his assumption that the novel would not go over well with East German authorities. Descriptions of members of the Russian secret service or Red Army are not always flattering; the poor state of the railroad system sug-gests the general technological backwardness of the GDR; the elegiac tone of the narrative creates a pessimistic atmosphere that intimates a general dissatis-faction with conditions in the "Workers' and Farmers' Paradise" as its citizens experienced it. Moreover, Jakob represents a positive, utopian figure in the cause for socialism, yet the author seems to imply that there is no possibility for his survival in the (socialist) world as it is. Even though Johnson includes an aspir-ing reformer in the story and two main characters of the book move to the West, in actuality neither Johnson nor his characters ever question the basic principles on which the East German state established its system of government. With the exception of Rohlfs, each character recognizes the social and economic prob-lems of the GDR. However, whether or not the characters accept the East German regime, socialism is their education and their preferred system of gov-ernment, rather than the capitalist West from which, in classic Marxist-Leninist conception, fascism had developed.

More than most other European people, the Germans have had a troubled and ambivalent relationship with history. A positive consequence of this relationship has been that many German intellectuals concern themselves intensely with history, value history for understanding the present and future, and perceive a direct connection between history and politics. The other, now canonical, German novels published in 1959, for example, both possess as their central themes a coming to terms with the guilt and suffering of German histo-ry, especially twentieth-century history. In literary form, Johnson presents in *Speculations* his own processing of the German past and his version of how that past might be viewed in connection with the development of German history through the 1950s. He couches fictional actions in historical events that can be objectively verified in newspapers or scholarly history books but that encroach directly on the lives of his main characters.[6] His invented persons act according to their acute awareness of historical events; they refer to history to explain themselves; and their personal scars obtained from historical conflicts constitute, in no small way, their identities. The atrocities of the Second World War provide moral categories against which Jakob, Gesine, and Herr Rohlfs project their views of their border crossings and legitimate their socialist convictions. But the continuum of history further informs and motivates Johnson's characters to consider their alternatives and make choices, or it impels them to uncertainty and bewilderment.

## The Historical Situation

Understanding the full action of the plot requires apprehending what macroevents couch the microevents involving the novel's characters. Thus one level of *Speculations'* plot elements consists in the historical events that frame the story. Those events of the autumn of 1956 around which Johnson centers the fictional story include the Hungarian uprising against Soviet domination, the attack on Egypt by British and French troops, and the fledgling political reform movement inside the GDR. Johnson's main characters play roles, however small, in each of these world events. The events also set the narrated time of the novel, approximately five weeks in October and early November 1956.

Jonas Blach and Herr Rohlfs operate within the historically grounded conflict of a group of intellectuals acting inside the GDR to reform the country's dogmatic regime. Blach works for the group, and Rohlfs, in the role of a self-proclaimed "dogcatcher," helps to crush it. Johnson depicts here in fiction the real activities of a group of intellectuals under Wolfgang Harich, who, like Johnson, was a student of Ernst Bloch (1885–1977). As critics have pointed out, the name *Blach* recalls Bloch, a committed Marxist philosopher and a guiding spirit for GDR reformers who were active in the mid-1950s. Bloch was professor at what was then named the Karl Marx University in Leipzig when his students were arrested at the time of the 1956 crackdown. Possibly because of his fame or his age (he was seventy-two at the time), Bloch himself was not imprisoned but rather was forced into retirement. He was also punished with a teaching and publishing ban until he moved to West Germany in 1961. Before the crackdown in both Hungary and East Germany, Khrushchev (1894–1971), the Soviet leader at the time, had delivered a secret speech denouncing Stalin that was leaked to the Western press. That speech encouraged the work of reformers such as Bloch and Harich. After Stalin's death in March 1953 and in the wake of Khrushchev's secret speech criticizing Stalin's extreme dogmatism, rule by terror, and cultlike persona, Harich and his group believed that the time was right to suggest reforms for East German socialism. Harich's group hoped to end Stalinist-style rule, democratize the government, cooperate with social democratic parties in the West, and introduce economic reform while ensuring strict observance of the GDR's constitution.[7] Walter Ulbricht, head of the East German Politburo from 1949 to 1972, viewed members of this group as a threat to his power and had them arrested in November 1956. Some were sentenced to long prison terms, while others found refuge in the West.

In Hungary, reformers led by Imre Nagy had taken power and begun a democratization process that aroused the suspicion of the Soviet Union. In November 1956 the Soviet leadership sent tanks and troops to crush the democratization movement. In the West, Great Britain and France threatened Egypt with air strikes because of President Gamal Abdel Nasser's desire to nationalize the Suez Canal, a move that would have deprived Western shareholders of profits from their investments in the canal. Gesine works for NATO and thus supports, through her labor, the attack of these wealthy Western nations and NATO allies on an economically struggling former colony striving for its independence. These volatile globally significant situations provide the tension-filled background to the equally tense and perplexing microsituation of Jakob, Gesine, Jonas, and Rohlfs in their personal and political dealings with each other.

## The Story Line

Narratologists differentiate between two parts of any narrated story. The school of theorists known as the Russian Formalists speak of *fabula* versus *sjuzet,* while the French Structuralists refer to *histoire* as opposed to *récit.* These terms discern between the story as it happened chronologically and causally (*fabula* or *histoire*) and the form or version that the writer produces in conveying it to readers (or listeners) in narration (*sjuzet* or *récit*).[8] In *Speculations* the story as it happened is almost as complicated as the story as it is told. If *Speculations* has a beginning, it would have to be the point at which Rohlfs, a member of the East German Security Force, enters the lives of the other main characters—in other words, the point at which the state intrudes into the lives of its unsuspecting citizens. Those individuals whose lives are affected by Rohlfs's state-sponsored interests include Heinrich Cresspahl; his daughter, Gesine; Jakob Abs and his mother, Marie; and Jonas Blach, Gesine's friend, lover, and erstwhile English instructor at the university in East Berlin. In early October 1956 Rohlfs receives Heinrich's file, sent by superiors in preparation for a spy recruitment operation code-named "Birdie in the Hand." Rohlfs finds nothing interesting in these documents until he discovers that Gesine had left the village of Jerichow for West Germany in 1953 and now works for NATO headquarters in Mönchen-gladbach, North Rhine Westphalia, a West German province bordering the Netherlands. Gesine's position attracts the interest of Rohlfs, whose mission is to win her over as a spy for the Warsaw Pact military alliance. He also ascertains that Jakob, a twenty-eight-year-old railroad dispatcher, lives with his mother in a section of Heinrich Cresspahl's large house in northwestern Mecklenburg. Jakob and Marie came to Jerichow in 1945 as refugees from Pomerania (now western Poland) and remained there until the time of the story. Rohlfs believes he can influence Gesine through the Abs family.

In his quest to recruit Gesine as a spy, Rohlfs initially approaches Marie, who has become Gesine's surrogate mother, to establish contact. He succeeds only in frightening Mrs. Abs into fleeing to the West, where she languishes in a refugee camp for the rest of the novel. He next turns to Jakob, Gesine's adopted older brother. But Jakob is a busy person, not only as train dispatcher, a position from which he can take little time off. Without understanding why his mother has departed, he must return to Heinrich's house in Jerichow to settle her affairs, sell her belongings, and take her name off the town's registration books. On the way to Jerichow to take care of these matters, Jonas, traveling to the same destination, encounters Jakob, and at this juncture it becomes apparent that Jakob possesses a distinct and intriguing personality. Blach is passionately involved with a group of intellectuals discussing changes to the socialist state that would allow more democratic processes. Though Jakob has not uttered a word as he sits lost in thought, for Blach he embodies the ideals of a socialist community that does not yet exist. As they disembark from the train, they discover their mutual friend, Heinrich, and come to know each other on this basis.

During this time, late October 1956, the global situation becomes dangerously complicated as historical events bear down on the activities of the characters. Gesine comes to the East in an American military vehicle; she is armed with a revolver and small camera, giving the reader the impression that she is possibly already employed as a spy for the West. But the novel is not clear about what motivates her trip to the East. Because each man—Heinrich, Jakob, Jonas, and Rohlfs—has his own special relationship to Gesine, her presence generates even greater tension and discord among the characters who live in the East. She visits Jakob, Jonas, and her father in Heinrich's house (the house of her youth), where Rohlfs and his assistant, Hänschen, approach her with their proposition. Gesine is not willing to take sides for the East or the West; no deal can be worked out. However, ideas concerning the nature of socialism are exchanged while the world around them threatens to explode in conflict. Rohlfs promises

Gesine safe passage to the West, a promise Heinrich enforces with Gesine's revolver.

In a sense, rivals of every sort are depicted here. Jonas and Rohlfs, a status quo man, represent political rivals whose relationship ends in the predictable arrest of the dissident by Rohlfs. Jakob and Jonas represent rivals in their common love interest in Gesine and in their opposing positions in society (intellectual versus working-class man). However, this potentially discordant situation does not develop in any predictable way, since no real antagonism develops between Jonas and Jakob on either ground. The two men represent no rivalry in any negative or unproductive way. In fact, Jonas actually comes to admire Jakob as a working man, a practical man, a man of integrity, and an individual who naturally harbors the concerns of the socialist collective in a noncompetitive, unproblematic manner. In the course of the story Jonas and Jakob enter into a curious friendship. Jonas is so changed by his encounter with Jakob that he feels compelled to visit Jakob at his job to learn about work that is practical and economically vital to the cause of socialism. In Jakob's control tower, Jonas witnesses the maintenance of train traffic in service to travelers, commuters, and the movement of freight. As Jonas observes Jakob at work on this particular evening, however, a drama of international significance unfolds. Certain freight trains are being sidetracked to allow passenger trains to pass. The trains being held back are loaded with soldiers and military hardware destined for Hungary, where they will be used to crush Nagy's fledgling reform government. It becomes obvious to Jakob that a colleague in another tower is holding up the military freight in protest against the troop movements to Hungary. Jakob, who also does not agree with the troop movement, is forced, however, to make a decision against his own moral stance on the situation. Recognizing the futility of delaying the trains for a few minutes, Jakob orders the colleague detaining the Soviets to allow them to continue south. At this point, Jakob decides he needs to visit the West.

Rohlfs self-servingly arranges for Jakob to visit both Gesine and his mother in the West. During his sojourn there, Jakob and Gesine fall in love, but he is unsuccessful at convincing either Gesine or his mother to return to the GDR. At this point, world affairs culminate in an almost simultaneous Soviet crackdown on Nagy and the Hungarian government and the bombing of the Suez Canal by British and French aircraft. Jakob remains in West Germany for a couple of days longer, until 7 November. The next morning, as he crosses the tracks to go to work, he avoids the approach of one train only to step into the path of another; his wounds are fatal. Rohlfs arrests Jonas while he is telephoning Gesine about

Jakob's death. On 10 November Gesine meets with Rohlfs in a bar in West Berlin, where they discuss Jakob and the events that led up to his death.

## Narrative Structure and Generic Affinities

Within the initial pages of *Speculations* it becomes immediately apparent to readers that Johnson expands the role of the narrator by combining the formal methods of dialogue, interior monologue, and third-person narration. Hansjürgen Popp considers the novel to have four narrators, Gesine, Jonas, Rohlfs, and the third-person narrator.[9] However, the unidentified third-person narrator, the type that traditionally has been omniscient, speaks only when needed (BU 139). The third-person narrator fills in only when the others falter in their memories or reach the limits of their knowledge. The novel is, thus, enrichingly diverse in its approach to an intricate story but consistent in a style that allows the diversity of voices narrating the story to emerge independently of each other. Individual voices, in fact, are so autonomous that Johnson deemed it unnecessary to mark the speakers. Indeed, by reading attentively, context, relationship to Jakob, and attitude toward the East German state are enough to identify the text's dialogue partners and monologue speakers.

But Johnson takes his expansion of the formal aspects of the novel much further. It is possible to discern specific literary features in *Speculations* that more or less outline some literary trends of the time in which this revolutionary novel was published. Although Johnson never admitted to representing any literary theory or school, Johnson seems to share an affinity with the creators of the *nouveau roman*. Despite Johnson's misgivings about the *nouveau roman,* it seems to have had some effect on his notion of the novel. It is incorrect to say that *Speculations* represents a prime example of this product of the 1950s; however, it is an undeniable fact that the antilinear, multiperspectival narrative structure of this novel, with its evasive plot line, absent denouement, and yet dramatically intriguing story demonstrates elements of the *nouveau roman.* In an efficacious and poignant manner, Johnson performed the general literary task of any newly constructed novel according to the *noveau roman*'s most prolific representative and theorist, French author Alain Robbe-Grillet: "Far from respecting certain immutable forms, each new book tends to constitute the laws of its functioning at the same time that it produces their destruction."[10] Johnson is primarily concerned with conveying the story in an accurate manner, thus making the preservation of any particular form a moot point. He did not tailor the Jakob story to fit a specific generally accepted, traditional form but allowed the story to evolve into its own form as the particular problems specific to its nature necessitated their own best mode of mediation. Johnson said, "As concerns my means or methods of narration, I have conducted no experiments. I waited until I knew and had the form that I needed for the story I was familiar with and wanted to tell."[11] In fact, Johnson admitted that he could not commence with the writing of *Speculations* until he had slaughtered the "sacred cow of chronology" (BU 139); Jakob, he said, refused a normal narrative approach (BU 132). Thus *Speculations* offers an antilinear collage of genres or forms as disparate as the murder mystery, the spy thriller, the socialist-realist novel, the stream-of-consciousness novel, the psychological novel, and the romance. Elements of these various types of writings come together to create a new form in their unique combination in *Speculations.*

In the GDR of the 1950s, Johnson's artistic practice of reinventing form to suit better the content of the story would have evoked the negative label of formalist, one of the more perplexing misnomers of the East German regime. According to the country's guidelines for aesthetic expression, a formalist was a writer who did not view form as primarily fixed and thus altered form as an expression of aesthetic significance on its own account. Proponents of official doctrine advanced the idea that such writers, who privileged the concept of form over content, obscured the content, which officially was the most important aspect of a work of art. In other words, authors obfuscated the action of the novels when they chose to write the story in a nonlinear, noncausal, or as Bertolt Brecht would say, "anti-Aristotelian" manner. Indeed, discerning the beginning, middle, and end of the story in *Speculations* is difficult, but this is a novel in which content has truly determined the form (a natural state of affairs for many twentieth-century artists). According to Walter Schmitz, speculation is a formal principle of the novel, and thus the form plays along with the basic speculative element of the story.[12] *Speculations* imitates life in its speculations about life. As such, Johnson, like many authors of his stature, is an antiformalist, so much so that no form is worth preserving over the integrity of the story as narrated in a manner appropriate to its nature.

Another aspect of *Speculations* that challenges the notion that a narrated story should be based on a linearly laid out, causally connected set of circumstances derives from Johnson's frequent use of paratactic sentence structures. Theodor W. Adorno, a theorist and philosopher whom Johnson read and admired, explains that paratactic structures evade or elude the hierarchical effect of subordinating or hypotactic syntax.[13] Implicit in the hypotactic structures of sentences—where there are grammatical items such as dependent clauses and subordinating word order—is a notion that some types of information can be privileged over others. Johnson, in something as unobtrusive as the grammatical structure of his sentences, undermines any hierarchical notion of the facts that he presents to readers. A paratactic narrative structure contains an abundance of sentences, phrases, and clauses that are situated in succession but have few conjunctive words that create logical connections between sentences. The paratactic structure has the effect of dispelling causal relations between the communicated facts of the story. In this form, grammar does not have a controlling effect on readers' understandings of the events. The tendency and purpose of the narrative are truly left to readers to decide for themselves and have no legitimation within the story. Thus on every level, Johnson retreats from constraining readers to think in any one direction about the story content.

Even in the late 1950s, when the East German regime began to relax doctrines governing aesthetic expression, certain basic formal principles needed to be observed to pass official scrutiny. The official doctrine for writing literature dictated a style of realism that harked back to the prevalent form of the nineteenth-century novel. The realist novel of the nineteenth century, no matter how perplexing its central conflict might have been, typically possessed an easily identifiable beginning, middle, and end to the story as well as a causally connected narrative delivery couched in an abundance of descriptive detail. The novel presented a gratifying resolution to the conflict of the story and was usually told from the perspective of an omniscient narrator. This traditional notion of realist narrative was sanctioned by the East German regime as the only acceptable way to write prose. Add to this the fact that the development of socialism was to be the central theme of all literature produced in the GDR—prose, drama, or lyric poetry—and authors were bound in both the form and content of their works. Thus, socialist realism, an artistic concept advanced by Soviet theorists in the 1930s, became the aesthetic doctrine in the early years of the GDR. The philosophical proponent of socialist realism after the war was Hungarian literary critic and philosopher Georg Lukács (1885–1971). In accordance with Lukács, Wolfgang Emmerich described some basic features of the type of realism that found favor with the Eastern bloc regimes of the 1950s. Works were to display a "totality of life" and had to be organic—that is, had to come to a reasonable closure while respecting the laws of reality in presenting special story material within that reality.[14] Needless to say, these official stipulations led to the production of literature that was stylistically wooden, aesthetically unimaginative, and predictable in its story line.

Socialist realism produced works that not only held to certain aesthetic rules but also dealt with specific themes consisting of the socialist workplace and the struggles in it to build or improve the economic and political strength of socialism. Thus *Speculations* fits into the socialist-realist understanding of literature as far as its positive stance toward socialism and the prominence of the workplace in the novel are concerned. But Johnson undermines the basic formal stipulations of socialist realism while maintaining certain other important aspects of it in his Jakob figure. With Jakob the story centers on a positive working-class hero who is committed to socialism and, in line with his commitment, performs his duties efficiently and conscientiously for the economically vital railroad industry. As will be discussed later, Rohlfs's interpretation of who Jakob is represents a classic example of the socialist-realist hero. Concerning the technical aspects of the novel, as a young man, Johnson often took his meals in a canteen for railroad workers. He was permitted to do so because his mother worked for the East German railroad in various capacities. The conversations that he overheard there enhanced the descriptions of Jakob's work. Johnson's technical descriptions are so authentic that the translator had to consult employees of the Pennsylvania Railroad for translations of the railroad terms. Thus, Johnson couches his action in many descriptive, often technical details that inform the reader about Jakob's world of work.

However, in opposition to the formal rules of the socialist-realist novel, *Speculations* possesses no satisfying closure, possesses little sense of linearity, and is fragmented into several perspectives, all with equal validity, each voice contributing to something that does not add up to an organic whole. If anything, the concentration of these different perspectives on the single topic, Jakob, results in an ungratifying void that is created by the inaccessibility of the truth as well as the inadequacy of language as a medium for expressing personal experience. The resulting chasm grows from a collection of imperfect material, including faulty memories, personal interpretations, and unreliable, ideological slants on the events. The irony of the form and content relationship in *Speculations* is that it is more like life—that is, more realistic than the novels of (socialist) realism published before and after it. Johnson is saying in form as well as content that no narrative of life is spelled out as clearly as in "realistic" novels or in Hollywood films, for that matter.

The mutually exclusive relationship that political ideology and the notion of objective truth share compelled Johnson to make certain choices of a formal nature where the depiction of specific characters was concerned. Ironically, the depiction of the dogmatic Stasi officer benefits from Johnson's aesthetic decision that contradicted the official doctrine for literary expression. Rohlfs may have appeared in an unfairly negative light had Johnson not chosen the inner monologue to provide Rohlfs's character its most authentic, individual unfolding.[15] One would expect, for example, that the East German security official might be a clearly evil, opportunistic, and ambitious person, designed specifically to be abhorred by readers. Johnson suffered at the hands of such people, and it would only be fitting that he depict them in a negative manner. However, Rohlfs, as readers learn, performs his duty with an understandable, reasonable, and deep-rooted conviction for his cause. In his inner monologues, we learn things about his past that do not make him a positive figure, but readers are also not inclined to judge him as purely evil and villainous. Readers become familiar with the novel's characters in ways that would not be possible solely with an omniscient narrator. In this respect Johnson employs the device of inner monologue with great skill, for through it readers come to accept all the persons of the novel on the basis of their own experiences in life. Despite ideological tensions in the novel, there is no right or wrong judgment placed on the regimes or characters who cross borders between the two Germanys. The novel is thus resolutely authentic in its depiction of circumstances as they are for real people, which again throws back in the face of socialist realism the notion of what it is to write realistic narrative.

The idea that *Speculations* possesses elements of detective fiction originates from the fact that the story begins with a dead body and an indirect question as to how the person died, "But Jakob always cut across the tracks" (SAJ 7). As Johnson explains, "The narrating begins when the story is at an end,"[16] which is a central generic characteristic of murder mysteries or detective novels. Johnson himself was an avid reader of detective fiction, as were certain writers and thinkers who exercised a notable influence over his intellectual and literary development, including Marxist dramatist and poet Bertolt Brecht and philosopher and literary and cultural critic Walter Benjamin (1892–1940). As Bernd Neumann points out, one of Johnson's mentors, Bloch, read detective fiction extensively and wrote that it begins at that point when the crime has already been committed, a claim that is equally valid for Johnson's Jakob story.[17] Indeed, *Speculations* begins with a corpse and describes a quest for the truth behind the story of that death. As stated earlier, the basic narratological principle of the author's approach to the subject matter is the speculation announced in the title. The inevitable discovery of the truth at the end while identifying with likable characters and relishing animosity against evil characters make reading detective fiction a delight. Johnson, however, radically breaks from the norms of the genre in this respect. The method of reading detective fiction presupposes that, through reading, one comes ever closer to the knowledge and truth of the story; readers acquire more knowledge as they register each sentence. Johnson's novel frustrates readers' expectations of becoming wiser as they proceed through the book. Reading does not illuminate what happened to Jakob when he crossed the tracks one foggy morning, as he did every morning, only to be hit and killed by a shunter. Reading, like life, becomes an exercise in speculation rather than the accumulation of definitive facts that lead to a concrete knowledge about the way things really are. As Neumann explains, readers are expected to figure out who Jakob really is.[18] To know who Jakob is is to know how he died, yet precisely this knowledge remains elusive. Readers are set off balance from the start by the indirect question that opens *Speculations*. By commencing with an apparent retort to an utterance that does not appear in the narrative, Johnson challenges, in general terms, the attitude toward reading as a quest for knowledge. Johnson compels readers to make connections and to participate actively in the speculations of the characters.

## Views of Jakob

One of the most interesting treatments of Johnson's text is Popp's introduction to it, which is especially helpful in understanding the attitudes of individual characters. Popp discerns the main characters according to their notions of freedom within their social conceptions of themselves and how they fit into their surroundings. Jakob, for example, recognizes no freedom in his actions but performs his duty as he must; there is no other possibility for him as an individual in his particular situation. For Rohlfs, freedom is tantamount to insight into the necessity of one's actions—that is, assenting to the obligations of one's duties to society. Rohlfs believes that freedom amounts to recognizing one's function within a societal whole. Gesine is driven to act in a way other than what societal duty or political necessity might dictate to the individual. She bases her decision to leave the GDR on her personal choice, something she thinks of as freedom. Thus, her reason for leaving is generated by her feeling of hopelessness that positive transformation is possible in socialist East Germany. Freedom for her represents a path of escape, a notion that is again substantiated in *Anniversaries*. Jonas, like Gesine, views freedom as the ability to think and act differently from what is socially and politically expected by the powers that be. However, his action varies radically from Gesine's in that he remains within the social and political system's constraints for its citizens. Jonas believes that the status quo can be ameliorated by recognizing errors and reforming from within and thus decides to remain in the GDR.[19]

Viewing the characters in this manner introduces a broader issue. Johnson depicts characters who differentiate between the value placed on individuals over the community in which they exist, versus individual desires made a subordinate second to the priorities of the community decreed and enforced by the state. Johnson addresses the tension between individual desires versus collective priorities and community harmony. From this perspective, Jakob and Rohlfs place less value on individual aspirations in light of communal priorities, while Gesine and Jonas place the individual in the center of their conceptions of social beings and their actions. These implicit political stances as well as individual hopes come to fore in their conceptions of who they consider Jakob to be. The other characters' discussions reveal an appropriation of Jakob that lies at the very base of the authority of interpretation, personal assumptions about the truth, and the vulnerability of the dead to be used by the living as it suits them.

The three main voices of the narrative belong to Rohlfs, Jonas, and Gesine. Each one possesses an individual standpoint on Jakob's death and, as it turns out, each one can claim a stake in his life. With these three persons the author explores questions of guilt, truth, and loss as they express the speculations that comprise the novel. To discuss these characters separately will elucidate their relationships to Jakob as well as their individual conceptions of socialism. In an imaginary meeting, Rohlfs, Jonas, and Gesine would agree with each other about the premises on which socialism is based. Their antagonism, brought out in their discussions of the events that led to Jakob's death, reveals disagreement about the implementation of socialism as well as about the role of the individual in a socialist society. Also, through the eyes of the various characters, readers gain insight into Jakob as a person. As readers find out more about Jakob, they realize that no reliable information exists; Jakob becomes merely a composite of these various perspectives with the real Jakob forever gone from grasp.

As a government official, Rohlfs's function is to insure the continued existence of the state in its present form. He is conservative by dint of his personal history and his profession, which accounts for his negative reaction to the activities of the small reform movement inside the GDR and the uprisings in Hungary. Rohlfs is, however, a committed socialist and not necessarily an unimaginative opportunist working his way up within the state apparatus. As with many of Johnson's characters, this personage represents an interesting conjuncture of historical experience and personal involvement in the large- and small-scale events of the novel. With his unwavering communist conviction, Rohlfs already opposed Germany's fascist regime in the 1940s, at a time when it was extremely dangerous to be antifascist. Because of his political beliefs, he deserted to Soviet troops in the winter of 1942, but, while escaping, was shot in the hand and leg by his compatriots. He is permanently crippled and carries with him those battle scars as he performs his function for the state. He believes unconditionally that the system for which he works is morally superior to the capitalist system out of which fascism grew in the 1920s and 1930s. Since Rohlfs has personally suffered for the cause, he defines himself or creates his identity around the existence of the GDR. Thus, anything that he perceives as a threat to the state is simultaneously a personal menace.

In viewing Jakob as a connection to Gesine, Rohlfs initially thinks of him in purely instrumental terms. Rohlfs actually profits from this connection because he is able to arrange meetings with Gesine through Jakob, although he does not secure her as a comrade in espionage. But Jakob is not only a device for Rohlfs. In becoming familiar with Jakob, Rohlfs's conception of socialism is enhanced. As the Jakob he knows from official documents comes to life before him, Rohlfs is edified by the genuine uprightness and propriety that Jakob emanates as an individual. These traits are not mentioned outright but are revealed to the reader in Rohlfs's reaction to Jakob's words, gestures, and demeanor. Rohlfs's agonistic behavior where world politics and socialism are concerned reflects a view of socialism that reduces its ideals to points of petty rivalry with the capitalist West. Rohlfs views the socialist state for which he works only in opposition to the West. This attitude is reflected in his cui bono formula, which measures remarks, situations, ideas, or personal attitudes only insofar as they support or impair the advancement and socialist development of the GDR. If any one activity or person is perceived as impairing the socialist state, the interpretation is that, directly or indirectly, the enemy is being aided. Jakob, conversely, represents socialism as intrinsically good, a principle of integrity; he therefore has difficulties with certain realities of socialism, such as the existence of Rohlfs's intimidating security agency and the GDR's dependence on U.S. dollars to buy coal from other socialist countries. Jakob takes the evolution of socialism in the GDR to a higher level simply by not recognizing it as the competition of one economic system with another. Socialism's intrinsic ethical value as a normative system by which an entire nation can exist is demonstrated in the consistent politeness with which Jakob approaches the many people who come in contact with him. In his nonagonistic demeanor, Jakob possesses a higher consciousness about socialism than those other characters of the novel who struggle openly with the East-West dichotomy.

Thus, encountering Jakob shakes Rohlfs's conception of socialism as a simple opposition to capitalism. Even though Jakob does not change the way in which Rohlfs must conduct himself in his position as a Stasi official, Jakob transforms Rohlfs's personal views, just as he does for the other three characters. Rohlfs expresses his admiration for Jakob after their initial chat: "Suddenly I sat transfixed, immobilized with suspense, something in his way of thinking struck a chord in me; by and by, it dawned on me that it was similar to my own" (SAJ 38). Rohlfs discovers that Jakob is a good worker and loyal citizen as well as a potential friend. Their views are similar, even though Jakob can allow himself truthful but negative observations from his position as railroader. Jakob points out that many tracks are missing due to reparations paid to the Soviet Union as a result of the war. He also mentions the government's emphasis on expanding heavy industry, thus neglecting the railroad system. In Rohlfs's cui bono measurement standard, these observations could easily be construed as disparaging remarks about the wisdom of the East German leadership and the Soviet comrades who liberated the Germans from fascism. Rohlfs thinks Jakob is taking liberties in his short speech about the state of the railroad system; however, it is apparent that Jakob's dedication to socialist principles is so definitive that his observations can be allowed and treated as useful information necessary for any citizen of the GDR to possess. Jakob can constructively point out serious problems with the system and still be committed to the cause, a new concept for Rohlfs. Jakob simply provides historical explanations in delineating what must yet be done to improve life in the GDR. In short, he possesses a historical scope that Rohlfs seems to overlook or view too narrowly.

Rohlfs constructs in his mind an image of Jakob that fits his own political perspective and, interestingly, recalls the hero formula for the socialist-realist novel. In his 10 November conversation with Gesine in West Berlin, Rohlfs contradicts her report of Jakob's behavior during his short sojourn in West Germany. Rohlfs admits, "But I can't listen to you without prejudice or else I mislay Jakob. I can no longer fit him into my memory" (SAJ 221–22). For example, Jakob encounters in his hotel West Germans who treat him in a condescending manner, taking for granted that he likes it in the West, supposing his poverty, and referring to communists as "traitors." Jakob has noticed that the "Badenweiler March," a favorite of Hitler's, is available on the jukebox. Rohlfs imagines Jakob punching out a bar patron who thinks the song is pretty and who had taken Jakob to task for his socialist convictions (SAJ 220). Jakob represents for Rohlfs a fighting antifascist when in actuality Gesine has just explained that Jakob, true to his friendly nature, had gained many (unwanted) invitations to dinner, to afternoon coffee, to more evenings of beer and singing in the bar. As Johnson himself pointed out, "This story with the jukebox, that one Herr Rohlfs invents, because it fits his way of seeing."[20] In a separate situation, Rohlfs imagines Jakob sitting in Gesine's apartment forced into a maddening idleness that makes him appreciate his activity at home in the GDR. Gesine has just explained to Rohlfs that Jakob did not move from her apartment during the long days she was at work, but Rohlfs contradicts her in his fantasy. To do nothing all day is not in Jakob's character as Rohlfs imagines it. To pass the time while Gesine is at work, Rohlfs imagines Jakob feeling compelled to fix furniture, shop for her, or prepare dinner. Emmerich explains that the hero of the socialist-realist novel, based on Goethe's classic Faust figure, was to be "the model of a continuously working person" in portraying fictitious champions of socialism in novels with the intention of "spread[ing] enthusiasm for work and increas[ing] production."[21]

For Rohlfs, Jakob is a continuously active antifascist who despises the West for its decadence. Thus Johnson demonstrates how the dead live on in the interpretations of the living. Readers receive a truly idealistic composite view of Jakob. Rohlfs's representations are not necessarily inaccurate, because indications are that Jakob might have conducted himself in these ways in these specific situations. Yet they fit Rohlfs's rather narrow political scope, which is an element of his imagination that raises suspicion where his view of Jakob is concerned. It is equally valid to say that Jakob is not as limited in his persona as Rohlfs's image of him would suggest.

Rohlfs's image of Jakob is especially perplexing considering that Jakob's personage equally enhances Jonas's very different conception of socialism. Jonas is attracted to Jakob out of a sense of deficiency that spans all aspects of the professor's life. He is dissatisfied with his work as a teaching assistant in English, he is dissatisfied with the real socialism around him, and he is dissatisfied in love since the woman he desires, Gesine, lives in the West and loves another man. When Jonas initially encounters Jakob on the train to Jerichow, he immediately senses the consummate power that this man possesses for him and his cause of a democratic, humanistic socialism. Jonas's construction of Jakob is somehow beyond language, for Jakob neither says anything nor does anything to attract Jonas's attention. Jonas "noticed" (SAJ 58) Jakob on the train to Jerichow, possibly in contrast to some young East German soldiers speaking loudly and excitedly about the weapons on which they had recently been trained. Here again are the intrinsic ideals of socialism that hover about Jakob like an aura, set against the socialism as opposition displayed by the soldiers with their enthusiasm for weapons.[22] But Jonas's encounter with Jakob goes deeper than the political opposition of capitalism and socialism. More than any other character, Jonas addresses a central but subtly treated issue of the novel, the inadequacy of language to describe inspiring experiences and visionary ideas: "If I remember correctly, I immediately began searching for words, which I discarded again, one after the other. They all described a characteristic; this man didn't seem to have any" (SAJ 59). In his contribution to the group of intellectuals that has set out to reform socialism in the GDR, Jonas attempts to put into words his desire for a utopian society. When he sees Jakob, Jonas perceives the embodiment of traits that could make up that ideal society of people but discovers that the words to describe it accurately, like the utopia itself, do not exist.

Jonas generally notes those items that are most foreign to his life. He has been a world traveler who comes from the middle class, and he presently performs his duties to the socialist society as an academician. Yet he is attracted to the simple life of the country, the beauty of its landscape, and the practical concerns (and wisdom) of working-class people. Within his field of vision abound activities of a practical nature, the range of which covers the simple preparation of a schnitzel or the tending of a garden right up to the operation of the nation's railway system. Jonas is not fascinated only with the tasks themselves but also with the sense of satisfaction that he attains in partaking in practical activities. To further complicate his position, Jonas is at this point testing the limits of what it means to be an intellectual in the GDR. He possesses his own progressive thoughts about socialism; however, the guidelines are unclear about how to proceed with their realization. In a sense tending to practical needs is service to socialism in a rather unpolitical or uncontentious fashion. In Jonas's case, tending to practical concerns represents an escape from his own potentially dangerous ideas. Yet Jonas is aware of the scrutiny and judgment that cover all activities as social beings in a community, which is why he admires Jakob and cannot see the other man as having any discernible characteristics. Unlike every other character in the novel, Jakob fits evenly and smoothly into his environment: there is no friction between him as a person and the demands of his surroundings. In his completeness as a person, he lacks delineation and therefore offers no basis on which he could be judged in any definitive manner. Jonas, conversely, exists in a constant state of judging and being judged. It is significant, then, that Jonas witnesses Jakob's only identifiable moral fall, when he allows the Soviet troops to pass under his control tower on their way to Hungary. As Eberhard Fahlke explains, Jakob's silent self-confidence breaks apart at this point.[23] Although Jonas is a professor and intellectual, there is a reversal of roles in which Jakob becomes Jonas's mentor, demonstrating work high in the tower above the railroad yard. Jonas cannot translate his beliefs or desires into action, which is yet another explanation for the attraction that a life of practical endeavors has for him. Jakob offers Jonas work with the railroad, while Gesine attempts to convince him to come to the West. In the end, Jonas is simply crushed between the two choices when Rohlfs arrests him for his activities with the reform group.

The fate of Jonas in *Speculations* parallels the theme of Johnson's short story "Jonas zum Beispiel" ("Jonah for example"), written in 1957 (BU 121) but not published until 1962. This story deals succinctly with the incompatibility between intellectual integrity and political power. Here Johnson adapted the biblical story of Jonah, who follows the Word of God to the letter only to be disappointed when God does not follow through. Jonah appears to be a fool and must spend his days resting under a tree separated from the community, disgruntled and dismayed by his misplaced trust in the Word of God. When God asks why Jonah is upset and obviously disappointed, he retorts, "Because you never do as you said and as is right according to your law!"[24] Jonas Blach too wants to contribute to the making of an improved form of socialism and does so by following a perceived softening of dogmatic positions on how the country should be governed. In short Jonas mistakenly trusts the sincerity of Khrushchev's speech and foolishly believes that his own contribution as an intellectual can make a difference. Like his biblical namesake and the historical group active under the leadership of Harich and Bloch, Jonas is deceived by signals from the powers that be and in the end suffers a banning from the very community to which he hoped to devote his life. After all, Jonas had the opportunity to escape to the West. In trying to remain consistent with his beliefs, he remains in the GDR, only to receive, like Harich, a ten-year prison term. The relationship between political power and thinking persons with genuine concerns about politically charged issues remains a thematic concern in most of Johnson's narratives, including his last novel, *Anniversaries*. Thus Johnson describes the intellectual's relationship with political and governmental power as one of suspicion, incompatibility, and discord, a negative connection that he came to know firsthand.

Having grown up with Jakob, Gesine's interest in him harbors aspirations of a personal nature. She was only thirteen years old when Jakob entered her life as a young man of eighteen. Gesine's mother died when she was five, and she had no siblings, thus making her desire for an immediate family quite ardent. Jakob and Marie Abs thus fulfill her familial needs, becoming like an older brother and mother to her while living under the same roof in postwar Germany's dire circumstances. As a model older brother, Jakob takes on the role of guide, protector, and teacher in Gesine's life. All three of these roles are evident in the way Jakob, in the black of night during a drizzling rain, leads Gesine, on paths she does not know, through fields and forests to her home in Jerichow. They take an alternate route to avoid Rohlfs and other members of the Stasi who are pursuing them. Of the three figures who were most directly involved with Jakob before his death, Gesine knew him the longest and was the closest to him emotionally. The love between Jakob and Gesine is based on the most important aspects of their lives: their common childhood, their common upbringing in a socialist society, and their common concern for global political issues. Her vision of an ideal life for herself includes Jakob and his relationship to the community that she knew in Mecklenburg, the landscape there, and her few but close family relations. Gesine dashes her and Jakob's hopes of a life together when she refuses to accompany Jakob back "home." In West Germany, Jakob "seemed like a complete stranger: and bewildered" (SAJ 215) and thus could not endure a life in the West. The utopia that Gesine dreams of with Jakob can, therefore, only be in the Mecklenburger sky, and it must retrieve a time in her innocent childhood, a time free of political and moral choices. The night before Jakob must leave to return to the East, he sits deep in thought at Gesine's side, thinking about flying kites, often a symbol of freedom, on a hill near Jerichow called the Rehberge.[25] The scene contains all the state colors of Mecklenburg; the kite itself, handcrafted in Heinrich Cresspahl's workshop, is blue and yellow, and the shining sun adds a red hue. The sky becomes a new realm as the clouds "seemed tangible, one might have walked on them" (SAJ 231). Gesine thinks to herself, "I'd like to be up there on those clouds" (SAJ 231). In other words, their utopia truly is no place on an earth that offers only two alternatives, East or West, both unattractive and unpromising in light of political developments in Egypt and Hungary. Each lover chooses the lesser evil for him- or herself, and they part ways. Jakob returns to his death in the East, while Gesine remains in her loneliness in the West. If Jonas makes the reader aware of the inadequacy of language as a true mediation of meaning, then Gesine, like Jakob, expresses the shortcomings of any existing social system as a guilt-free, morally pure society in which to live.

Jakob, in the perceptions of those who describe him, is a person for whom traits and actions exist in harmonious unity with each other. He is not alienated from himself or his society, meaning that he cannot distinguish his beliefs and morals from his actions. Gesine observes, for example, that "things always have a way of fusing with" Jakob (SAJ 206). Those who have observed Jakob in life demonstrate that his inherent personal traits include politeness, respect for colleagues and other citizens, unwavering fairness, and consideration for the comfort of others. He represents a man of his word, possesses an admirable sense of responsibility, and demonstrates a reasonably sophisticated understanding of history; he harbors no selfish ambitions and desires only to do his best at work in service to the socialist state. Whether it is an unfamiliar landscape in which he moves without error or the ideals of a socialist society, Jakob intuits everything that for others must be laboriously learned or that represents received knowledge. His dedication to the socialist society in which he lives and works is demonstrated by his voluntary attendance at planning meetings after work, by his thorough knowledge of the stacks of regulations about his profession, by his tutoring young apprentices in his spare time, and by the fact that he does not complain about the high expectations or long hours at work. His wish in life is not for his own happiness but for the modernization of the railway system to better serve the people who use it and the economy that depends on it. Jakob's relationship to work is unalienated; he knows all the aspects of his work quite well and works with pride in support of the socialist state. He understands fully that his labor is vital to the economic health of the fledgling GDR. In light of recent German history, Jakob is convinced of the moral superiority of socialism as an organizing principle of society, but he recognizes that socialism has its problems (SAJ 38–39). This amalgamation of traits and actions becomes the basis of readers' understanding of Jakob as a person.

Jakob is often described as *ebenmässig,* literally meaning "evenly measured" or "well proportioned." A figurative definition renders a sense of harmoniousness, symmetry, and balance. *Ebenmässig* is an adjective that condenses all the traits mentioned above and describes how Jakob exists in his world. "Symmetrical" is the harmonious manner in which he moves about in his environment as well as the emanation of an inner equanimity detectable in his gaze. No other figure in the book possesses this quality, and it is the one affect that Rohlfs, Jonas, and Gesine lack, a deficiency that undermines their own quests for satisfaction in life. Although memories of the dead can fade and change, Jakob possesses unique elements that reveal a constancy in life that all characters associated with him notice and cannot forget. For each person who encounters him, Jakob becomes an object of envy and desire; Jakob is steadfast, consistent, and never altering in life, and thus he remains "even like eternity" (SAJ 152). His position as dispatcher for the railroad shows how a person with an uncompetitive nature can quietly and confidently impart order and harmony to the movement and circulation of power. Jakob's polite, respectful demeanor implicitly judges the self-interested, agonistic powers of the world. In novel form, Jakob's singular, respectful, community-minded demeanor looms up larger than the self-serving interests of nations. However, his exposure to power as competition and weapon so jumbles his harmonious dance with locomotives such that the trains he once controlled from his tower become dangerous, and the railroad yard, once a natural part of his environment, becomes unknown territory. Whether his death was an accident, a suicide, or a political murder, he falls victim to the oncoming locomotive because he now knows too much. His unblemished character and his ingenuous comprehension of his space in the world are permanently lost and out of synchronization with his environment. This exposure to the divisiveness of the world brings about his fatal misstep.

## Leitmotifs

The figurative power of the novel's principal leitmotifs—the elusive cat, the ubiquitous fog, and the insufficient light—effectively imbricate the more comprehensive ideas of the novel. These motifs help to create an atmosphere in which readers discover the limits of knowledge and the inability of any one person objectively to know the reality of a given situation. Johnson employs these objects in correspondence to the novel's basic narrative stance as a search for truth that falls well short of any conclusiveness. Johnson's novel thereby implicitly undermines an authoritative stance on any subject, be it a historical perspective, the ideas upon which a political system is based, or an ideological belief system. The fragmented and refracted narrative structure contains an important lesson about a real-life condition: "What is then the truth?"[26] The assumptions with which one works on any level are thus always already lacking in their absoluteness. Johnson's formal standard, one that portrays the memories and interpretations of the characters involved, pits opinion against opinion, which in turn reflects an authentic approach to the reconstruction of any event in narrative. The event is not depicted in an artificial causality or described from a single third-person perspective. To claim to possess the truth already implies an ideological posture toward a specific incident, which in turn calls into question the integrity of the claim to the truth. This is where Johnson's motifs are most efficacious in accenting some central thematic issues of the novel.

The cat is mysterious, aloof, independent, unpredictable, and beautiful. She represents elusive truth in service to nobody as well as the unfulfillable desires of the individuals who encounter her, most notably Jonas and Gesine. Her presence underscores the complexity of relationships between characters while embodying the lack of correspondence between what characters think they know and how circumstances reveal themselves to be. The cat observes Jonas working on his paper about the virtues of democratizing socialism. Her presence signals to readers how intangible and unattainable his goal will remain and fills the space in which Rohlfs and Jonas argue about their conceptions of socialism, a discussion that will ultimately end with Jonas's arrest. The power of the political apparatus to take away an individual's freedom is the only obvious "truth" between Jonas and Rohlfs. The cat is in the house as the Gesine-Jakob-Jonas love triangle sorts itself out, as Gesine admits to Jonas whom she really loves and who can honestly make her happy. Gesine's bliss, however, is cut short by Jakob's refusal to remain in the West and his ultimate death.

The fog, mentioned in the first lines of the novel, is a motif that directly challenges the view that there are distinct right-wrong, black-white, good-evil dichotomies where human affairs are concerned. It fittingly warns readers from the beginning that no such clarity should be anticipated in this narrative. Germany's October–November fog is a real weather condition that shrouds choices in uncertainty, just as the novel's changing circumstances shake the characters' belief systems at their bases. Confidence in the facts does not resonate with any clarity of vision, which in turn brings into question the clarity of facts as such. The ubiquitous fog and rain obfuscate clear vision and thus create the symbolic link to the limited perspectives of the characters. Amazingly, even readers who take in all of the characters' perspectives are none the wiser at the end of the narrative since the fog never clears and the light is never quite bright enough to illuminate all aspects of Jakob's death.

The continuously recurring motif of controlled light exercises a similar effect on the knowledge of what really happened to Jakob. Days in northern Germany in November are short, and the daylight hours are often overcast. The light in *Speculations* is artificial and sparing, provided not by the sun but by headlights, lamps in rooms, light from cigarettes, or Jakob's control panel. Johnson's use of light, which is never enough to brighten the entire scene, actually clarifies little.[27] As much as it may reveal, it reminds readers that, in its limited scope, much more remains in the dark. Johnson utilizes these common items to elucidate the basic stance of the novel, which leaves the reader no other choice but to speculate along with the characters about what really took place.

The author treats Jakob's death from the perspectives of Rohlfs, Gesine, and Jonas, each of whom ponder the central question that generates the narrative. How could Jakob have possibly perished in a shunting yard that he knew better than any other railroad worker? In other words, was it really a tragic accident? Possibly Jakob did not notice the locomotives coming his way. The yard was foggy and the tracks were slick with rain; already that morning another railroad worker had been crushed by a train due to poor visibility. Could these elements have added up to a tragic accident? Or was it a political murder? Jakob was unsuccessful and not particularly willing to help Rohlfs recruit Gesine as a spy for the Eastern bloc countries. Was Jakob's death arranged by the East German security forces as a simultaneous act of revenge and a cover-up? Or was Jakob so despondent about his personal situation that he willingly stepped in front of the train that killed him? After all, his mother fled to the West, Gesine, his newfound love, chose to remain in the West, and Jakob knows he can never convince either one to return to the East. While visiting both women, he witnessed certain vestiges of fascism as well as the superficiality of the West. Despite the obviously better living conditions, on moral grounds alone he cannot remain in the West; he is a worker who believes wholly in the principles of socialism. This belief, however, was shaken when he became part and parcel, through his position as train dispatcher, of the deployment of Soviet troops in Hungary, which eventually crushed the reform government there. Were these personal and political tragedies too much for him to continue living? The characters, and thus readers, must grapple with these basic questions. There is no group of facts that point overwhelmingly to one interpretation of Jakob's death over another. Was Jakob a sentimental idealist, a champion of individualism and self-determination, or simply careless? The interpretation that readers choose as the most plausible essentially determines who Jakob was. Thus, the most frustrating or intriguing—that is to say, the most lifelike—aspect of the novel is the lack of definitive answers. Life is revealed as the fictions people tell themselves to make sense of their lives; life is indeed pure speculation.

# CHAPTER 5

# The Frustrated Biographer

## *The Third Book about Achim*

In *Speculations* Gesine Cresspahl asks the dogmatic state security officer, Rohlfs, "What do you do with facts you don't like?" (SAJ 222). In his next novel, Uwe Johnson delivers a story that centers on exactly that problematic question. The main characters' varied approaches to the circumstances of the facts and their use in narrative create the tension and conflict in *Das dritte Buch über Achim* (1961, translated in 1967 as *The Third Book about Achim*). Certain themes carry over from *Speculations* into the Achim material, and they are reflected in this line from *The Third Book:* "Does one have to be convinced, after all, and each time, does one really?"[1] Although the question is asked of a film and is addressed to Karin, Achim's girlfriend, this short, unassuming line underscores the central issue of *The Third Book.* Karsch, the main narrative perspective of the novel, discovers that one does have to be convinced every time. Karsch must reckon with a serious discriminatory power as he goes about his work. Accosted with discrepant facts he must choose those that support Achim's desired loyalty to the Communist Party's political line. As in *Speculations,* the search for the truth is a thematic focus of the novel, but its main character, Karsch, must consider how to present the "truths" he finds. Here Karsch experiences a direct encounter with how seriously the East German regime takes publications and how much confidence it places in books as tools of persuasion and ideological conditioning. There does indeed have to be a lucid and well-delineated political point in all narratives published in the country where Achim lives and works.

Again, even though Johnson wrote this novel in the West, the challenge of socialist-realist guidelines (and realism in general) continues in Johnson's work. In fact, one critic maintains that all of Johnson's work, up to this point, can be characterized by his implicit contestation of the principles of realism and an attempt to demonstrate their flaws in narrative fiction.[2] As in *Speculations,* the subjective nature of truth, conceptions of personal identity, and the individual's relationship to greater political forces constitute the novel's central themes. In *The Third Book* Johnson again takes up the issue of the political border separating the Germanys, unique to his work even in the year of this novel's publication, 1961, when the topic had still not received serious attention from any other literary talent in Germany. It was also the year that the East German regime erected the infamous wall between the communist and capitalist sectors of Berlin. The significance of this coincidence rests in the fact that Johnson's second novel, published before the building of the wall, deals with "the border: the difference: the distance and the attempt to describe it" (TBA 246). Of course, with the building of the Berlin Wall, that distance and difference grew even greater and became even more profound in the ensuing years. Upon publication of *The Third Book,* Johnson, to his great annoyance, was more liable than ever to be called the "author of the two Germanys," which he felt was nothing more than a trendy, even restricting, marketing label. Johnson took every opportunity in interviews and public appearances to dispel this classification, one that, on the surface, seemed so appropriate to his work. Despite Johnson's aversion to this label, the reality of the matter was that no other author publishing in the West was in quite as good a position to describe the East with such care and passionate authenticity. In 1960 Johnson had, after all, spent most of his life in the East, while he had only recently (and reluctantly) attempted to make a home in the West.

## The Story

Despite the title, the main character of *The Third Book about Achim* is Karsch, a West German journalist who resides in northern Germany in the port city of Hamburg. In the early spring of 1960, he receives a telephone call from an ex-girlfriend with whom Karsch had lived for eight years in West Berlin. Karin is a twenty-eight-year-old actress who now resides in a large East German town in the state of Saxony, presumably Leipzig, the city in which Johnson himself attended university. Karin telephones Karsch and asks him to come to the GDR to visit her. On receiving Karin's call, Karsch immediately travels to the East.

Karin has a successful film career in East Germany, but even more successful is her boyfriend Achim T., a bicycle racer with a highly recognized profile among the masses. More significant for the story is the fact that Achim is also a favorite—more so than Karin—with the East German state. Her reason for wanting Karsch to visit may have something to do with her relationship with Achim. In a fashion typical of Johnson, her motivation for inviting Karsch and Karsch's eager response remain vague and open to speculation for the entire novel. Does she believe that Karsch may help her relate better to Achim and his contradictions? Or does she hope to make Achim jealous? Does she want Karsch to help her move to the West? Does she wish to use Karsch as a comparison to Achim? Will Karsch help her understand why she remains in a relationship with Achim? Readers may choose one of these reasons or discover their own explanations about the impetus for Karin's curious action.

Although Karsch had planned to stay only a week in the GDR, the intriguing street life of the people and Achim as the people's hero entice him to stay considerably longer, approximately three months. In the very beginning of his sojourn Karsch is so fascinated by Achim and his success that he writes a four-page article about the cyclist. When an East German state-owned publishing house discovers the article, representatives of the house ask Karsch to consider writing a book-length manuscript about Achim's life. The two representatives, Mr. Fleisg and Mrs. Ammann, meet with Karsch on different occasions and encourage him with an advance for the publication of the book. Two books already exist about Achim, but implication is that these books have not served their purpose in the eyes of the state.[3] Karsch's assignment is to produce a different kind of book that will contain the communist revision of history to suit better the didactic intention of many of the books published in the GDR. Fleisg works for a publishing house that specializes in youth literature. In this respect, Fleisg and Ammann believe that a third book about Achim is a worthwhile idea since it fills in areas of Achim's life neglected in the other two books. Furthermore, the implications for Germany's figurative unification in a project that involves a West German journalist writing about an East German sports idol are tantalizing. However, Fleisg and Ammann have specific notions about what should be included in the book and how it should be written. The political ramifications of Karsch's misreading of the situation are immediately clear to readers, for there is no way that Karsch can write his book about Achim without an ideological conflict with his benefactors. Ingenuous as ever in his demeanor, Karsch accepts the terms that, in the end, set him up for a personal and political crisis.

As one is apt to do in a biography, Karsch starts at the beginning and thus enters into the arduous task of seeking out information about Achim's childhood. But Karsch runs into immediate difficulties when he discovers that Achim belonged to the Hitler Youth. This fascist youth organization was bitterly anti-communist and performed an important function in the ideological indoctrination of the youth in Nazi Germany. Achim, like many at his impressionable age, accepted this indoctrination with complete and unwavering conviction. Achim's father, conversely, was a Social Democrat who illegally listened to foreign radio broadcasts, worked in a factory, and introduced Achim to the bicycle. He is thus a possible positive influence in Achim's life from the socialist point of view. But his grandfather was the Nazi mayor of a small town, a fact that further complicates Karsch's work on Achim, who is to be portrayed as a socialist hero. These uncomfortable realities in Achim's life could be excused, attributed to the impressionability of youth, the overriding historical circumstances of the time, or the misguidance of his home environment (his father never tells him that fascism is wrong because he fears that his son will turn him over to the Gestapo). However, the final blow to Karsch's project comes when he anonymously receives a photograph with a person that looks like Achim at the forefront of a group of angry bricklayers, marching in a violent demonstration against the government of the Socialist Unity Party. After confronting Achim with this photograph, Karsch abandons his project, realizing that he will never be permitted to tell about the real Achim. Too many considerations regarding the preservation of Achim's position as socialist poster boy, youth idol, and representative of the people in the East German People's Chamber hinder an authentic portrayal of his life. Frustrated by this dilemma, Karsch returns to Hamburg, where he tells an unidentified listener about his visit to the East and his attempt to write a biography about Achim.

## The Historical Situation

Before a discussion of the structural features of the novel can begin, it is essential to understand the significance of Karsch's discovery of Achim's possible role in the uprising. As with *Speculations,* historical macroevents couch the microevents of this interesting novel. In the case of *The Third Book,* the most significant historical event is the uprising in East Germany on 16–17 June 1953, which is central to the Achim query because, from the official communist standpoint, it was instigated by Western agents and led by neo-Nazis, putatively the two greatest enemies of the East German state. In actuality, the uprising was spontaneous and popular and was less political than it was a reaction to frustration with high production quotas, low wages, and exorbitant food prices. With the lack of legal or structural recourses to combat these pressures an uprising was inevitable. The uprising developed so quickly and haphazardly that no clear political demands were ever formulated by the striking workers. Items such as free elections, the establishment of a pluralistic political system, and democratic freedoms were not initially issues for the protesters, although some of these demands were raised in the course of the uprising. Achim cannot admit to having been involved with the uprising because, as Karin explains, most people viewed it "as a new way of counting time, before and after" (TBA 223). Like the French Revolution, it meant a new age (a new calendar) in East Germany for the people who witnessed a day when their hard-line government faltered for a moment. In fact, in West Germany, 17 June became a national holiday called "Day of National Unity," a commemoration that became an annual aggravation to East German–West German relations.

The end of the novel contains a clear description of the uprising as it occurred in the town in which Achim was working as a bricklayer. Johnson includes items that characterize the uprising, taken from historical accounts of the event (TBA 236–41). The revolt began in Berlin on the Stalinallee on 16 June 1953 when approximately forty construction workers marched to the office of Walter Ulbricht, then *Staatsratsvorsitzender* (head of the Politburo), to protest his domestic policies and demand a meeting with him. Ulbricht never appeared in public or addressed the people's demands during the crisis. The next day, violent dissatisfaction manifested itself in most other large and medium-sized East German cities. The revolt spread to construction sites and factories in most industrial centers. The intelligentsia played no role in the uprising, a fact that underscores its spontaneous nature and lack of formulated political demands. Although the protest spread rapidly to industrial areas, it had little effect on the agricultural sector. Without clear leadership and broad support, the rebellion disintegrated due to a lack of sustained initiative. On the afternoon of 17 June Soviet tanks moved in to crush what was left of the rebellion and restore order on behalf of Ulbricht and the Socialist Unity Party.[4]

Achim's alleged participation in this uprising is problematic because historically, though the revolt lacked a clear political agenda, the aggression of the protesters was vented against offices and functionaries of the Socialist Unity Party, Achim's party and the leading party of the state that he represents. If Achim did in fact participate and Karsch's book publicized that fact, it would represent an inexcusable political fluctuation in the eyes of the state and would thus be inappropriate behavior for an East German national hero. As is typical in Johnson's writings, the picture that supposedly shows Achim at the front of the marchers does not indicate with absolute certainty that Achim was involved. The person in the photograph only looks like Achim—after all, seven years have passed since the uprising. But Achim's negative reaction when confronted with the photograph leads Karsch to believe that Achim at least participated, even though he may not be the demonstrator in the picture. Achim's reaction to the possibility of his participation implicates him more than the photograph. Does the picture underscore the impression that Achim is easily persuaded by a group, or can he not discern one raucous and cheering crowd from another?

## Form and Content

The general setting of the action and the constellation of characters in the novel give rise to certain reader expectations. Karsch's dialogue partner, due to particular scenes described by Karsch, is moved to ask, "Is this going to be after all the story of a lady and two gentlemen?" (TBA 95). This question and others, including "Is this your idea of suspense?" (TBA 113) and "Did Karsch feel that he was being watched?" (TBA 18), signal that the narrative could, because of its subject matter, represent an established genre such as the romance or the spy thriller. Through these questions, the built-in recipient of Karsch's story, the person inquiring into Karsch's experiences in the East, anticipates and dispels any readers' expectations of genre. A story involving a woman who lives with a man and who has invited her ex-boyfriend for a visit must necessarily be about a love rivalry. A westerner in the East dealing with a politically sensitive issue will necessarily attract the attention of state security agents and live there under surveillance. It would only make sense that the westerner would receive a visit from men in dark trench coats, a visit that is meant to intimidate him and thus to contribute to the suspense of the spy thriller. But the narrative is neither a suspense novel nor a romance.

As with *Speculations,* the driving force of the story in *The Third Book* is an investigation, a quest for the truth.[5] Karsch becomes the story agent through the act of gathering information and proceeds in full awareness of the end of the story: "The book in which a visitor named Karsch wanted to describe how Achim became famous and how he lived with his fame was to end with Achim's election to his country's parliament" (TBA 34). The novel really has two beginnings, because two stories intertwine in this narrative, the story of Karsch's investigation and the story of Achim's life.[6] The two narrative strands of the story intersect at the point where Karin takes Karsch to see Achim at a bicycle racing arena where an enthusiastic celebration of Achim's thirtieth birthday is taking place. Karsch's presence at this celebration possesses a double significance for the narrative because it represents both a narratable beginning and ending. The festivity in Achim's honor is a beginning because this is the point where Karsch first encounters Achim. This is the first scene that Karsch describes over the phone to the unidentified caller who questions Karsch throughout the narrative. The discourse time—the time of Karsch's exploration of Achim's life—commences, more or less, at this point. This initial encounter also represents an ending to the narrated time or story time, the time of Achim's life from approximately 1939 to the spring of 1960. Karsch witnesses a climactic display of enthusiasm for the sports hero, which inspires the question that begins all investigations: "How come?" (TBA 30). The encounter also signals the beginning of a series of frustrations as Karsch attempts to research and write the description of Achim's life. Karsch sees before him the task of describing how Achim came to this point of popularity, fame, and material success. Riding his bicycle around the arena and responding to his cheering fans, Achim becomes the inspirational image of Karsch's work on the sports idol.

But the novel does not begin until Karsch has left East Germany. Karsch has returned to Hamburg from his frustrating three-month sojourn in the other Germany and receives, almost immediately upon his return, a phone call from an acquaintance curious about his trip. Here Johnson creates a dialogue that contains one story within the other. The narrative structure of the novel presents the ironic situation of an unidentified narrator describing Karsch describing Achim. The primary narrative of the novel is the telephone conversation and the caller's subsequent questions, which appear in italics, about Karsch's trip. These questions motivate the description of how Karsch investigated Achim T.'s life. Essentially, Karsch's book was meant to be a historically grounded biography. However, due to the impossibility of its completion and due to the recounting of Karsch's material by this unidentified person, the novel represents a unique case study about the implications of the border for German-German relations on the level of two individuals. The unidentified caller finds Karsch's narrative interesting and significant precisely because it points to a larger problem—that is, the misunderstandings that typify German-German relations. Although instruments and forums of communication abound in this narrative, in which typewriters, telephones, conversations, films, meetings, photographs, letters, travel, questions, and answers play central roles in the telling of the story, the novel is about a breakdown in communication. The manifestation of a many-leveled misconception of one Germany for the other is the violent border that runs between them. Thus, a description of the border by the narrator opens the novel in an attempt to introduce the underlying reason for the series of miscommunications that follow. The novel discusses the border in the guise of a central problematic life, in which its description pits opinion against opinion and ideology against ideology to demonstrate just how complex and jaded the notions of truth are for the two Germanys and the people who live there. This multileveled, ironic, continuous questioning and evaluation throughout the three hundred pages of the novel forces readers to come to conclusions about the German situation on their own.

*The Third Book* is, as Johnson himself said, the "description of a description," which was, in fact, the original title of the novel (BU 173–74). Thus the description of a description constitutes the overriding structural principle of the novel. Even though the narrative is written primarily in the third person, the individual asking the questions serves as a reminder that an actual dialogue has taken place at some point in the past. Note, for example, this change in person: "And that is why you stayed? Why Karsch stayed?" (TBA 26). The record of this conversation with an introduction discussing the German-German border as the central theme of the novel comprises the contents of the book and leads into the narratized discourse of Karsch and his endeavor. In other words, Karsch's intention to write a biography is unintentionally realized as the record of an informal interview about the original intention and why the original project failed. In a general way, the first question leads into the second description, the description of Karsch's experiences in East Germany: "How was it?" (TBA 5). The narrative reflects Karsch's discussion of his own notes as he responds to questions and interjections from his conversation partner. Readers are thus thrice removed from the material.

Questions serve as a method of reorienting a narrative that fluctuates frequently in its focus, but they also have the potential to exhaust Karsch as he talks about his experiences. Early on Karsch demonstrates his frustration with the material as he breaks off one answer to demand, "Ask me something else" (TBA 7). The final question of the novel is simply a rephrasing of the opening question, "And how was the trip?" (TBA 246). The cyclical nature of the narrative becomes evident as the novel ends where it began, with Karsch's return from East Germany, demoralized and disillusioned, answering a telephone call from his acquaintance who wants to hear about the trip. The narrative goes nowhere; the contents of its sentences reveal no telos. Again, as in *Speculations,* Johnson approaches the material from various points of view, employing first-, second-, and third-person narrative stances to portray the material as authentically as possible. As Karsch speaks his piece (or peace), his conversations with Achim, Karin, Fleisg, Ammann, Achim's father, Mrs. Liebenreuth, and others reveal themselves in their points of view but by no other means. Their individual voices are smoothed over by the singular style of the inquirer recounting Karsch's experiences in what is ultimately a third-person perspective. Moreover, there are very few quotation marks or other markers that indicate the exchange of speech between various characters. Thus, with the questions and the inquiring narrator, readers cannot be certain whether there is a straight third-person, dialogic, or monologic narrative in *The Third Book.* It appears as though Johnson has accomplished an amazing narratological feat, writing all three types of narrative in the same words.

## The Truths of Achim

When Karsch commences with work on his book about Achim he does so in an honest and deliberate manner. Karsch appears to be extremely naive and politically unaware as he enters a pact with two officials from the socialist publishing industry. Karsch will have no choice but to politically locate his narrative about Achim's life. Karsch seems to want that kind of a challenge. Furthermore, he is interested, with his official function as Achim's biographer, in traveling about the country and becoming familiar with the GDR unencumbered by restrictions normally placed on Western visitors. It is important to keep in mind that Karsch contributes to the travel section of his newspaper at home, something learned from a related story called "An Absence" that is discussed later in this chapter. Karsch has professional reasons for remaining in the GDR that go beyond his work on Achim. His opportunity and desire to explore "the other Germany" also correlate with the narrator's suggestion that the novel concerns the border and the differences between the two German states, not exclusively the failed biography.

Even though Karsch has freedom to travel within the GDR, the two publishers are state representatives who expect service to the state in return for Karsch's advance. Karsch has freedom but they are interested in a "useful book" (TBA 90), which implies other more onerous kinds of restrictions. With the introduction of the state into the project, the question of the true authorship of the book becomes obscured. Johnson already indicates with the nomenclature of the officials, Mr. Fleisg and Mrs. Ammann, that they harbor special plans for the way in which Achim's life will be used once it appears in narrative form. The name *Fleisg* reminds readers of the German word *fleissig,* meaning "industrious, diligent, active," definitive characteristics of the socialist-realist hero (see chapter 4). The name *Ammann* ("Amen") reflects the sacredness of Achim as a symbol of the socialist covenant that can make a humble background an advantage in the new society established by the Socialist Unity Party.

The state recognizes that Achim possesses the potential to influence the masses in the ways that no party official, teacher, or other civic leader can. The use of Achim's life that Fleisg and Ammann have in mind contains a narrow but important didactic function.[7] Essentially, Fleisg and Ammann do not wish readers to learn about Achim's life but rather from Achim's life: "His mistakes are not important, only the things that link him to our new era" (TBA 106). In this respect the state appears more forgiving of Achim's missteps than the public might be. The difference of approaches, represented in the preposition *from,* where the state places its emphasis, and *about,* where Karsch would like to place the emphasis of his book, is where the project meets a disastrous impasse. There is no room for Karsch's undiscriminating honesty in a project that possesses a function beyond the mere task of writing a description of a person's life. Conceptions of truth that carry ideological baggage create decidedly different criteria for the selection and organization of information.

The misunderstanding between publisher and writer revolves around the differing roles that journalistic writing plays in the respective Germanys. Karsch states from the beginning that he is a journalist, a profession that had a special function in the GDR. As a Western journalist, Karsch seeks to locate, from various sources, as many facts about a given story as possible and to report them in a manner that diminishes him as the subjective force behind his report. Ideally, his goal in reporting information is to obtain as great a level of objectivity as humanly possible. Journalists in East Germany performed quite a different function. As one student of journalism at the Karl Marx University in Leipzig said, journalists in the GDR sought to "take the facts and paint them red." Indeed, a major part of the journalistic curriculum centered on instruction in Marxism-Leninism, and only those students most loyal to the state were admitted to the university to study journalism. Karsch is expected to adopt a similar posture as he writes the third book about Achim T. Obviously, all narrative is the result of a selection process and subjective synthesis of material. The authentic Achim can never be depicted, no matter how resolutely and honestly the task is attempted. Karsch will also, if left to his own devices, work in a fashion that perforce suppresses or privileges some kinds of information over others in creating order out of them. It is ironic that Achim reminds Karsch of this fact in an attempt to use one of his journalistic attitudes to the athlete's own benefit:

—You can't put in everything anyway, right? he said.
—So you've got to make a choice, right, so naturally you pick the most important, right? the thing that's essential, man! Now Karsch was supposed to ask what was essential. (TBA 141)

Karsch's threshold of permissible, "essential" material, as an independent writer and journalist, is much lower than that of the subject of his inquiry and the Eastern patrons of the work. Fleisg and Ammann demand that Achim should represent the GDR as someone who has benefited from the socialist system and also as someone who must present a consistent, unwavering belief in those advantages. No matter how improbable (or how untrue) it may be, the book must reflect that Achim has always had his socialist convictions. Described in this way, his life will create in popular memory the revision of history that the state seeks to construct. Fascism and capitalism will have always been wrong for this individual; the Communist Party under the leadership of the Soviet Union will have always been right. It is a dualistic approach to the past with no in-between. The construction of history expected of Karsch must possess, then, clean ideological lines that prevail in the description of this socialist hero.

Both interested parties, Karsch and the Fleisg-Ammann team, demand some level of control over the meaning that Achim's life will take in book form. For Fleisg and Ammann, if certain facts are included, their power over the ideological signification and pedagogical value of the biography will be undermined. For Karsch, if certain facts are suppressed, his meaning will lose its independence and will not be true to what he knows: "Incompleteness is a lie" (TBA 171). He will compromise his integrity as a journalist and biographer if he follows the ideological guidelines set down by the East German publishers. Karsch grapples, then, with a problem that permeates German life, especially since the atrocities of the Second World War: the disastrous effect on the psyche of knowing that you know without any real avenue to work through what you know. Karsch is not willing to contribute to such a repression of information.

Fitting the narration of a person's life to propagandistic formulas is bound to fail with any author committed to impartiality and with the goal of being informative. Moreover, the chimera that objective truth will always remain is ever further from Karsch's grasp when he encounters the East German sense of biographical narrative. He cannot produce a life in narrative so ideologically polished that inner conflicts, self-contradictions, ambiguity in convictions, and political ambivalence do not exist. An implicit reminder to readers here is that no person leads such an uncomplicated existence. The rough edges, the uneven textures of an individual's life will always create difficulties for biographers seeking absolute clarity and uncomplicated linearity. Writers who seek to transmute the multifariousness of an individual's experiences to political means and who depict, with the described life, a single overriding meaning will perforce forfeit the truthfulness of the work. Contradiction is endemic to human existence; the most earnest biography will portray contradictions in some balanced manner.

When Fleisg and Ammann approach Karsch, it becomes apparent that the historical events of the GDR are to play a primary role in the description of Achim's life: "The whole man consisted of the arrival of the Soviet army and the building up of a new economy and the new satisfaction in life plus all the cheering fans along the tracks" (TBA 42). Karsch is thus constrained to work in two areas, history contemporary to the life of Achim and history of the individual life of his inquiry. It is evident in Fleisg's guidelines for the project that Achim as bicycling champion and individual comes last in the list of items to include.[8] Collective concerns, ideological formulations of history, and Achim as a figure of prestige for the state all take precedence over the real life of the individual

Achim T. The life of this professional cyclist is to connect with and be subsumed into greater historical events, such as the liberation from fascism by the Red Army and the growth of the GDR's socialist economy. Fleisg and Ammann assume that Achim's life will serve as a vehicle for historical material with which every citizen of the GDR can, then, more readily identify.

In the end, ideology thwarts the project because Karsch cannot locate the proper balance between fact and fiction that suits himself, Achim, or the commissioners of his work. It is not that Karsch is a stranger to invention or that he is reluctant to manipulate the facts of Achim's life within his own narrative prose (TBA 171–72). Karsch is aware that Achim will necessarily become a construct of the author's own design. But two axiomatically incompatible designs are vying for Achim's life story. The diametrically opposed meanings of Achim's ideological purposefulness versus his individual singularity reveal a struggle in which Achim-Fleisg-Ammann wish to control as closely as possible the depicted meaning of Achim's life while Karsch seeks to allow Achim's life story a greater level of authenticity and autonomy. Autonomy in the presentation of Achim's life coincides with readers' greater independence in reaching an understanding of Achim. Karsch wants to be sensitive to the uniqueness of Achim's individual life experience: "Karsch didn't want everything about Achim, he only wanted to pick what distinguished him (in Karsch's opinion) from other people, from other bicycle riders, for that was the purpose of his choice among the different episodes of a life" (TBA 172). Achim views his own life, as does the government, in an instrumental fashion, thus rendering inappropriate all aspects of his life that dispute his purpose as socialist role model and symbol of national pride. Toward the end of the novel Karsch explains the various ways in which he could organize "the scraps on which he had stored pieces of Achim's life" (TBA 193). Juxtaposing Karsch's inclusive version of Achim's biography against the monolithic version desired by Achim and his benefactors shows that truth and meaning are genuinely powerful not on their own merit but by virtue of the power of the Red Army, the state security apparatus, and the Socialist Unity Party, with its three million members. Here Achim's life must shed its unique aspects and become part of the socialist master narrative with which all citizens are expected to become familiar. Karsch's only recourse is to counter with his own sense of objectivity and his conviction that a genuine selection process of the past requires the views of as many persons as possible. Karsch thus proceeds with an approach to his work that values inquiry over imposition, creative reconstruction based on testimonies over ideological guidelines, discovery, and open interpretation over the predetermination of meaning. Karsch seeks the truth despite the fact that his search leads him to uncertainty and creates in him a sense of vulnerability. However, these feelings of discomfort are normal by-products of a search for the truth.

## Achim T.

Though he does not represent the main narrative perspective, the central figure of the novel is Achim T. To a certain extent Johnson based his invented person Achim on a historical person, a champion bicycle racer from the former GDR named Gustav Adolf Schur, nicknamed Täve. Two books about this cyclist, written by Klaus Ullrich, were already in existence at the time Johnson commenced the writing of *The Third Book, Unser Weltmeister* (*Our World Champion*) and *Unser Täve: Ein Buch über Gustav Adolf Schur* (*Our Täve: A Book about Gustav Adolf Schur*). Johnson borrowed limited material from the latter, which was published in 1960. Karl Pestalozzi discusses the similarities between Achim's career and Schur's in an article that explores how Johnson worked with this historical material.[9] As Pestalozzi shows, passages depicting some of the problems that Johnson's famous cyclist encounters in his daily life were inspired by Ullrich's book. Johnson, however, devoted several pages of *Begleitumstände* to refuting Pestalozzi's claim that Schur resembled Achim T. Although both men were successful bicycle racers, Johnson cites, for example, their different places of birth, ages, and professional training to prove his point (BU 179–80). Johnson admits, however, that he used "on the whole twenty-seven words from books about the athlete Gustav Adolf Schur" (BU 171–72). Bernd Neumann claims that the two books prior to *The Third Book* were those by Ullrich (which Neumann considers to be two versions of the same book) and another called *Täve* written by Adolf Klimanschewsky and published in 1955 in East Berlin.[10] Whether Pestalozzi or Neumann is correct is not important here; either way, Johnson certainly based his novel loosely on historical material and a historical person. The fact that three books exist about the same person—in reality or in fiction—already throws open to debate the notion that any one biographer can claim to have captured the real person.

As in *Speculations,* the relationship of the three protagonists represents a strange manner of love triangle that shows no signs of tension-filled rivalry. Karsch, as westerner and Karin's former boyfriend, presents no discernible threat to Achim as far as the relationship to his girlfriend is concerned. Achim interests Karsch as the object of his biography. Karin is in a position to be the person closest to Achim, the one who potentially knows more about him than anybody else, a position that Karsch could envy. But such is not necessarily the case. Distinguishing features of the three main characters are frustratingly lacking, and those that come through in the text pale before the process of gathering and evaluating information about Achim's life. One critic outlines the relationship of the three characters as follows: Karin performs a mediating function between Karsch, the Western observer, and Achim T. the Eastern point of view.[11] In other words, Karin, as the self-confident counterpart to the misguided and confused Achim, represents the connection between him (East) and Karsch (West).

Love interests may not play a crucial part in the novel because little love seems to actually exist between the two main GDR figures. Achim and Karin's relationship evidences no passion or emotion but instead seems to be based on their common functions as role models for the state. Both of them lead staged and constructed public lives that entice Karsch, with his natural inquisitiveness as a journalist, "to lift the façade" (TBA 30). Karsch represents a set of Western eyes, a man who takes in and strives to understand what he observes. One critic claims that Karsch possesses no discernible individualizing elements at all: "Karsch, on the other hand, is a medium without individual characteristics."[12] The potential distinguishing attributes of his character are so enmeshed in the overriding narrative voice of the novel that a rounded personage seldom surfaces in the book. In the course of the novel, Karin comes to reject Achim and the state he represents, but little is known about her beyond her profession, her popularity, and her sense of responsibility for her actions. Karin is in certain instances an antagonist to Achim since her relationship to the state is more confrontational. Unlike Achim, Karin recognizes a direct correlation between her actions and their consequences. For instance, as Karin travels with Karsch to a local village where the collectivization of private farms is underway, they visit the grave of a farmer whose land was taken. The farmer had been coerced into signing his land over to the state and saw no reason to continue living. On discovering this injustice, Karin describes how she had voted for Achim to represent her and others in the People's Chamber. Because Achim voted for the collectivization of the farms, Karin, having voted for Achim, sees herself as bearing some responsibility for the farmer's suicide. At this point she leaves Achim. It may seem like an extreme reaction given the rather distant connection between Karin and the deceased farmer, but it is a distinguishing element of Johnson's female characters to possess this heightened sense of responsibility, social awareness, and guilt. Karin takes the position that individuals must decide what is right, while Achim is willing to allow the party to make such decisions for him. But the discussion of individual persons in the novel is potentially a moot point since, as another critic correctly observes, "description of the attempt and the background of the failure of the action" stand as the thematic focus of *The Third Book*.[13]

To the second question, "Who is this Achim?" (TBA 7), Karsch describes his first encounter, Achim's thirtieth birthday celebration sponsored by the state and held in a velodrome. Karsch answers the question of Achim's identity by describing his powerful effect on a crowd (TBA 7–10). Otherwise, Karsch answers this question in a conventional manner and even possesses a preconceived, rather Western, capitalist idea of the genre in which he works: "Does it also make you think of the rich old man in the warmth and quiet of his house that was built for him and him alone, as a boy he used to sell shoelaces on windy street corners, now he has made it?" (TBA 41). The biography of a thirty-year-old presumably should not present the pitfalls or require the effort of researching the life of a much older person. Exactly the opposite is true. Achim insists on striking descriptions of his life from the manuscript with the reminder that "his life didn't belong to him" (TBA 141). This reminder that Achim does not exist as a private person underscores the fact that, as is the case with most prominent people, he has separate public and private personages, which, if not held separate, threaten to destroy each other.

To somehow mesh Achim's public and private selves in a biography, a genre that purports a relatively high truth value, becomes an increasingly bewildering task for Karsch. The so-called foreman of the publishing house desires a "complete book" (TBA 42) but in actuality is only interested in Achim as a public figure and instrument of government power. As Mark Boulby states, "Achim is . . . the creation, not to say the creature, of his society."[14] Johnson was concerned with such a figure because he stands in a patently awkward and volatile position between the government and the people: "He is loved by the people and loved by the rulers, but since the people and the rulers are somewhat separated, he is a mediating figure. And that made him interesting to me."[15] Due to his strict separation of public and private selves, Achim represents a person afflicted with a chronic case of "opportunistic self-alienation," as Pestalozzi called it.[16] This self-alienation is just the measure Achim needs to prevent his own social, psychological, and emotional implosion. Self-deception here is a mechanism of self-preservation, and it never becomes clear whether Achim is aware of this fact beyond the level of self-preserving intuition. Since he represents a person caught between the limiting interests of the state and the arbitrary realities of his individual existence, self-alienation is another form of Achim's ruin as a complete individual. His public and private selves cannot be reconciled in a public form (the socialist biography) that, in turn, cannot accommodate private content due to its coerced didactic function aimed at legitimizing the state's control of power and desire to shape the convictions of its collective society. In his research, Karsch encounters a situation where the public image literally upstages the private, a state of affairs that pleases Achim and the publishers. But as Karsch explores his object, he discovers a potential for the private to over-power the public, a situation that Achim and the publishers deem threatening. In fact, Ammann's criticism of certain areas of Karsch's work in progress illustrates the threatening nature of the material: "Too private. Too private" (TBA 103). Karsch discovers that Achim presents himself as human putty to be molded as the prevailing ideology deems suitable for its purpose of control and domina-tion. For the East German state, he is the package in which its ideological mes-sages can effectively be delivered. In exchange, Achim lives materially well. For example, in the GDR of 1960, the average citizen did not own an automobile, the housing shortage was acute, and very few people were permitted to travel to the West. Achim has a chauffeur-driven car at his disposal, lives by himself in a spacious, well-furnished apartment, and races in the West. In light of these spe-cial privileges, the motivations behind Achim's activities appear opportunistic. Achim has become, in essence, a political prostitute.

On the bicycle Achim enjoys a secret existence for himself, one that is impenetrable by either the East German state or Karsch: "Only when he'd con-centrate all his attention on the relationship of body and bicycle (the sensation of motion) and speed up his pedaling, carefully breathing, until he'd experience a bearable and pleasant feeling of exertion, would his contentment be complete. He'd feel in tune with himself" (TBA 130). Some critics view this relationship between Achim and his bicycle as a metaphor for the unproblematic relationship between individual and society.[17] Even though this interpretation is feasible, ideas of advancing the cause of socialist society seem to have no place next to the personal pleasure that Achim extracts from riding the bicycle as fast as he can. Riding lends itself more as a metaphor of escape. On the bicycle Achim enjoys a sense of freedom that he can find nowhere else in his environment. While racing or training, he transcends the limitations placed on him by the regime and his past history. If Karsch could talk to the riding Achim, the one "in tune with himself," he might locate the genuine person. Karsch could then dis-tinguish the ideological icon Achim T. from the Achim of individual desires and feelings, the person with his own history.

In his conventional approach to the biography Karsch commences his research at Achim's birthplace and childhood sites to learn about the man's par-ents and adolescent experiences in wartime Germany. Karsch discovers that although Achim represents a model in his present socialist society, he was a par-adigmatic figure in the fascist society of the past. Achim belonged to the Hitler Youth, which all young people were more or less coerced to join. But Achim admits that he participated with conviction and with an enthusiasm for weapons, war games, and uniforms that was not necessarily required. He was involved in organized military exercises and was inculcated with fascist ideology such that his father, an erstwhile Social Democrat, became apprehensive and cautious around his own son. The Nazis brought misfortune and death to Achim's family and destroyed their home. Still, Achim did not comprehend the extent of the iniquity of the fascist regime whose ideology he readily accepted. When Achim lost his mother and sister in an Allied bombing attack, he still believed that the Jews had caused the war. When Gestapo agents ransacked his house on the suspicion that Achim's father had sabotaged a prototype remote control airplane, Achim continued to believe that the Germans were at war because they needed living space. In other words, the fourteen-year-old Achim did not show that he critically questioned fascist norms as he later grew to understand them. As Karsch researches Achim's later life, the events of the past that make up the private self become increasingly problematic for the depiction of a socialist role model.

In the throes of Achim's paradigm shift from a fascist to a socialist consciousness, Karsch must take his information about Achim's life and measure it against the state's stipulations about whether the material is permissible or restricted for publication. As far as the selection of material for the book is concerned, Karsch must proceed with an extraneous set of guidelines that follow the societal premises of the GDR (TBA 38). The following examples demonstrate the process of elimination that Karsch must work through to write the biography according to official guidelines. Achim received his first bicycle (literally) by accident when a soldier of the occupying Soviet army fell off of one in front of him. He helped the injured soldier to his feet and received the bicycle in return for his good deed (permissible material). Achim also describes how three Soviet soldiers later steal the bicycle back, exercising their prerogative as the victorious power over the Germans, a prerogative they take with women in Achim's town as well (restricted material). While he had the bicycle, he practiced riding it to increase his speed and endurance by experimenting with riding postures and breathing techniques (permissible material). However, he did so not to improve as an athlete but to visit his girlfriend every weekend in a town four hours away, traveling time that it is in his own self-interest to reduce (restricted material). The Red Army liberated Germany from fascism, so stories of Achim hiding his bicycle from Soviet soldiers contradict official history (restricted material). Achim's initial reluctance to join the Free German Youth, the socialist youth organization, contradicts his image as a lifelong socialist. Once in the Free German Youth, Achim uses this membership to his advantage by stealing away to capitalist West Berlin during one of its functions to buy a bicycle gearshift not available in East Germany. With this incident not only does he throw his true commitment to the cause into question, but, by paying for the gearshift in East German currency, he breaks a law stipulating that no East German money be taken to the West (all restricted material). Yet when he returns from West Berlin, he genuinely feels that he is again at home (permissible material). Achim speaks of his short sojourn in the West to compete in a bicycle race with convincing detail. He tells how alienating life in the West was for him and how the West German family with which he resided condescended to him. He resents this treatment despite the cornucopia that the West provides in material things (permissible material).

Achim lived through historical events but did not consciously experience them with the ready-made political awareness he now possesses—an awareness provided by the Socialist Unity Party. Of the time directly after the war when Achim should have been learning the difference between fascism and the occupying powers (first the Americans and then the Soviets), the novel says, "He lived as though he couldn't feel. He saw everything, but he couldn't put it together in his mind" (TBA 126). Even when Achim speaks of the June 1953 uprising, "he spoke like a blind man. As though he didn't know what he had once seen. As though the words didn't contain meaning" (TBA 238). This detached stance toward his life's experiences is an indication that he possesses no historical consciousness of his own and demonstrates a self-designed, repugnant distancing from the historical events that are a part of his identity.

In psychological terms, Achim has set up an effective defense mechanism against his history to maintain his present status. Thus the question marks covering Karsch's notes indicate that he is not dealing with a self-made man but with a made man, constructed by exterior forces. Achim's convictions and principles did not develop, they were received, paid for with his fame and willingness to represent the government. His public appearances are staged according to the political goals of the Socialist Unity Party. The meaning of his existence is controlled and one dimensional in that it portrays a simplified formula of static, timeless socialist conviction coupled with an adeptness in bicycle racing. A prime example of Achim's constructed image is his protest against the playing of the West German national anthem at a bicycle race in which he placed. The narrative account is re-created on film by producers working for the East German state. Several takes of the same scene show Achim stepping down from the platform at the sound of the West German anthem and resolutely walking away, insulted and determined to make the race organizers aware of their mistake. This knowledge causes readers to wonder whether Karin or Achim is really involved in professional acting.

Yet Achim's life is to be couched in a hero's narrative. Achim, as Karsch discovers, does not possess the agency that a hero needs to affect his environment. Achim experienced a life marked more "by sheer coincidence or persuasion" (TBA 173) than by self-determination and inner conviction. As becomes evident at various points in the novel, Achim is not always the winner of the race, and he has only been a committed party man for the past five years. He is not universally popular because many have become skeptical of his new government position and jealous of his lifestyle (TBA 163–64). The relationship between the East German government and the people was based on mutual mistrust, a fact to which the employment of hundreds of thousands of people in the state security service attests. The idea of a state that prided itself on its service to its people, as the GDR regime did, was an inflated notion indeed. The more Achim adopts the policies and the phrases of the "administrator" (Ulbricht) as his own, the further he grows from the people. As Achim's life story emerges from the memories of those who know him, it becomes evident that Achim is more a product of history than an agent of it. Although Achim might exist in a state of self-alienation, his denial of the past takes on the same instrumental quality that his function for the state possesses. His past is strange to him, an embarrassment, or even dangerous to his position because none of the socialist convictions that he presently supports can be detected in it. Should Achim's status come into question, his usefulness to the state will diminish and with it most certainly his privileges.

Ammann's demands concerning the contents of the book would also not allow for a description of Achim's evolution into the socialist order. Rather, she expects a narrative that portrays a person with a steadfast, unwavering socialist conviction that has always existed. Achim's story, however, in its most charitable form would be the tale of a young man who develops through the stages of his life to adopt a socialist consciousness. A biography that depicts how a great athlete had come to believe in and become committed to socialism could be as inspiring to readers as a figure that "is with us must have been with us for many years, must have defended the socialist order already in the criminal days" (TBA 98). Whether Achim actually believes in what he says in support of the Socialist Unity Party is up to the reader to decide. However, Karsch's material, as reflected in the novel, depicts a young man's development to a socialist consciousness. As the literary historian Wolfgang Emmerich points out, Johnson, in his early publications, parallels (or preempts) East German aesthetic development with his own development as a writer in the West.[18] In other words, Johnson offers readers a sense of how East German literature might have developed without the artificial and retarding restrictions placed on it by the GDR's political climate. In this respect, *The Third Book* parallels a form of East German literature called

*Ankunftsliteratur,* loosely translated as "arrival literature." Interestingly, this class of literature is named after a novel published in the same year as *The Third Book, Ankunft im Alltag* (Arrival in the Everyday), by influential East German author Brigitte Reimann (1933–73). This subgenre of East German literature depicts the transformation of the main character, who eventually learns the value of the socialist system for humanity; the main character, introduced as an uncommitted or even self-centered nonbeliever, thus "arrives" in socialism after a process of self-exploration and coming to terms with personal doubts. The character comes to recognize and fully support the principles of socialism and the norms of socialist society. *Ankunftsliteratur* involves pragmatic adjustments of the main character to the realities of socialist society.[19] Achim's story could be written to depict a similar development where a private individual, initially uninformed, indifferent, and disinterested in his socialist environment, eventually takes on the highest responsibility of his society in the People's Chamber and represents his nation at international competitions. As arrival literature, Achim's biography could be a pedagogically effective story, a tool for converting the unpersuaded rather than a static, impersonal depiction of a sports idol turned party functionary. Even though there is a suggested title in the novel for just such a depiction of Achim's life—"My Development toward a Political Conscience" (TBA 174)—neither Achim nor the East German publishers are ready for a new genre that allows for hesitancy or faltering in the socialist perspective of the central figure.

When Achim intervenes in the work, the biography stands to become an autobiography full of wishful thinking, with Achim essentially dictating to Karsch what should be written to fit the narrow political framework of the project. Achim "corrects" Karsch's rendition of the Free German Youth story in this manner: "After initial hesitation I realized (Of course you'd have to write: he) that one must not confine oneself in one's private life, but that one must take part in society, and asked to be admitted as a member—it was up to Karsch to realize that Achim's memory of owning that button moved faster than the entire year he had spent in (initial) hesitation" (TBA 138). Achim thus holds his politically damaging past at arm's length, separate from the image that he represents for the government and the populace in the present. Karsch must be willing to write Achim's life in a continually corrective mode to produce an ideologically enabling fiction that will legitimate Achim's continued existence as an idol and national hero. Conventional thinking would say that Achim is the single best source of information for his biography, but his meddlesomeness discredits the project in terms of Karsch's methodology. As counterintuitive as it sounds, Achim's participation in the project detracts from its authenticity: "He wanted to have lived all along the way he lived now, as a member of the administrator's party for the last five years: at last convinced and committed to the justice of a State which had shown him nothing but pleasant aspects. He was looking for indications of this tendency in his life and not for the other trends, that's what he wanted of his truths, and they were his after all" (TBA 174). When a secret detractor of Achim's character sends Karsch a photograph of someone who looks like Achim in the front lines of an antigovernment demonstration during the June 1953 uprising, Achim denies participation. He claims to have been elsewhere training for his next race. Karsch can only say, "I can't think of anything more" (TBA 242). Karsch means that he has exhausted his capacity to invent, ignore, overlook, recast, structure, order, select, and understand information for the biography. The government representative is in the ironic position of not being himself representable in narrative. In other words, Achim has become too sublime for representation. At this ludicrous impasse Karsch succumbs to the impossibility of the situation, recognizing the futility of working cooperatively with Achim and the publisher on the project.

## Border

Karsch's seemingly well-defined project is a special experiment that possesses a doubly significant ideological importance, "reunification for two people, etc." (TBA 108). The book, if completed, would not only package Achim's life in revised history but would stand as an affirmation to the possibility of German unification, as the West German Karsch and his East German publishers work jointly on a project of mutual cultural significance. Holger Helbig notes that unification was still the official goal of the East German regime in 1960, so the project was proposed in the spirit of and supported by this political sentiment.[20] But the depiction of Achim as standing "for all of Germany" (TBA 31) turns out to be a farce; in reality, Achim is sole property of the Socialist Unity Party. The symbolic unification that could have occurred in the successful completion of the project is sadly unrealizable.

When Karsch crosses the border into the GDR, he discovers a land that meets his Western eyes with an unanticipated strangeness (TBA 15–16). Never before had he traveled to another country where, despite knowing the language, he felt so out of place or disconnected from his surroundings. His sense of alienation permeates the narrative. When Karsch entered East German territory he became an instant stranger relegated to the position of outside observer (TBA 21). In other countries he could rely on certain superficial trappings of capitalism to help him relate to the culture. The brand names of consumer products, the conduct of waiters and waitresses, and the automobiles were the same as in his native West Germany (TBA 15–17). In the East, although he knows the language, he cannot communicate as someone who understands the lifestyle and culture in which his book will necessarily have to be set. In this respect it is odd that an East German publisher would propose to a West German visitor the project of writing a book about one of the GDR's greatest sports idols. However, Neumann correctly views the entire novel as delineating an East-West dialogue in the central conflict that arises between Achim and Karsch.[21] Of course, understanding can only begin by crossing the border and making an attempt, as Karsch does. Boulby cites this as the reason for the person asking the questions of Karsch, for this nameless inquirer provides a "thoroughly western standpoint, one that is ideologically conditioned."[22] The questions of the unidentified recipient of Karsch's story are thus an ideological starting point for Western readers that Karsch himself can no longer provide.

Karsch's observation that "Only occasionally . . . did he [Karsch] feel reminded of the past history both Germanys had in common" (TBA 16) indicates that Achim's life lacks any threads common to both Germanys. Such connections will need to be constructed according to the ideological guidelines of the Socialist Unity Party. Karsch resists the party's blatant functionalist view of history and the contemporary political situation in Germany to remain with what he deems a truer and more balanced belief system that weighs the Western and Eastern perspectives equally. Interestingly, Karsch is not completely successful at withstanding the ideological "hailing" (*Althusser*) of the East because he returns to the West a changed person. His long sojourn in the GDR has made him "incomprehensibly distant" (TBA 7) from his friends at home. He understands the Eastern point of view better than do the vast majority of his fellow citizens and thus draws attention to the fact that the West is tragically and inexplicably naive about its compatriots in the East.

At the beginning of the novel, the narrator stresses the importance of the border for the story that follows: "But Karsch, the way he looks, the reason for his trip, are far less important at this point than the absolutely natural suddenness with which streets break off in front of earthworks or in ditches or before walls" (TBA 3). The prevalence of the border appears to be misplaced and is difficult to comprehend because it is barely mentioned after this page. The placement of the border, however, is taken out of its physical manifestations and reflected consistently in Karsch's experiences in the East. It manifests itself in the minds of the main characters and the same language but different vocabularies that they use. The East and West's common language, history, and cultural tradition actually damage Karsch's project because they provide him with a false sense of familiarity with the Germans on the other side of the border. Johnson portrays Karsch and Achim in such a way as to project the mutual incomprehensibility of the 60 million West Germans and the 17 million East Germans. Lack of understanding contributes to the failure of the project as much as the unreconcilable emphases and levels of interestedness in its contents and purpose. Toward the close of the narrative, Achim reproaches his biographer: "Do I have to go on telling you. You just can't understand" (TBA 230). Johnson was the first German intellectual to predict that the border was more than politics and geography. In this vein, *The Third Book* is one of the first cultural manifestations of the idea that the border between East and West Germany was a spiritual, mental, and emotional phenomenon in the minds of individual Germans as well as a violent physical presence.

## "An Absence"

In 1964 Johnson published a collection of short stories entitled *Karsch, und andere Prosa* (Karsch, and other Prose), one of which, "Eine Reise wegwohin, 1960," translated as "An Absence," again takes up the Karsch story.[23] Interestingly, intimated in "An Absence" is the notion that Karsch was not primarily interested in Achim's life as book material and used the biography as a pretext to remain in the East to enable a sojourn of exploration. Thus, Karsch also utilized the three-month stay to gather material for the travel section of his newspaper in Hamburg: "Gradually he told the story of Achim's whole life— along with his efforts to describe it, merely not to be giving away his planned article" (AA 44). "An Absence" provides more detail about Karsch's trip to the GDR. The alienation between the people of East and West Germany is further accentuated with a scene in which he visits a family in Mecklenburg that had hidden him when he deserted from the German army toward the end of the war. The man with whom Karsch speaks is actually Martin Niebuhr, Klaus Niebuhr's uncle from *Ingrid Babendererde*. Karsch discovers that he has no meaningful connection to his erstwhile protector, who shows signs of uneasiness at the journalist's presence. The common history between the Germanys that Karsch sought in Achim's life does not even exist between two persons who experienced Germany's criminal days together in solidarity against the Nazis. But more importantly, "An Absence" takes up in greater detail Karsch's difficult reentry into West German society.

When Karsch arrives back in Hamburg, he finds his bank account empty and no prospects for work. Furthermore, he is emotionally exhausted, morally dejected, and infinitely better informed about Germany. In fact, he returns home with a level of informedness that proves detrimental to his psychological and emotional well-being, for his enhanced knowledge of Germany becomes like a disease. Günter Blöcker writes, for example, that this fifty-page piece introduces readers to the psychological side of Karsch.[24] Karsch moves into a different apartment to seclude himself. He also visits with his son and sees his ex-wife, encounters that emphasize his disconnectedness from life. Through these interactions readers learn a lot of background information about Karsch that elevates him from the level of a Western gaze in the Achim novel to a person with his own alienating past. Norbert Mecklenburg correctly claims that "An Absence" shows a person undergoing a "learning process," albeit at its devastating conclusion.[25] Midway through the narrative, Karsch encounters a group of refugees from the East just arriving in the West: "they did not yet belong here, as they no longer belonged there; and in this moment of indecision Karsch was closer to them than a West German" (AA 39). Thus, the initial stages of Karsch's education about Germany take place in the Achim novel, while the final stage of his learning process is the completion of his alienation from both Germanys, described in "An Absence."

"An Absence" can be viewed as Johnson's way of adjusting the critical gaze set on East German society in *The Third Book* by providing an equally candid discussion of West German ideological idiosyncrasies. His ingenuous outlook where objectivity, truth, freedom of speech, and the integrity of his work as a journalist are concerned has been severely challenged by his experiences in the East. Readers witness how that challenge continues in the West. In "An Absence" the West German government, putatively democratic and pluralistic in its scope, cannot tolerate some of Karsch's political views. Karsch makes public, in print and on television, his opinion that the GDR should be recognized by the Federal Republic of Germany as an autonomous state. This opinion directly contradicts government policy and, more seriously, challenges the central premise of the West German Basic Law, which stipulates the existence of a single German state under a democratically elected government. After Karsch's public appearances, West German police enter his apartment and confiscate years worth of photographs and notes from his personal working files. Although the police of the Federal Republic of Germany are neater, the action reminds readers of the Gestapo's search of Achim's house when he was a boy. Karsch discovered the East German population's healthy suspicion toward the state, an attitude that is best delineated in Karin. In West Germany Karsch notes that the state's interests are more pervasively and efficaciously equated with the noble ideas of free speech, equal rights, and political freedom. These citizens' rights are more closely aligned with the political agenda of the West German state in the minds of its citizens. For example, on hearing Karsch's political stance on the East German issue, his landlord calls him an "unpatriotic scoundrel" (AA

54); he receives threatening and insulting phone calls from people who never identify themselves (AA 53); and he is only moved to act independently on his opinion after a newspaper editor says, "An independent newspaper directed to middle-class subscribers cannot in the middle of July suddenly and without instructions from the board of directors depart from the guidelines of West German government policies" (AA 46). Knowing both German states from the experience of having been checked, limited, suspected, scrutinized, used, and violated in his profession as a journalist, Karsch learns that Germans on both sides of the border have not mastered their common past.

Germany is a place Karsch can no longer call home without either living a lie, like the opportunistic Achim, or denying what he knows, which is impossible for a man of his integrity. He now lives in Italy and "can be persuaded to come to West Germany only on the most essential business" (AA 58). As a sign that Karsch will never come home again, the author informs us that he will contribute to the travel sections of newspapers in West Germany. Travel articles require, after all, continuous travel, but more importantly, Karsch is only responsible for descriptions of beautiful places that people wish to visit. Karsch has decided that such unproblematic descriptions constitute the limit of his ability. In the end, he leads a life of self-imposed exile (not unlike his creator, ten years later) and can reconcile himself with Germany much better at a distance.

# CHAPTER 6

# Of Sports Cars and Private Spaces

*Two Views*

Considering that the titles of Uwe Johnson's first two published novels include the terms *speculations* and *third book,* it becomes clear, even superficially, that he does not approach a topic or story in a straightforward fashion or from a single angle. In either the plural forms of nouns or the numerals in each title, Johnson indicates the lack of an authoritative center in his narratives. With his focus continually on divided Germany, Johnson claims that his disjunctive and antilinear approach to narrative is the symptom of the extremely complex situation in Germany. On the soil of a single nation, the two states, representing two opposing ideologies, could lay claim to a common cultural tradition. Until 1990 these German states maintained a troubled relationship compounded by the superpowers that occupied them: "Under such circumstances as they are in Germany one cannot actually say that the author is making things difficult out of so much obstinacy."[1] Johnson's next novel remains thematically with the division of Germany, characterized in the two persons of the story. The story speaks of the trepidations involved in crossing the German-German border, the difficulty of relations between compatriots who live on either side, and the experience of a significant historical event that has an impact on the lives of millions of people. Although Johnson does not break with his established thematic focus, he does undergo a stylistic change in this next book. He himself acknowledged that *Zwei Ansichten* (*Two Views*), published in 1965, demands less of its readers than *Speculations* and *The Third Book about Achim.* As Johnson once stated in an interview, this story presented fewer complications and required less thought about form than his previous novels: "We are not dealing here with the explanation of a death and with various persons who pursue various interests in this explanation. Rather, in *Two Views* we have only two persons who each present their view of the development. That is a simpler story."[2] Where *The Third Book* both begins and ends with a border crossing, *Two Views* merely ends with one. Where *Speculations* involves border crossings that go both ways and end in tragedy, *Two Views* describes a crossing from East to West and ends on an uncharacteristically optimistic note, or so it seems. *Two Views* also evidences an approach to narrative different from Johnson's other novels, texts that warranted the generally accepted opinion that Johnson is a difficult author to read. One might say that *Two Views* is decidedly more user-friendly.

Despite the modern setting, the substance of the story is centuries old, as Johnson admitted, and is quite familiar to all who read stories. In short, Johnson recasts the plot of *Romeo and Juliet:* lovers are separated against their will by conflicting ideologies and the German states that propound them. Family loyalty will not hold them apart but rather the violent border that separated the two Germanys for forty years. Johnson explained the narrative's story material as follows: "Even some of the old motifs appear modern: the family feud that resists the union of the children is nowadays replaced by the feud of the states that want to hold their citizens for themselves; the understanding between the two is so impeded and accordingly defective that it can be compared to the wrong letter that Romeo obtained in Alexandria; and the absolute separation by death presents itself as contemporary as four or fourteen centuries ago in the mere risk of death."[3] The center of the tragedy in this version of the story of separated lovers does not rest upon the death of the "star-crossed" lovers but rather on the miscommunication and misunderstanding that exists between their respective states. The lovers have not died, but any aspiration of a unified Germany—or at least a German nation that can communicate normally between its two states and their respective populations—has perished. As in *The Third Book,* Johnson demonstrates the impossibility of East-West German unification in the form of an ill-fated relationship between two individuals. Johnson, in a sense, provided West German readers another cultural manifestation that the wall and border had planted themselves in the minds of East and West German citizens as well as constituting a menacing presence.

## Plot

Johnson often maintained that writers can only write about that which they know. Thus, the story in *Two Views* is a conglomeration of several autobiographical factors. Johnson's wife-to-be, Elisabeth Schmidt, crossed the border in early 1962, about six months after the building of the Berlin Wall. After her escape, Johnson remained in contact with members of the Girrmann Group, whose activities helped many East German citizens cross the seemingly hermetic border. Johnson describes details of their activities in *Begleitumstände* (BU 255–64). In fact, the dedication at the front of *Zwei Ansichten,* "für S. B.," refers to a married couple who worked with the Girrmann Group and provided

Johnson with information about its smuggling methods. The engagement of Johnson's sister-in-law, Jutta Schmidt, to Dietbert Busch was broken off in 1964 as a result of their long separation created by the Berlin Wall. Furthermore, Johnson was in regular contact with women who worked in health care in the East. He collected extensive information about Beate's working environment from a source known only as "Nurse Renate" and a friend in Leipzig familiar with the East German health-care system.[4] Johnson's diverse experiences come together in this narrative about two people who are united in spite of the wall only to separate again once they are together in the West.

As the title suggests, the story has two perspectives, one of a man living in the West (Dietbert Ballhusen) and the other of a woman living in the East (Beate Dusenschön). The story of the West German, a professional photographer, revolves around the acquisition and subsequent loss of an expensive sports car. While on a local assignment, he discovers the unfortunate vehicle being salvaged from a canal into which its owner had plunged it. The photographer buys it for a low sum, has it refurbished, and drives it to Berlin with the intention of showing it off to his East German girlfriend, Beate. Instead, despite an elaborate security system, he wakes up one morning to find only an oil stain in the place it had occupied the night before. The stolen car throws Dietbert into an emotional frenzy that precipitates a series of trips among West Berlin, Hamburg, and his small town in Schleswig-Holstein in search of comfort, distraction, and consolation. He travels in order to obtain another sports car, to meet with Beate, and to attempt to turn opportunity into cash. He photographs the newly built wall and attempts to sell pictures of it, an endeavor that meets with mixed success. Four activities ultimately provide the framework of Dietbert's life in this narrative: commuting between Schleswig-Holstein and West Berlin, opportunistic sexual exploits with various unidentified women, heavy drinking, and pining for his East German lover.

One afternoon in West Berlin, while searching used car lots for another automobile like the stolen one, Dietbert stops at a bar whose proprietor catches his eye. His no doubt sexual interest in this young woman brings him back to the establishment on subsequent evenings. He discovers that the bar is the meeting place for a group of young people who help East German citizens cross the closed border. One evening, after many drinks, the West German "hero" writes his East German girlfriend a love letter implying that she should come and join him in the West. In his drunken stupor he forgets the letter, sealed and addressed, lying on the bar. Someone in the group discovers the letter and delivers it, thus opening the opportunity for the group to help two people reunite. Dietbert

acquiesces to the group's plans to bring Beate over. Even though the group operates at less than cost, Dietbert hesitates when asked to contribute to the expens-
es involved. He feigns poverty and offers an amount equal to "the tenth part of
the value of a compact car at that time. When the man drew his face into dubi-
ous folds, wiped his brown hair with a troubled air, Dietbert raised his offer by
a fifth, hoping this would make him seem credibly poor."[5] When Beate decides
to join him in the West, he does all he can to obtain another sports car, seeking
to greet her in a style befitting a successful westerner. The thief turns out to be
a young West German man seeking to run with his East German girlfriend
underneath the provisional crossing gate into the western part of the city. This
attempt misfires due to the young man's failed estimation of how low to the
ground the automobile actually sits. The ensuing crash totals the car, and the
West German man is taken off to an East German prison. To avoid embarrassment to their family, the car thief's wealthy parents have paid Dietbert a lump
sum of money to get a new car. Dietbert travels to Stuttgart to purchase a new
car directly from the factory. He races the car back to Berlin, but the brand-new
motor is not broken in for fast driving. Dietbert stalls on the autobahn, loses precious hours with a mechanic, and must continue his trip driving slowly because
of the sensitive engine. He is forced to travel to Hamburg, where he can catch a
flight to Berlin to make up lost time, but he fails to reach the rendezvous point
at the prearranged time. On the final leg of his journey, in a mad dash to see
Beate, he crosses a street without looking, is struck by a bus, and lands in the
hospital with a concussion. After much coaxing from the barmaid, Beate eventually visits Dietbert there and gives him an evasive answer to his proposal of
marriage.

Beate is a nurse at a state-operated hospital in East Berlin. She has settled
willingly into a life in the East German republic even though she has previous-
ly been treated unfairly by the government. Her father was an officer in the
German army in the Second World War; when the Red Army occupied the eastern part of Germany, the Soviets arrested him because of his status in fascist
Germany, and he was never heard from again. Because of her father's affiliation
with the previous regime, the new socialist government punishes her by denying her the opportunity to take university preparatory classes. Beate originally
wanted to become a doctor but goes instead into nursing in a quest to become
independent—that is, to escape the constraints placed on her by family and
state.

Upon receiving her job in East Berlin, the hospital management offers her
a double room in a dormitory located in a wing of the hospital, but she turns it

down on a pretext, preferring to illegally arrange a private room in the city. The closing of the East Berlin–West Berlin border directly affects the young nurse. Of all her family members, she is most attached to her youngest brother, whom she mothered during the difficult years after the war. Beate is thus devastated when he manages to cross the closed border. His illegal emigration represents a genuine emotional loss for her, and she again suffers government reprisals due to the actions of a member of her family. In a quest to find out how her brother prepared his escape, East German Stasi officials discover her private room and interrogate, harass, and finally evict her, forcing her to take a double room at the hospital. At work she is demoted, treated poorly, and given menial tasks to perform. One day a member of the smuggling group visits her to deliver the letter from Dietbert, introducing into her cheerless life the possibility of her leaving the GDR. Many visits from members of the group follow as Beate performs certain tasks for them in exchange for Western medicines for her patients. She also prepares mentally and emotionally for her own departure. Via hand-carried note she replies to her West German suitor that she will come across the border, but not necessarily or primarily for his love. She crosses the border in the north posing as an Austrian tourist in transit to Scandinavia. To her deep disappointment, moments before she is to cross the border, she discovers that her false papers have the wrong color eyes. She now questions the sincerity of Dietbert's love but cannot turn back. She travels first to Copenhagen, from there to Hamburg, and then on to West Berlin, ending up just a few blocks away from where she started but in a completely different world. She visits Dietbert in the hospital, where she says that she will "think over" (TV 183) his proposal of marriage and leaves with a newspaper under her arm. She wants to find work and a room of her own.

## Historical Circumstances

As with Johnson's other novels, *Two Views* centers on a significant historical event that directly affects the characters' lives. Although the border between the German Democratic Republic and the Federal Republic of Germany had been sealed soon after the war, an open border existed between the two parts of Berlin until 1961. East German citizens could still travel relatively unhindered to West Berlin, where they could easily obtain West German citizenship. East Germans visited West Berlin for a variety of reasons, to "go shopping there or visit friends, go to the movies or enter the refugee camp and be flown to West Germany, into the open world and another way of living" (TV 34). From 1949, when the GDR came into existence, up to 13 August 1961 more than 2.6 million of the GDR's 17 million inhabitants left. In August 1961 alone, 47,000 citizens crossed the border from East to West Berlin, enticed no doubt by higher wages, better living conditions, and the opportunity to become West German citizens with access to all the advantages (and drawbacks) of a Western society. Of the magnitude of the exodus, Johnson says, "Daily now over one thousand persons threw away their East German papers, a township in a week, a small city in a month" (TV 31).

Many of those who crossed were like Beate, under twenty-five years of age and trained in a skill or profession vital to the economic viability of the socialist state.[6] As reprehensible as the building of the wall was, this social "bloodletting" or "brain drain," as it is sometimes called, had to be stopped. Training citizens in vital skills at great expense only to lose them across the border severely undermined the GDR's economic and social stability. Thus, the "Anti-Fascist Protection Wall," as it was officially known in the East, or the "Wall of Shame," as it was unofficially known in the West, became a symbol of cold-war confrontation and an amazingly lucrative tourist attraction in West Berlin. Hereafter a map of Berlin available in the eastern part of the city displayed *Westberlin* printed as one word on a yellow field minus the designation of streets or neighborhoods. For citizens of the GDR, the western portion of the city officially did not exist.

## Narrative Structure

In *Two Views* Johnson reinforces and substantiates his belief that the nature of the story determines the form of the work in which it appears. Whereas *The Third Book* and *Speculations* were both labeled "novel," *Two Views* carries no generic designation. This book seems to defy any such classification, although the label "novel" could be applied without stretching the generally accepted limits of its definition. *Two Views* could also be considered a conventional piece of prose compared to the works published before and after it. More than any other of Johnson's novels, *Two Views,* as its title indicates, possesses a highly symmetrical structure, which is reflected in the initials of the protagonists (D. B. and B. D.). The two perspectives, represented by two main characters, are divided evenly on the western and eastern sides of the Berlin Wall. The book is 243 pages long (German version), 183 pages in translation, and comprises ten chapters, five devoted to the perspective of each character, starting with Dietbert. The narrator recounts the tale in the third person and enters into the characters' most private realms and thoughts, making him the most omniscient of all of Johnson's narrative voices. Yet the narrator has a small moment of doubt where he questions his information and thus reminds readers that omniscience is still a chimera in Johnson's mind: "She did not start up until three (three? yes) younger men in proper suits, on which the badge of the government party would not have stood out so prominently yesterday, pulled the man from his seat, and surrounded him at the car wall with general menaces such as: 'We've put up with your kind long enough, now things can be done'" (TV 40). Johnson has obviously retreated significantly from his previous radicalization of narrative stance to take up a more traditional, almost nineteenth-century realist, narrative view. It is necessary to say "almost" because, as in *The Third Book,* Johnson depicts the two sides of this story as the report of another person, a third person, as it were. At the conclusion of the two parts of the story the narrator encounters both main figures within the narrative itself, thus depicting them as the sources of the story. After the accident with the bus, the narrator helps Dietbert to his feet and accompanies him in the ambulance to the hospital: "I helped to pick him up and rode in the howling ambulance to the emergency station with him" (TV 180). The implication is that the narrator learns Dietbert's story after meeting him in this unusual manner. The narrator knows Beate personally because she stays with him, his wife, and their daughter for a week after crossing the border: "Later she made me promise. 'But you must make up everything you write!' she said. It is made up" (TV 183). Beate provides the story about herself and her crossing, and she thus represents the source of her own story.

Herein lies the real authority and authenticity of the narrator's stance, not in the gestures of authoritative reporting inherent to his third-person, seemingly objective stance. The narrator is revealed in the text in such a way as to show that he is just a mediator of the two views being presented. He has not witnessed the unfolding of events but rather has learned of them in conversation with the participants, a situation that alerts readers to the fact that the views are, in turn, the invention of yet another subjective recounting of the events. The narrator constructs the chronology and structure for the readers, but the material has been "discovered" by the storyteller. The appearance of the narrator in his own representation of the story affords the narrative a measure of authenticity and credibility exactly because it simultaneously throws into question the absolute omniscience of the narrator.

## Dietbert Ballhusen and Beate Dusenschön

Unlike *The Third Book,* in which the story centered on clashing interests in a single and singular project, it is advantageous in a discussion of *Two Views* to concentrate on the characters. In this story, psychological traits drive a narrative about an apparently political topic that revolves around a putative romance. Basically, to understand Dietbert and his activities requires thinking in psychological terms. The driving force of Dietbert's character is his constant attempts to compensate for his sense of inferiority compounded by his low self-esteem. His reductive sense of self results from his provincial origins; furthermore, he works at a low-level position as photographer for the local news section of a small-town newspaper. Dietbert is opportunistic but has little ambition; he fears flying, is daunted by the big city, is intimidated by people with more financial power, and is overweight. He seeks to rectify these aspects of his identity by playing the big spender (exclusively on himself), driving a red high-status sports car, and traveling frequently to the big city by airplane. Furthermore, he attempts to make up for deficiencies in his life by playing around with fast women and fast cars, by putting on airs, and by consuming alarming amounts of alcohol. These activities reveal the image of a character who is self-indulgent, self-pitying, ungracious, unappreciative, materialistic, and indecisive. These adjectives describe a person whose goal is to create the cinematic scene in which the suave and debonair West German man drives in his sports car to the airport to whisk away to her ultimate happiness the young, beautiful, and materially deprived East German woman. Dietbert seeks to impress Beate merely by the aura of his material trappings. His entire worldview focuses on making an impression, especially on those to whom he feels, for one reason or another, superior. East Germans are, in his mind, vulnerable to his airs. He exercises his profession as a photographer on the same ephemeral effects as he sells images that speak most readily to the public's lust for sensation. In other words, whether privately or professionally, he needs to make a superficial but extraordinary impression.

Deprivation and insufficiency characterize Dietbert's aimless, hapless quests on both sides of the border. His activities center on regaining items that have been lost, ostensibly the sports car and Beate herself. For example, of his stolen car, the book says, "He was deprived of a great deal" (TV 5). Although he can, as a westerner, travel to East Berlin to see Beate, "he did not like the thought of meeting her there because he would have to leave her behind again, because such a trip seemed to him like going to see a sick person for whom there is no longer any hope" (TV 19). Dietbert has lost the important objects or properties of the image that he projects of and to himself.

As Bernd Neumann points out, Dietbert defines himself through consumption rather than production.[7] Due to his basic posture as a consumer, he seeks to possess everything he desires, even those qualities that are not consumable and thus possessible. In an encounter with an East German woman to whom he has just delivered a letter for a nineteen-year-old acquaintance, Dietbert is impressed by the young woman's appearance and demeanor. He says, "'May I take your picture?'—thoughtlessly determined to have the photograph, also coveting to take her intensity with him" (TV 61). The intensity that he observes is this young woman's love for her boyfriend in the West, a love he is incapable of feeling. Dietbert's desire to possess even personal traits such as emotional intensity underscores the idea that he seeks merely to possess Beate as an addition or accessory to his sports car. Dietbert's actions and personality reveal that he lacks traits that should otherwise be evident to explain his desire to have Beate in the West. There is no genuine concern for Beate's well-being, no sincere inquiry about how she is doing, and no authentic expressions of love for her. When he receives the check from the parents of the young man who stole his car, the narrator says, "Young Dietbert could have been well out of the affair" (TV 71). He could have had any beautiful woman for his sports car, but he wants the one whom he has just rescued from an evil government, one who is unfamiliar with the riches of the West, one for whom he can play the hero, and one to whom he can feel superior. Without Beate his compensatory, inflated image of himself is simply not complete.

Beate, conversely, is defined more by who she is socially—that is, we know her by virtue of her performance as a nurse, her role as nurturing sister, and her interaction with colleagues and friends. She works in the health-care system, serving the state by exercising the duties of her profession, but she is not absolutely committed to the state's principles. In a diligent and highly efficient manner, she performs a function useful to the entire society in aiding the sick or injured. She is depicted as a devoted sister and daughter. Her past is revealed only insofar as it might explain how she came to decide finally to leave the GDR. Social circumstances explain that choice. The state that she serves has treated her unjustly in practically every aspect of her life as a social being. Her quality of life has been negatively affected by the breakup of her family and the loss of her private room; her life at work has been harmed and her friendships severely impaired by the state's exercise of its absolute power over its citizens. After the wall goes up, Beate believes, "The only ones who have a right to bawl are people like me who thought our system was some kind of strange strict teacher; now it's shown that it is our owner. It's put up a fence around its property" (TV 46). This sense of being owned, of being property in the view of the government, makes living in the East extremely uncomfortable for Beate. She has struggled for most of her life to become more independent in her immediate surroundings, and she always valued the freedom to choose the other side if she wished. She could not choose her profession, she cannot choose her political leaders, she cannot choose where she wants to live, and she cannot freely choose her friends. Now that the wall exists, she cannot even choose West Berlin, but ironically, as a reaction to the wall's creation, she does just that. On the surface her border crossing looks like a political move. It might be the quest for a better life or a search for love, but in the end it is a definitive gesture of self-determination.

On more than one occasion, Johnson clashed with literary critics, and the controversy about the interpretation of *Two Views* was intense. The debate developed around the names of the two main characters and what they represented. In the original German version, the West German man is referred to only as B and the East German woman only as D. Critics wrongly assumed that B personified society in the Bundesrepublik Deutschland (West Germany), while D stood for the Deutsche Demokratische Republik (East Germany). *Two Views* seemed to undermine the image of the West German protagonist as representing the better Germany. This perspective brought to the fore critics' suggestions that Johnson's capacity to create positive Western characters was deficient due to his preference for East German society. Even after years of Johnson's adamant rejection of this simple equivalency, interpreters of Johnson's work continue to find it irresistible to make this association in their treatments of the novel.[8] Moreover, the fact that the characters were identified merely by initials indicated to critics that B and D were stereotypes rather than rounded, highly individual, and carefully wrought characters. Many authors have, after all, used this technique to underplay the individualistic element of given characters and thus to enhance their function as archetypes; Heinrich Böll and Franz Kafka, whom Johnson read and held in high esteem, are prime examples of writers who used this technique with great efficacy. But the criticism did not go unanswered. *Two Views* represents one of those rare occasions when critics' misunderstanding exercised a direct effect on the work. In the translation, Johnson chose to reveal the characters full first names, Dietbert and Beate, as a response to the critics who insisted on such a simple association. Moreover, the autobiographical details of the book's conception and publication history release the author from negative intentions in the area of archetypal depictions of East and West German society.

And yet revealing the names of the main characters in the translated version does not completely cancel out the notion that Beate and Dietbert represent their respective societies on some level. Knowing the personalities of the two main characters enables an understanding of why West German critics would not take well to Dietbert as a fictitious illustration of their society. Horst Krüger claims that the West German part of the story possesses a "strangely pale and superficial" image, arguing that the narrator advances only one view of Germany (the Eastern one) because the depiction of the West is so typical of East German propaganda. The West German figure is thus an East German political construction, created by an East German who is "homesick" and lacking a sense of rootedness in the West.[9] The fact that Dietbert, with all his deficiencies, can be understood at all as a distinguishing figure of an entire society is ironically what makes him a possible representative. It must be stressed again that this was not Johnson's intention, and yet Dietbert possesses enough Western attributes that Western readers can see a piece of themselves in him. Dietbert is not met with incomprehension but with disdain and apprehension. Because of Johnson's sensitive and authentic portrayal of a person who is obviously the product of an advanced capitalist society, Dietbert's character conveys certain unattractive truths about life in the West. In Western eyes, Beate is a more sympathetic character, but she reflects positively on what was propagated in the West as a society brutalized by its Stalinist regime.

Thus, on some level the figures are only imaginable in the societies in which Johnson portrays them. Each character reflects concerns that have been conditioned by their social and political environments. Western advertising has worked on Dietbert; he concerns himself with an image that he partially creates by means of an expensive sports car, the "consumer product fetish par excellence."[10] Dietbert attempts to correct psychological and emotional disturbances with activities pleasing to the senses, an overt or subliminal message in most advertisements. He grants himself every excess without concerning himself with the destructive impracticality, exorbitant expense, or unnecessary risk of such indulgences. Dietbert naturally responds to the consumer expectations of his society to satisfy his desires, while Beate can follow her desires only through what is illegal behavior in her state. As long as his finances hold out, Dietbert can remain relatively content; with Dietbert, readers receive the impression that money really can buy satisfaction, another consistent advertising message. Beate displays a greater number of variables in her life that affect her emotional and mental balance. She concerns herself with her private sphere, the area of interest that requires the most protection and offers the best refuge from the intrusive nature of the East German state. There is no aspect of life that the state does not affect or, in Beate's case, besiege: "When she closed the door behind her now, to the room where no one knew she lived, she felt something like pride. She had something to defend; she had stood up for it, and successfully" (TV 8). Beate considers the concern for material goods an alienating attribute exemplified by the dysfunctional relationship she maintains with her oldest brother, who is constantly saving for his next middle-class acquisition: television, automobile, house. If she desired an image that had an effect in her society, she would need to join the Socialist Unity Party and wear a suit with the party emblem prominently displayed on the lapel of her jacket. She would also need to agree with state policies and use the language of the state to advance professionally.

Instead, Beate seeks private space, independence, and individual choice, privileges that Dietbert takes for granted and squanders on his side of the wall.

## The Views

Although the objects of each character's desire—symbolized by Dietbert's sports car and Beate's room—comprise revealing aspects of their respective societies, the comparison of East and West is not as prevalent an issue as it may appear. Throughout his works, Johnson invariably operates with views on specific issues as narrative problems. He explored and presented the varying perspectives on the biography of a famous athlete in *The Third Book* and on a fact-finding quest in the death of an exemplary individual in *Speculations.* The Eastern and Western points of view in these novels delineate important variables in deciphering what occurred in the story. Johnson does not allow his narrator or, more importantly, his readers the satisfaction of confidently choosing the side with the absolute truth. Anyone who reads these novels with care is left incapable of making such a choice. The same can be said of *Two Views.* In the title, *view* refers to the "old meanings of the word view, the vue, the prospect, 'seen from one side,' up to the simple difference of opinion."[11] In other words, *view* should be considered to possess a great semantic diversity in this book. The term applies to the novel's opinions, descriptions of land- and cityscapes, and hopes for the future as well as its perspectives on the past, on life in two different economic systems, and on obtaining what is desired out of life. No matter how the novel is approached, Dietbert and Beate provide two distinctive points of view even if readers receive them filtered through the third-person narrator. The artistry of Johnson's work lies in his creation of the possibility of simultaneously viewing the global issues and unique historical settings within the private realm of his characters. The two views in this novel are the perspectives on the incident of Beate's crossing the border, but they also contain the capacity to illuminate the two spheres into which the world was divided at the height of the cold war. To put it differently, the narrator describes how each person, from his or her side of the wall, views the events that lead to Beate leaving East Berlin for West Berlin. However by virtue of telling a story about individual lives in which the wall plays a prominent role, the narrator concurrently and surreptitiously discusses critically the dysfunctional manner in which East and West relate to each other.

Interestingly, Johnson chooses to describe the effect of the actual building of the wall from Beate's point of view but not from Dietbert's. Dietbert's story begins when he acquires his sports car in July 1961, but the next narrative-worthy event in his life occurs when his precious car is stolen. To describe Dietbert's reaction to the news of the wall's building is probably less than interesting, since Dietbert himself is disinterested in its existence. The young thief's passion and desperate response to permanent separation from his girlfriend allow Dietbert's lack of response to the building of the wall to appear all the more absurd. Is Dietbert, after all, not in the same predicament as the unfortunate young man who risked his life to reunite with his lover? Moreover, the wall is an abrupt end to any normalization of relations between the two parts of Germany; it is a sign of political failure on the part of the East and West German regimes. Millions of people have been separated from their loved ones and must pay for the consequences of this failure. Yet for Dietbert, the wall stands as an annoyance to his private desires: "He felt personally offended by the confinement of Beate in her Berlin; he had a private anger against the forbidden zones" (TV 18). One of his most realistic Western attributes is that he never asks himself why the wall was built. Instead, he reacts solely to its sudden physical presence. That response involves perfunctory consternation, but in other ways the wall presents financial opportunities. Dietbert and his compatriots in the West turn the physical reality of the Wall into a sellable, exchangeable commodity in the images they take of it: "He was able to market one of his pictures of the Wall that had been built between the two Berlins" (TV 16). Later in the book, the wall's positive economic impact on West Berlin is intimated as Dietbert arrives and is unable to find a hotel room because of the influx of tourists who have come to see the spectacle of East-West confrontation (TV 102). At one point in Dietbert's quest for sensational views that he can capture on film and sell, he rents an apartment window high above the wall from its tenant. From this vantage point he is able to photograph the various elements that comprise the border: watchtowers, barbed wire, military personnel (TV 108). On the Western side, in one of Johnson's most cynical insights, the reprehensible communist wall has produced its own example of capitalist trickle-down economics.

The wall does not affect the collective psyche of West Germans depicted in *Two Views*. In the East, however, Johnson creates the notion that there is a sense of life before and after the erection of the wall. Unlike the West, where life continues relatively unchanged by the barrier, each East German citizen will need to make psychological, social, and emotional adjustments to new circumstances. Some of these adjustments are reflected in Beate's observation of numerous inebriated people on the day the border was sealed and the report of increased suicides in the days that followed. Interestingly, Beate's reaction to the wall reveals what it signifies about her government, her future, and how she has lived her life up to that point: "She had lived under this state as in her own country, at home, trusting in an open future and the right to choose the other country. Locked in this one, she felt cheated, deceived, deluded" (TV 35). For Beate, the wall is a sign with a referentiality that reaches beyond its mere physical presence. It forces her to think differently about her life in the GDR since she now has no alternative but to persevere in the East.

## Severed Identities

Placed as a boundary—to restrict movement, to modify behavior, to contain desires, to thwart plans, to separate people, to divide a city—the wall exerts a debilitating effect on the identity formation of the two main characters. In a sense it represents an ego boundary as much as it determines a political, geographic, economic, and even cultural border. Thus, the unnaturalness of the wall is illuminated by the main characters' identity changes to adjust their views of each other and of themselves. Beyond the obvious necessity for Beate to cross the border with falsified identification papers—Beate becomes Martha for a few pages—the wall has precipitated for the characters the loss of items that significantly contributed to the composition of their identities. In an unusual series of causal relationships that begin with the building of the wall, Dietbert loses his sports car and Beate must relinquish her private room. Projections of personal space and outlooks on the future for the two main characters have always involved the other side of Berlin in some capacity. With the other Berlin severed, they have lost their sense of agency because an entire realm of opportunity and possibility has been cut off from them in one fell swoop. The smuggling group in the bar at Henrietta Square fills this void. While Dietbert languishes in bars in a state of self-pity and doubt, members of this group continually cross back and forth across the border as messengers and couriers. Dietbert's questionable desires become intertwined with their idealistic energy.

Dietbert's and Beate's first encounters with the smugglers are characterized by descriptions of an omnipotent force that metaphysically steers their actions. Thus, the introduction of the group into the narrative is akin to the deus ex machina that enters the plot to resolve the difficulties of the main characters. The language that describes Dietbert's discovery of the bar out of which the smuggling group works is most telling. Dietbert starts out the day "haphazardly" looking for another car in an area where he encounters people and places "unexpectedly." He walks about the neighborhood where the bar is located in a "planless" fashion thinking about his "blunderings" (TV 54–55). Exhausted and frustrated, he sits down at an outdoor table in front of the bar, which he thinks is just any bar: "Someone or other placed a beer in front of him" (TV 55). With this consecrating gesture Dietbert is unwittingly pulled into a highly organized and carefully planned process that ends in Beate's crossing to the other side. The matter-of-course air with which the group works, believing that it is uniting separated lovers, stands in marked contrast to the indecisiveness, reluctance, and feelings of guilt with which Dietbert approaches the procedure of getting Beate out. He explores other opportunities for helping Beate despite the fact that she has not asked for help. He foregoes one possibility for organizing her escape because the cost to him required "half the price of a compact car" (TV 120), making the financial commitment too high in proportion to his emotional investment in the project. Here Dietbert cannot even describe to the smuggler the reason he wishes to help Beate and only thinks of "love" after it has been suggested by the smuggler himself. In a drunken conversation with the barmaid on Henrietta Square, he mentions in passing that he wants to help an East German girl over the border. The proprietor of the bar takes his wish in earnest and writes on his tab that he should come by on Wednesday at 2:00 P.M. for a meeting. He receives the note on Sunday but does not discover it until Wednesday (by accident), after he has arranged a flight to leave Berlin. Again, where Dietbert's enthusiasm about the prospect of a reunion with Beate in the West is concerned, the descriptive words are telling. As instructed, he returns to the bar on his way to the airport. When he discovers that the bar is locked and there is nobody inside, he is "rather relieved" but looks "perplexedly" at the barmaid as she approaches from down the street and stops him from getting back into his cab (TV 128). He considers the image of daily life before him "incredulously" (TV 128) because this young woman, loaded down with shopping nets full of groceries and accompanied by her dog, claims to be able to outmaneuver the power and technology of East German security forces and border police to bring Beate to the West. Changing his plans, he goes "resignedly" (TV 128) to the man who will create the false papers for Beate. There is no indication that Dietbert's will is unequivocally behind the undertaking.

Beate, too, is not as resolute about crossing the border as she should be, given that she risks being shot or imprisoned if she is caught. The smuggling group seems to exercise the same power over Beate as it did on Dietbert. In her first encounter with a female member of the group, before realizing what this person wants to do for her, Beate "walked along as if she were being pulled" (TV 140). She receives Dietbert's drunken and forgotten letter but needs weeks to decide on her three-sentence answer because she wants no misunderstanding: she seeks to devise her response "so that not a word committed her to too much" (TV 146). At one stage in the preparation of the crossing, Beate displays regret at having the opportunity to move to the West; the freedom to choose one system over the other is apparently no longer her desire (TV 155). In one moment she experiences an intense sense of "homesickness" at the prospect of leaving, while in the next she cannot stand another day in the GDR. As far as their "love" is concerned, her feelings for Dietbert "won't be enough for a whole life, it's not nearly enough for coming over" (TV 148). On her ride to the northern border, she feels "trapped" in the train that is taking her away from the GDR. Strangely, in all the feelings she expresses about not having West Berlin open to her, "trapped" is never one of them. Her outright refusal to cross the border—probably the only time she expresses her true feelings about the undertaking—comes too late in the process. She has reached the border only to discover that Dietbert gave the creator of her new identity the wrong color for her eyes. On discovering this dangerous mistake, the narrator says, "She did not want to go on. . . . She wanted to turn back" (TV 175). She was not concerned about the possibility of being caught but rather was dismayed that her lover did not know her as well as she thought and thus could not really love her as he had claimed. Her reticence to cross sheds an intensely ironic light on the document she must sign in the West, which states, "I came of my own free will" (TV 182).

One of the greatest curiosities of *Two Views* is the fact that the love story does not make its full impact until the wall is present. Neumann says that the "love" between the two characters gains its "durability" only after the permanent separation becomes a reality.[12] Dietbert's intense desire for Beate grows out of his memory of her, which becomes magnified, intensified, and highly distorted by the knowledge that he cannot have her where he wants her (TV 26). Dietbert convinces himself first through Beate's inaccessibility and forced absence that he loves her. To use a cliché, absence and separation make the heart grow fonder because the wall forces individuals to use their imagination to create fantasy images that replace reality.[13] In explaining this phenomenon, Johnson retells a short piece by the French novelist Stendhal (1783–1842) that likens the psyche of a person in love to a branch tossed into a salt mine. After months in the mine the branch is covered completely with "shining diamonds" and it is no longer recognizable (BU 323). Stendhal's salt mine is the Berlin Wall, which compels the characters to create fictions that guide their activities. Dietbert creates delusions about Beate from the very beginning, as he believes that she will be impressed by his sports car and the material life of the West. In fact, some of Beate's hesitation to come to the West results from feeling alienated by westerners and mistrusting the capitalist system (TV 156–57). Dietbert drinks heavily, but alcohol makes her sick. On the one occasion that Beate receives a large amount of money as a work bonus, she generously gives it away, while Dietbert's spending is frivolous and always only on himself.

Beyond these rather minor contrasts, there are important differences, such as Beate's dedication to her family, her professional attitude toward her patients as caregiver, and her sense of responsibility, none of which Dietbert possesses or is inclined to appreciate in another person. Beate walks about the streets inventing Dietbert in her mind, partially from memory but mostly from her own idea of what traits an ideal conversation partner might possess. She creates "tedious dialogues" (TV 146) in her mind, trying to formulate a response to Dietbert's desire that she cross over to the West. She speaks with Dietbert silently as a product of her fantasy, but this imagined Dietbert is "a tall, reassuringly strong young man who fitted her idea of expressions like prudent, superior, patient, loyal; he was reticent, often too earnest, but she could easily make him smile just with a child's pout" (TV 147). Given what readers know about Dietbert, very little of Beate's imagined person is accurate. The characters transcend the wall by imagining the person on the other side without the interference and subsequent contamination of the actual person's presence. They create, in effect, false identities to figuratively cross the wall. If love exists in the story, it does so only in the main characters' imaginations.

Dietbert and Beate separately ask themselves the same question about the young students helping them. Dietbert "could not imagine why anyone should help him; he had helped no one" (TV 131–32). Beate "felt she had not deserved their help. It was not easy for her to imagine their reasons; she could not ask them" (TV 156). Although the answers are not available in *Two Views,* Johnson intimates in a related story called "Eine Kneipe geht verloren" ("A Tavern Vanishes") that the bar's proprietor enters into the smuggling affair initially to help a good friend to cross the border. She and some students continue with their activities to combat the sense of frustrating powerlessness that concerned individuals feel in the face of overwhelming political forces. Johnson here displays people who do something, within the scope of their own limited resources, against the reprehensible act of a national government. In particular, the bar's proprietor acts on her anger about the building of the wall while staving off feelings of individual powerlessness.[14] But the members of the smuggling group also work from an assumption. They execute their activities in this case trusting in ideal love while they supply logistics that lead to getting Beate and Dietbert permanently on the same side of the wall. Since the group possesses its own view on the matter, another acting subject or agent is introduced into the story as Dietbert and Beate are rendered passive by the construction of the wall. Thus Dietbert and Beate's fantasies as well as those of the group motivate the border crossing and thereby the narrative. Fictions beget fiction. The reticence of the two main characters and the inexplicable motivations of the smuggling group demonstrate that the dangerous border crossing takes place on the basis of imaginary constructs wrapped in misunderstanding, miscommunication, and false identities and generated by ideological assumptions. Beate's crossing is therefore a sort of accident.

## Cinematic Trappings

Because the novel portrays Beate more sympathetically than Dietbert, Manfred Durzak considers her the main character.[15] Patrick O'Neill claims that the narrative is more "focalized" on Beate, thus making her more sympathetic and a character with whom readers can readily identify.[16] These critics mention an important aspect of the novel, for Beate is, in many respects, a character who is better developed and "rounder" (to use E. M. Forster's term) than Dietbert. However, readers do not come to know Beate until Dietbert's cinematic delusions about his love for her beg the question of who she is. The scene that he seeks to create with her in his sports car, the spy-thriller trappings that he imagines in bringing her across the border, and his faulty information about the GDR (TV 121) all contribute to his filmic sense of this undertaking. These images fit into Dietbert's playacting in a master fiction of danger and intrigue. Dietbert's constant state of self-ironization, self-alienation, and self-delusion is, in essence, the germination of the story. Because of these traits, his desire for Beate grows into narrative movement.

Dietbert creates a film in experiencing his activities vicariously through internally projected cinematic scenes. As a photographer, he lives life as the two-dimensional and pure representation of film, moving or otherwise. Like the passive stance taken when watching a movie, life is there before him, but he does not need to interact with it. Dietbert has, however, partially created himself out of popular films. He derives his rules of love relationships from "movies" (TV 18), and he expresses his love in "moviephrases" (TV 147). He seeks out help for Beate with a "movie actor's poker face" (TV 119) and views himself as in a film when he receives Beate's letter asking him to help her come across the border: Dietbert "also felt as if he were looking at himself from outside, watching as in a movie a Dietbert who was acting unhappiness" (TV 124). He approaches the problem of his separation from Beate like fiction; he acts out his ordeal in a plot-driven movie that screams for a Hollywood-style resolution.

Dietbert's anticipated final scene, in which Beate climbs into his expensive red sports car, is the best imaginable conclusion of the film from a westerner's point of view. Such a scene represents the triumph of the West over the East. It is also an indication of how Dietbert views Beate not only as a woman but as a citizen of the underprivileged GDR. Dietbert perhaps does not accurately portray Western society in his personal attributes, but he does represent West

German society in his condescending attitude toward East Germans, which is characterized by a feeling of superiority and arrogance: "When he learned of her East German citizenship, his self-assurance increased sufficiently for him to invite her to dance" (TV 69). He operates from the notion that by virtue of his being from the wealthy West, he is impressive to a person from the poor East. That attitude goes for Dietbert as a person and for any material trappings he uses to create his image. When his car is stolen, he is forced to rent an older model that "not even an East Berlin girl would admire" (TV 12). He assumes that Beate's motives for leaving the East center on his own sense of status and self-esteem, which he, in turn, projects onto Beate. These constructions of Dietbert's that comprise his relationship to the East and to Beate are all shattered when she arrives in the West to ruin the end of his film by leaving him alone in his hospital bed. The happy ending of political freedom and marriage after the vagaries of escape and the emotional upheaval of separation are straight out of Hollywood, a plot structure and predictable denouement of which Beate wants no part.

## Freedom

Once in the West, Beate attempts to regain some of what she lost in the East: "In her coat pocket she had the weekend newspapers, which are so fat with advertisements, job offers and rentals; she wanted to look for a room" (TV 183). Having crossed the border, she wants to establish herself in a new, independent life in West Berlin. Her introduction into the new world at the beginning of a new year (January 1962) reveals itself to be a bittersweet experience. Government officials are as intrusive and intimidating in the West as they are in the East. Her fear of being caught with false identity papers intensifies again on her border crossing into West Germany from Denmark. She must enter a refugee camp in West Berlin, where a camp doctor examines her for sexually communicable diseases and agents interrogate her for military intelligence useful to the Western allies. The camp employees treat her like a criminal, as someone capable of infecting the West German society that she is about to enter. These annoyances aside, the optimism with which the novel ends is a bit uncharacteristic of Johnson's work. However, Johnson's characters continue to exist beyond the narratives in which they are depicted. In a later interview, for example, Johnson explained that after three years Beate is no longer happy in the West and regrets her decision to cross the border. If given the opportunity to start again, Beate would choose to stay in East Germany. In any case, the group that helped her escape no longer operates.[17] The bar that served as the group's base helped fund many of the crossings and thus eventually went out of business.[18] The disenchanting reunion coupled with the knowledge of an East German who made a wrong choice dashes the apparently optimistic ending of the book. The West is not the best.

# CHAPTER 7

# The Poetization of History

*Anniversaries: From the Life of Gesine Cresspahl*

More secondary literature has been devoted to the explication of Uwe Johnson's *Jahrestage: Aus dem Leben von Gesine Cresspahl* (*Anniversaries: From the Life of Gesine Cresspahl*)[1] than to any of his other novels, which is no surprise considering the massiveness and thematic richness of the novel. *Anniversaries* represents theoretically, philosophically, and aesthetically one of the most complex and important novels in all of German literary history. Even before the novel's completion in 1983, *Die Zeit,* Germany's most influential weekly newspaper, included *Anniversaries* in its 1979 list of the one hundred best books ever written. *Anniversaries* is the most ambitious work Johnson ever produced. He utilized the full potential of his insight into human desire, his uncanny sense of historical development, his extensive knowledge of philosophy, and his meticulous research skills to write a novel of epic proportions. With *Anniversaries,* Johnson finally unpacked his East German bags, for existence in northwestern Mecklenburg in the fictitious village of Jerichow reveals itself in lifelike totality.[2]

Johnson essentially reconstructed Germany's history through the portrayal of a small farming village as well as of the extended family of Heinrich Cresspahl and the surrounding community. Johnson always possessed this material, retaining it for an appropriate context in which to recount it. He explained in an interview that the lives of Heinrich and others were "known to him" at the time he wrote *Speculations* in the late 1950s and that it was difficult for him to "leave" Heinrich "out of *Speculations,*" because doing so reduced Gesine's father to a secondary character in that novel.[3] Many persons from Jerichow were either left out completely or appeared in a secondary role in *Speculations.* However the miniature Mecklenburg that Johnson stored in his imagination for more than a decade fully emerges in *Anniversaries.*

There are several indications that Johnson thought about Gesine Cresspahl during his working sojourn in New York City. His *New York Times* clippings contain notes as early as 1966 that Gesine was in New York. The idea for the novel was set as Johnson noticed her "on the southern side of 42nd Street heading for

Sixth Avenue" (BU 406). After all, none of his other characters could have ended up in New York in the same capacity as Gesine (BU 406–8). Johnson admits that he might have been the only person who saw Gesine there. Having made this discovery, his novel could begin. The former resident of Jerichow, who also appears in certain stories in the collection *Karsch, und andere Prosa,* is thirty-four years old and at a point in her life when it becomes important for her to know "Where do I come from, and what made me into what I am."[4] These deceptively simple questions are the germinating seed of this monumental novel, which stands, even in its massiveness, as only a partial answer. Thus, the main narrative perspective in *Anniversaries* is accorded to Gesine because the novel's contents, as the title assures us, indeed come "from the life of Gesine Cresspahl." Everything in the book can be measured against how it fits into Gesine's family, its history, her experiences, her political beliefs, her worldview, her professional world, and her circle of friends and acquaintances. As Manfred Durzak points out, Gesine is both the subject and the object of the narrative, creating thus the varying points of view that shift between first person, dialogue forms, and third-person narration to yield one of the most interesting and poignant lives in German fiction.[5]

## Plot and Historical Circumstances

Readers' extensive introduction to Gesine's life begins in August 1967 in New York City, where she works as a secretary and translator of French, Italian, and German correspondence for a major bank. She lives on Manhattan's Upper West Side with her ten-year-old daughter, Marie, at 243 Riverside Drive, Apartment 204, overlooking the Hudson River (BU 411). Jakob Abs is Marie's father, the result of a short love affair between Gesine and Jakob alluded to in *Speculations.* The novel runs along two time lines: one entails the narrated time, beginning with the Kapp putsch in 1920 in Germany and ending in August 1968 in the United States, and the other represents the time of narration, from 20 August 1967 to 20 August 1968 in New York City. Of course the time of narration leaves narrated time in its wake as each calendric entry closes and the next recorded date signals a new chapter. The narrated time in Germany contains a description of Jerichow as the villagers lead their lives and conduct their business against the backdrop of the greater events of German history. Johnson has populated the small community with a diverse group of people, including farmers, townspeople, nationalists, socialists, Protestants, Jews, landed aristocracy, large- and small-business owners, Nazis, communists, educated and uneducated people, skilled and unskilled laborers, and various families with individually developed prejudices, interests, and secrets. The globally significant historical events against which the village's activities are cast include the German depression of the 1920s, the rise of fascism in the '20s and '30s, life under fascism in the '30s, the Second World War, the British and Soviet occupations, and the establishment of the German Democratic Republic in 1949. In 1953 Gesine leaves East Germany for the West, which means readers too lose touch with Jerichow. She eventually moves to Düsseldorf, where she works as a secretary for NATO, but she resigns from the position to protest the British and French attack on Egypt as a result of its attempt to nationalize the Suez Canal. Since Gesine is a single mother, motivated by a heightened concern for job security, she chooses to apprentice in banking. In April 1961 Gesine and Marie move to New York City, where the narrative eventually catches up with itself in 1967. In the course of 1967–68, Gesine's work for the bank undergoes a qualitative change when its executives perceive an opportunity to profit from the reforms being implemented in Prague. The vice president of the bank, De Rosny, Gesine's boss, assigns her two missions: she must learn the Czech language, and she must prepare for a business trip to Prague in August 1968 to offer the reform government a hard-currency loan to help its fledgling economy. Readers also learn about Gesine and Marie's daily life. Their New York City is like New York City for many people; it includes the *New York Times,* the subway, diners, parks, rush hour, congestion, cultural diversity, security concerns, office culture, life without an automobile, and the South Ferry, all of which receive attention from Gesine's assessing gaze as a foreigner.

This massive work treats many historical events. The year 1968 rivals 1918, 1945, and 1989 in their significance for twentieth-century history. Besides the German past, Gesine concerns herself with the U.S. involvement in Vietnam; the assassinations of Martin Luther King Jr. and Robert F. Kennedy; civil strife in the United States, West Germany, and France; and other events as they appear in the novel through Gesine's reading of the newspaper. The most important of all the events for Gesine, overshadowing more than 50 percent of the narrative, is a period of reform in the former socialist Czechoslovakia known as the Prague Spring. Because of the country's stagnating economy, the Czech government under Stalinist leader Antonín Novotny had considered some limited economic reform. Reforms did not begin in earnest, however, until 4 January 1968, when Novotny was voted out of the position of first secretary of the Communist Party of Czechoslovakia. Alexander Dubcek was voted into power and immediately instituted basic democratic rights in the cultural, political, and economic spheres of Czechoslovakian society. It is interesting that *New York Times* stories describing this period read like reports about Mikhail Gorbachev's Soviet Union in the late 1980s. Dubcek sought to continue with necessary and desired reforms without arousing the consternation of the Soviets and of other conservative Warsaw Pact allies. In other words, he had to promote reform while simultaneously retarding the general population's desire for change that could go too far and too fast for the USSR. Thus, Dubcek was constantly in a position of internally implementing reform while externally reassuring the USSR of the Czech commitment to socialism, to the Warsaw Pact, and to the Eastern bloc's economic association, the Council for Mutual Economic Assistance (COMECON). Dubcek did not succeed at allaying his allies' concerns. Of all the Warsaw Pact leaders, including Soviet Leonid Brezhnev, East Germany's Walter Ulbricht was the most vocal opponent of Dubcek's liberal line. In late June a letter entitled "Two Thousand Words" was published in the Czech media; it called on the entire population to implement change freely and independently, thus creating the impression that the government was losing control of the reform process. The letter was translated and printed in full in the *New York Times* and in the German version of *Anniversaries* (and is an irritating omission in the translation). By mid-July the Soviet Union stopped the withdrawal of its troops from Czechoslovakia and commenced consultations with its allies as a form of intimidation. In August high-ranking members of the Czechoslovakian government who opposed reforms called on the Warsaw Pact to stop what they considered a dangerous counterrevolutionary development in their country. Late on 20 August and early the next morning, Eastern bloc troops led by the USSR occupied Czechoslovakia and put an end to the reform movement.[6] The last entry of *Anniversaries* is dated 20 August 1968: Gesine, Marie, and an old friend from Jerichow, Dr. Kliefoth, are walking on a beach in Denmark before the Cresspahls are to fly into the turmoil of the invasion of Czechoslovakia.

## Narrative Structure and Form

In numerous critical reviews and articles, *Anniversaries* has been referred to as a "family novel," a "historical novel," a "big city novel," a "provincial novel," a "homeland novel," and a "novel of the twentieth century." These labels are both correct and incorrect since each one touches on a portion of what makes *Anniversaries* a great novel while excluding many other significant aspects of its contents. In other words, no one label or combination of labels can capture the thematic richness of this piece of literature. This novel is a complex and sometimes perplexing mixture of all of these thematic concentrations along with implicit social commentary, political critique, didactic intentions, and perspicacious insights into humanity's grim tradition of oppression and violence. The form of *Anniversaries* is highly structured in its layout as a calendar, but it nonetheless follows the path of Johnson's other novels in its radicalization of narrative voice and withdrawal from any sense of denouement or narrative telos. The 367 calendric entries (1968 was a leap year, plus there is an undated opening entry) create clear breaks in the narrative with the recording of each new date. The recorded date simulates the masthead of the newspaper with which Gesine begins every day; it possesses the double function of beginning the next entry and closing the previous one. Johnson utilizes the space between the recorded days as a unit of narration in which all types of material from the past and present can exist under the heading of a single news date. The compactness, rigidity, and chronological progression of the calendar thus stand in marked contrast to the truncated and confused narrative progression within the single calendric entries. Johnson fooled himself with what he hoped would be a limiting effect of the calendric design of the book. He originally envisioned the days of a single calendar year at two pages per entry, adding up to a little more than seven hundred pages for the entire novel. He foresaw the material fitting into three volumes, one of which he planned to finish every two years. When the book was finished in April 1983, the German version had four volumes and 1,891 pages, which the American editors abridged and fit into two volumes totaling 1,147 pages.

With the prominence of calendric entries and division into volumes, critics have mistakenly referred to *Anniversaries* as a diary or a tetralogy (German edition). In numerous interviews Johnson rejected both generic categorizations. He corrected those who insisted on calling *Anniversaries* a tetralogy by referring to the various volumes of the novel as continuations, which in fact they are. The first volume appeared in 1970, the second in 1971, the third in 1973, and the fourth in 1983. The volumes do not individually represent varying themes surrounding a single concept but rather manifest a continuity in plot structure, pagination, narrative voice, and character identity. It is not possible to read one volume without the others because no single volume constitutes a self-sustaining narrative entity. If it were not physically awkward to handle and technologically cumbersome to produce and if the publisher could have waited more than ten years to publish *Anniversaries,* the book could have appeared all at once in a single volume. Of course, publishing the novel in installments made its reading a less daunting undertaking and thus eased the way for its reception by a public less and less interested in reading long, complicated novels.

*Anniversaries* cannot be categorized as a diary because the contents of each entry are not nearly as private or limited as they might be in that type of narrative. Much of the novel is in the third person, and the diary form should be, by definition, in the first person or at least reflect a consistent subjective first-person perspective. Much of *Anniversaries* contains descriptions or interpretations of events that Gesine did not experience directly or at which she was physically present but experienced as a child—that is, with little or no awareness of what was taking place. Johnson steadfastly maintained that Gesine commissioned him to write this text for her, which constitutes yet another reason why *Anniversaries* should not be categorized as a diary: people write diaries by themselves. Probably due to his frustration with obstinate critics, Johnson addressed the issue in the novel by explicitly stating, "This is not a diary" (Jt 4:1474).

In *Begleitumstände* Johnson explained that it was perhaps a manner of midlife awareness that caused Gesine to begin looking to the past with such intense interest. The point of her search is to learn about what constitutes her life besides the chronology of particular events (BU 415). Where chronological points of time in the distant past become too impersonal as structuring principles in the novel, Johnson substitutes bodies of water that have meaning for Gesine's life. Bernd Neumann explains, "In this element above all, in the substance of eternal transformation, the various times and their landscapes encounter each other in *Anniversaries*."[7] The lengthy descriptions at key, structurally symmetrical points in the novel attest to water's significance for the narrative. The novel's contents are bracketed within water motifs that have metaphorical intensity for readers and biographical significance for Gesine as a native of Mecklenburg and an avid swimmer. A description of the playfulness, vastness, and mystery of water initiates the narrative on the beach in New Jersey and ends it on the beach in Denmark (the Baltic Sea) on the same date, one year later. Volume 2 of the German version begins at a swimming pool with descriptions of the water's turbulent movement and the echoing sounds caused by the divers and swimmers who displace, disturb, and move through it. Volume 3 (the original final volume) starts at Lake Patton in northern New York State with a discussion of all the lakes in which Gesine had swum and representing various stations in Gesine's life. Add to these instances the continuous mentions of the Hudson River, the address on Riverside Drive, the Baltic Sea, and all the lakes in Mecklenburg and it becomes evident that water possesses biographical importance for the main character.

Water represents the substance of narrative: "What is valid for time is also valid for water as its epic image."[8] From time eternal, water has been a symbol of the source of life, a meaning that carries over to *Anniversaries*.[9] Like water, narrative is the stuff of life. The waves created in the ocean are allegories of lived moments whose authenticity will never be regained, try as an author or even a fictional character might. These moments are concealed as secrets of the dead past, brought back to a fragmentary and tenuous existence in narration: "The taut roll, already streaked with white, enfolds a hollow space of air that is crushed by the clear mass as if a secret had been created and destroyed there" (A 1:3). The essence of water for Gesine is its associations with the past while representing the murky, fluid, and unstable situation of narrative recollection. The prevalence of water in the narrative suggests that something larger than Gesine's personal outlook is the source of her life story. It therefore symbolizes the singularity of Gesine's narrative perspective as it enhances and broadens her point of view with an atmosphere of mystery and an air of omniscience that does not disclose secrets.

Johnson seems almost legalistic in insisting that, in writing this novel, he is fulfilling a contract with a person named Gesine Cresspahl. This motivation raises questions about Johnson's relationship to his creation. As in *Two Views,* Johnson appears in his own novel, demonstrating that he exists both inside and outside the narrative. The name *Uwe Johnson* appears on the cover of the book as the author of the novel (definitely outside the narrative); the person Uwe Johnson appears in the novel as fictionalized reality (definitely inside the narrative), but he negotiates with Gesine in the narration of the novel (simultaneously inside and outside the narrative). Johnson appears in the novel as another narrative authority who seems to know more than Gesine about the contents of the novel and yet depends on Gesine for information about her life. One of the most quoted lines in *Anniversaries* makes obvious the interdependence of the author and the fictitious person who ostensibly is the focus of the narrative:

Who's telling this story, Gesine?
We both are. Surely that's obvious, Johnson. (A 1:169)

Gesine seeks to answer questions about her life with the aid and cooperation of her author while her credibility as a person rests on her independence (BU 443), which she often demonstrates to her creator. Yet this narrative strategy should not be taken as a destabilizing element. *Anniversaries* possesses a narrator, like any piece of literature, and the narrative voice, though it creates the illusion of multiplicity, is still Johnson's product. There is an authoritative third-person narrator who describes places, people, and events as well as Gesine's consciousness in all its complexity.[10] This is the most reasonable explanation for an involved narrative stance that is thickly coated in irony and utilizes multiple levels of reflection to negotiate the polyvalence of voices in the novel. In other words, there is one narrative authority who, not unlike a ventriloquist, throws his own voice behind the many different voices in the narrative.

## History, Montage, the *New York Times,* and Memory

*Anniversaries* is a unique novel in its complex and intricate patchwork of historical, factographic material interwoven with fictitious characters. Johnson fills their lives with information that both presents historical events in human dimensions and authenticates fictitious lives. In this respect, *Anniversaries* represents the results of an extensive research project as much as the product of imaginative, literary creation. Johnson was obsessed with historical authenticity in his writing and thus treated his fiction as reality recast in novelistic form. More than any of his other novels, *Anniversaries* required hours of exploration and enormous amounts of research to provide the necessary historical framework in which his characters come to life. Johnson extensively used sources generally accepted as possessing a high level of factual reliability, including legal documents, history books, guidebooks, pamphlets, documentaries, and, of course, newspapers. Catalogued and stored in the Uwe Johnson Archive in Frankfurt am Main are the 10,000 volumes of Johnson's private library, 4,000 of them in his reference and research section alone. His research library included 160 reference works, three hundred volumes of journals, and four hundred works on German history. Johnson also possessed 650 volumes on the culture, dialects, and history of Mecklenburg-Vorpommern as well as twenty-five books on the events of the Prague Spring. In addition, he used selected articles, organized and notated in ten files, from the *New York Times* between 5 July 1966 and 29 August 1968.[11] Thus, archival research was an important aspect of Johnson's creative process.

A measure of self-referentiality evidences itself at various points in the novel when Gesine obtains information for her stories about the past. Gesine's own research sources include, among others, her letter to the resort area Rande (A 1:4); the *New York Times* for characterizations of the time in which she lives; and the *Richmond and Twickenham Times* for knowledge about Heinrich Cresspahl's life in Richmond, England. In general she uses

"Books, you know"
"Old movies, The exhibition at the Jewish Museum."
"Letters from Kliefoth." (A 1:437)

These are Johnson's tools of narration, sources of nonfiction that become fiction while the actual process of collecting information too becomes fiction. Johnson's creative process entailed locating for the "bare skeleton" of the story "the flesh to cover it" (A 1:103), flesh taken from these various sources. Thus, Johnson's formula for authenticity combines factual materials from putatively objective recountings of human experience with the subjectively produced fantasy world of his invented persons. In Johnson's work, fact plus fiction equals authenticity.

Johnson also drew substantially from his surroundings for his fiction. It is fair to assume that the events included in Gesine's life in New York City actually occurred, meaning that a time and place can be attributed to most utterances or actions in the novel. For the New York City portions of the narrative, Johnson drew on his own personal experience as well as incidents involving friends and acquaintances. To describe authentically Marie's days in a Catholic school, Johnson masqueraded as a German journalist writing a report on parochial schools in the United States. He was permitted, on that pretext, to visit a Catholic school, interview the mother superior, and observe classes.[12] Given this dense textual combination of invention and historical material, it is not possible to know if the novel's events were obtained from a conversation overheard in a store, borrowed from another person's life, taken from another printed source, or experienced by the author. Johnson's method of writing fiction represents a composite of many experiences and preexisting texts written into one person's life. The fictitious element lies not in the source material itself but in the fact that it all pertains to Gesine's singular experience and subjective apprehension of the world. In other words, all material, no matter what its origin, was selected only if it suited the logic of Gesine's personality and biography as Johnson invented her.

Like many of his contemporaries, Johnson considered history to be an area that no German author could disregard.[13] Thus, he begins his story with "how it was when Grandmother married Grandfather" (A 1:103). Any German author who writes a story in the late twentieth century and reflects back on two generations of Germans begins narrated time before the fascist takeover of Germany. To begin a story with grandmother means to explore the conduct of individuals before German history took its disastrous turn in 1933. The implicit question in Johnson's text is how it happened that nobody stopped the Nazi rise to power. Was the Nazi permeation of German society not visible, or were other concerns at the forefront of people's minds? By exploring two generations, Johnson's fiction includes times that remain in living memory for many Germans and focuses on individuals in family settings. In *Anniversaries,* family history continues to exist in the form of stories passed along from one member to another, from Heinrich to Gesine and from Gesine to Marie. *Anniversaries* begins in earnest with Gesine's parents, with stories that describe Gesine's and Marie's family identity. When Gesine's parents meet, Heinrich Cresspahl has just left his mother, having set up a pension to support her while he works in Richmond, England, and Lisbeth Papenbrock is with her parents on an outing in Lübeck. This innocuous scene is the beginning of a family history as complicated and enigmatic as the political, economic, and social developments of the country in which they live. Like a sociologist, Johnson depicts the family as the smallest entity in which to explore social behavior, and as a humanist, he believes that history takes place in the activities of the individual. Starting with the meeting of Heinrich and Lisbeth, Johnson presents readers with episode after episode of great and small events that eventually become a comprehensive composite image of the twentieth century.

Before a discussion of Johnson's sources and their interaction can begin, it will be helpful to look more closely at the significance of the *New York Times* for the novel. More than any other factographic source, the *Times* provides the basis of a montage effect that harks back to famous examples such as Alfred Döblin's *Berlin Alexanderplatz* (1929) and John Dos Passos's trilogy, *U.S.A.* On the one hand, the *New York Times,* as a source of recent and ongoing history, is merely a part of Gesine's daily routine. On the other, it is a daily reminder of the deplorable state of depravity and inequity in which the world finds itself. In yet another role, the *Times* connects Gesine's personal history and life in New York to larger societal, global, and historical trends. Gesine has a genuine addiction to the daily newspaper. We recall that in *Speculations,* while on vacation in the West, Gesine bought more than two pounds of newspapers every day (SAJ 98). In *Anniversaries,* while she lived in Düsseldorf she went to the municipal library and read the news, starting with 1929, four years before her birth, and reading onward to recover the news she "missed" (Jt 4:1865). When she leaves town on vacation, she has a neighbor keep all the issues of the *Times* for her so that she can return and read them on weekends, "recouping lost New York days" (A 1:9). If she fails to buy a copy of the *Times* on a particular day, she recovers one from the trash (A 1:10). Gesine's news-hungry gaze feeds itself on events that possess time and place to counterbalance a consciousness that gropes frequently in the blurred and vague world of remembered past. It is no wonder that the *New York Times* represents for this news-hungry person the sole proof that the day actually occurred (A 1:10). Gesine locates her connection to the world through the newspaper as she verifies the unchanging yet always newsworthy fallen state of the world just as a nurse might continually check the pulse of a terminally ill patient. The fact that Gesine views the *New York Times* as a wizened old aunt indicates that the newspaper is one of her daily personal contacts. This image recalls the trope of the older female relative as the keeper of history, the repository of stories both about the family and the community, and accords the newspaper a personality suited to human interaction, a basic condition for a dialogic approach to textual expression (A 1:27–29). Furthermore, the *Times* acts as a tool that jogs the memory and frames the narratives of the past.

To see how Johnson's creative method incorporates news reports and historical events to enhance Gesine's fictional life, the entry of 6 September 1967 is instructive. This example shows how the historical and the fictional conjoin to mutually enhance their respective narrative stances and increase the associative capacities of the past to present events, capacities that are applicable to each entry of the novel. For example, Gesine knows nothing about the behavior of her mother and grandfather during the Kapp putsch in Mecklenburg; Johnson, commissioned to write her story, locates the information for her: "Then it is my task to find that out for her, how it was back then."[14] It is not enough to simply locate the event; it must also demonstrate a direct connection to Gesine's family history. In one of Gesine's many coversations with the dead, Lisbeth tells her daughter how she experienced the Kapp putsch, about the family's life near Güstrow, and about Robert Papenbrock, Gesine's uncle. The following quotation, initially discovered by Peter Pokay, comes from one of Johnson's many sources for the novel:[15]

> When Kapp was being forced to bend to the will of the working class, on 18 March, Baron le Fort had the town of Waren bombarded with a cannon. . . . This junker war cost five inhabitants of Waren their lives, and eleven others were injured, some of them seriously. When farmhands heard of the misdeeds of the murderous baron, about sixty men armed themselves with shotguns, scythes, and pitchforks and met in the woods of Schmachthagen. They wanted to hurry to the aid of the workers in Waren. They took the guns from Georg Lemcke, the landowner of Groß Dratow (2,454 acres) and Bocksee (2,320 acres).[16]

Johnson reconstitutes the history text as follows:

> In 1920, during the Kapp putsch, Baron Stephan le Fort, retired cavalry captain, owner of the Bock estate (6,479 acres), fired a cannon at the town of Waren-on-the-Müritz because the workers had taken over the town. The shell hole in the wall of the town hall can be seen to this day. When the farm laborers in the area heard tell of the five dead in Waren, they set out with shotguns and scythes and searched the surrounding estates for the rifles, machine guns, and ammunition supplied by the Reichswehr at Güstrow to the estate owners (A 1:41).[17]

Johnson makes a few minor changes in keeping with his belief that narrative, fictitious or otherwise, should not deliver morals but only the story: he elides the reference to the "will of the working class" and offers no value judgment about the baron himself. By the same token, he does not allow the baron's deed to remain in the passive construction of the original text. In Johnson's recounting, the baron possesses definite and clear responsibility for the perpetration of the fatal action. As a person who places a great value on traces of historical activity, Johnson provides the travelogue information concerning the shot fired into the town hall that can still be seen "to this day." More revealing than the comparison of texts, however, is how Johnson couches the historical incident in the context of 6 September 1967 and Gesine's family history.

As in most of the entries of *Anniversaries,* Johnson places documentation of past and contemporary historical events side by side. These events are temporally unrelated but in their juxtaposition bring out associative aspects of past and present. Even though the entry revolves around the Kapp putsch in Mecklenburg, it opens with *New York Times* reports about Vietnam, rioting in Brooklyn, and a random shooting in the Bronx (A 1:41). The Kapp putsch incident lines up with these stories almost as if it too had been found in that day's newspaper. The temporal distance between the events collapses in the juxtaposition of their kinetic similarities and statistics. Particulars of the report from Vietnam mesh with those of the unrest in Brooklyn and then blend with a shooting incident in a bar, which in turn combines with particulars of the 1920 violence in Mecklenburg. Strands of commonality include the instruments of death and destruction as well as statistics of the dead and wounded, all of them victims of disturbed social order and senseless violence.

Johnson creates the transition from the historical situation to his world of fiction merely by interchanging historical figures with his invented person. The landowner who loses his weapons to the workers is not the historical Georg Lemcke but the fictitious Albert Papenbrock, Gesine's grandfather. The event befits Gesine's family history because it occurs near Güstrow and explains the reason behind the Papenbrocks' move away from the area to Jerichow (A 1:44). Moreover, the historical incident provides Johnson the opportunity to demonstrate Lisbeth's unfortunate "Christian's love of truth" (A 1:42) and sense of uprightness that will later prove fatal to her in Germany's emerging fascist society. The adolescent Lisbeth carries out the function of the farmhands, who, according to the historical source, "performed . . . an essential function in showing their comrades from the towns the hiding places where the landowners had stored their weapons and ammunition."[18] The scene depicts Lisbeth's father, Albert Papenbrock, lying to the angry farm laborers—"Gentlemen. I give you my word as an officer. There are no arms in my house." (A 1:42)—until Lisbeth, fourteen years old and uncomfortable with the falsehood, tells the workers, "In there" (A 1:42), pointing to a secret door in the children's bedroom. There the farmhands discover nine infantry rifles and 210 rounds of ammunition. What in the historical source was the farmhands' show of solidarity with the workers in the town of Waren becomes for Johnson's text an act of family betrayal. Johnson retains the farmhands' show of solidarity with their helping agent in an utterance that the dead Lisbeth relates to Gesine: "While the house was being searched one of the farmhands said to me: 'Put something on your feet, child'" (A 1:44). For Albert, the farmhands represent "the enemy's approach" (A 1:42), while to Lisbeth one of them makes a kind, fatherly remark showing his concern for her health and his appreciation for her help.

In the subsequent conversation between Gesine and her deceased mother, Lisbeth describes examples of fascist behavior in Robert's conduct and reputation in the area. Robert's activities not only connect to the particulars of the Kapp putsch and *New York Times* reports (Johnson loops Robert into the semantic field of senseless shooting, saying that he would "shoot at sparrows and hit windowpanes [A 1:43]) but also foreshadow the imminence of a way of life in which his personality type will set society's norms. Despite the varying social and historical contexts of these events, the description of Robert's way of life calls forth images of vulnerable victim and pursuing oppressor that characterize the Kapp putsch, the Vietnam War, and the plight of African Americans in the United States. It is thus not surprising to discover that Robert is a war criminal on the run when he appears on Heinrich's property in 1947. Robert's activities reflect, on a personalized level, the chauvinistic and politically conservative nature of the historical events that lead into this particular entry.[19]

The Papenbrock family's social standing is also conveyed in revealing images. The fact that Papenbrock receives weapons from the army to keep order in case of a workers' revolt establishes that the Papenbrocks are well to do and have a vested interest in the status quo. Johnson implies a long tradition of privilege while hinting at the greater history of Mecklenburg in these few lines about Gesine's great-grandmother: "Henriette was her name. She came from an aristocratic family. She would use French expressions like: bureau, bain-marie. Or: wash-lavoir" (A 1:44). These words of French origin that list the amenities of a large estate not only serve as signs of high social standing but also represent the vestiges of an earlier occupying force, Prussia under the occupation of Napoleon's troops in the early nineteenth century. While the entry does not veer from its central focus, the Kapp putsch, the conversation foreshadows the province of Mecklenburg's future existence under fascism and later under occupying British and Soviet armies: "The town command, the Kommandatura, was set up in the brickyard villa across from Cresspahl's house. There they hoisted the fourth flag of the century. That one stayed" (A 2:146).

The essence of *Anniversaries'* novelistic ethos rests on how readers relate to the novel in all its complexity. No discussion of *Anniversaries* can avoid addressing Johnson's poignant juxtaposition of past and present events, which is a basic structuring principle of the entire novel. Many critics speak of parallels between the past and present, but Johnson dispelled that notion in an interview when he retorted, "Parallels do not meet each other."[20] Johnson viewed the past in direct relation to the present because the past contains events that in some manner meet with those of the present. As Johnson said, events of the present "call up" items of the past that find their way into Gesine's narrative.[21] To understand the meeting of past and present in *Anniversaries* enables insights into the history of the twentieth century in a way that only the novel as genre can provide. The unique structural scheme of *Anniversaries* supports four theoretical descriptions of how events of the past and present converge.

The incorporation of so many different sources, a large host of characters, and the interaction of historical time periods as well as various social classes creates a story that reveals an effervescent dialogization of past and present events. In Mikhail Bakhtin's sense of the concept, Johnson dialogizes history through the personal discourse of characters by creating varying contexts, intentions, motivations, and conditions in which their utterances occur and their decisions are made. Norbert Mecklenburg writes of the related short story, "Versuch, einen Vater zu finden" ("In Search of a Father"), that Johnson's "text consists of a richly varied spectrum of speech forms and polyphonically contrasting voices."[22] The same can be said of *Anniversaries,* for the entire novel is steeped in dialogized interactions. Instead of reducing history's mass of human activity to the single thread of his own narrative voice, Johnson allows data, documents, and persons their many voices because varying voices comprise the (hi)story that he narrates. History is related in its novelistic depiction through the abundance and sonority of dialogue between invented persons, both living and dead, various texts, both contemporary and historical, and the crisscrossing interplay of their varying speech patterns and significations. Despite the disparateness of the voices in the novel, they converge in, and thus delineate, Gesine's consciousness, which constitutes an essential element of the dialogical relationship between them: "The consciousness of others cannot be contemplated and analyzed and defined like objects or things—one must *relate dialogically* to them. To think about them means *to converse with them; otherwise they immediately turn their objectified side to us:* they fall silent and grow cold and retreat to their finalized objectivized images."[23] In the detailed description of Gesine's consciousness, Johnson unfolds the entire contents of the novel in the dialogization of its material.[24] Although the varying voices and texts present in the novel are not beholden to her, as the main person her consciousness resonates in every word of the narrative. The voices and texts, despite their origin, are subsumed under Gesine's consciousness because, for Johnson, her life establishes the selection criteria for material in the novel: "And then wait to see whether that suits her, as she is, or whether it does not suit her."[25] Even though items come together under Gesine's single consciousness, all texts and persons retain their independence and demonstrate their own dialogical relationships with one another. At the intersection of individual voices and texts in the consciousness of a single person, Johnson offers history to readers in a dialogized manner.

In a sense, Johnson obscures the events of the novel by portraying them tangled in a variety of discourses: journalistic prose, historical narrative, travelogue language, conversations between family members (both living and dead), and interactions of various social classes. Otherwise, the more perplexing the descriptions of events, the greater the possibilities of meaning. Johnson introduces a significant measure of interference into the direct comprehension of historical material by placing it in new contextualizations. In *Anniversaries* the juxtaposition of historical and contemporary events creates an ahistorical coextensive existence between seemingly unrelated events as he poses the contemporary view of the newspaper against the evaluation of past events in history books.

Johnson creates a theoretically complex juncture between past and present that can be characterized in other ways with the dialogization of the material as its first basic element. Neumann, for example, has referred to the connection between past and present as "correspondances," a concept that he adopts from Theodor W. Adorno's essay "Über Tradition" ("On Tradition").[26] Neumann quotes a passage in which Adorno says that tradition, "as something emerging as new, throws its light on the current and receives its light from the current. Such correspondence is not one of insight and direct relationship, rather it needs distance."[27] Here the old (past) and new (current) reveal their similarities in correspondences that present tradition as continual sameness, as past and present mutually reflect and illuminate each other. As Ulrich Fries points out, from here it is possible to appreciate the value of Walter Benjamin's idea of the dialectical image for the interpretation of Gesine's processing of current news within the history of her life story: "It is not so that the past throws its light on the current or that the current throws its light on the past, but image is what, in a lightning flash, merges with the now into a constellation. In other words, image is the dialectic at a standstill."[28] In this respect, paradigmatically arranged events collapse temporal categories in an image that contrasts them yet reveals a synthesis of them that divulges the essence of human tradition. In a similar vein it is possible to see the validity of Ludwig Wittgenstein's concept of family resemblances to explain the relationship between past and present events. In their mere juxtaposition, past and present evoke what Wittgenstein wrote about his endeavor to locate one element that all games have in common. Because he cannot discern a single such element, he concludes that all games possess resemblances such as those that run through a family. Wittgenstein comments on how these "similarities crop up and disappear" in the discussion of games: "And the result of this examination is: we see a complicated network of similarities overlapping and crisscrossing: sometimes overall similarities, sometimes similarities of detail."[29] The similarities that appear and disappear, he says, are like those traits that run through a family because there is no one characteristic that all members must have in common to belong. The same concept applies to the events of present and past as depicted in *Anniversaries*. The tradition of violence, oppression, social injustice, conflict, human agony, and guilt that Gesine perceives in the past and present also possess similarities like in a family. Accenting the resemblances of events makes flexible the selection of events on strands of commonality that are not stringently exclusive but also do not fall into a mode of boundless and groundless association. As a narrative, *Anniversaries* presents resemblances between disparate events that evoke revealing connections in readers' minds. War in Europe in the 1940s possesses certain similarities to war in Southeast Asia during the 1960s; 1930s and '40s racial discrimination against Jews in Germany demonstrates an uncanny likeness to discrimination in the United States against African Americans and Hispanics. Human relations in the social context of the village of Jerichow harbor germane, though surprising, affinities to how nations relate to each other, with their specific interests and designs on global power. In other words, *Anniversaries* depicts a seminal and continuous shifting between images of microcosm and macrocosm to reveal complex correspondences, dialectical and dialogical relationships, and family resemblances. All four items inform the extremely important interplay of past and present for the integration of the narrative in Gesine's consciousness.

Although Johnson possessed works by Bakhtin, Adorno, Benjamin, and Wittgenstein and avidly read philosophy, it is improbable that Johnson had these theorists in mind when he wrote *Anniversaries*. And yet this theoretical combination lies at the basis of the montage effect utilized in *Anniversaries,* an effect for which these authors' theories serve as elucidations. Applying the criteria of chronology, causality, logical sequence, or the contiguousness of geographic space and political circumstances would render events depicted in *Anniversaries* hopelessly disparate. Using these criteria, the Vietnam War has little to do with the Second World War; U.S. civil and racial strife in the 1960s possesses no connection to the treatment of German Jews in the 1930s and '40s; even positive historical trends, such as Heinrich Cresspahl's and Johnny Schlegel's establishment of democratic socialism and Alexander Dubcek's Prague reforms, display no convincing connections. Although in a causal, logical, close chronological way these items do not relate, they do correspond in theoretical fashion. Integration of disparate elements is the basic function of all montages; a potentiating effect on readers' insights into the human condition is its didactic usefulness and objective in *Anniversaries*. As discussed earlier, the montage effect brings readers to make associations among the text's disparate elements. However, with the montage structure in *Anniversaries,* the audience is drawn in various directions. Readers can create the distance between themselves and text mentioned by Adorno because of the paradigmatic juxtaposition of past and present. By the same token, these disjointed items from past and present fuse together in the texture of the narrative. Readers participate in this simultaneous distancing and fusing of past and present in their reception of the narrative, which constitutes the montage structure at work as it, in Ernst Bloch's words, "separates that which is close and brings together that which is furthest apart."[30]

The montage's effect resides in its eclectic material blended with the integrating story of Johnson's invented person. Benjamin explains that a newspaper's layout is intended to enable the disremembering of its contents: "If it were the intention of the press to have the reader assimilate the information it supplies as part of his own experience, it would not achieve its purpose. But its intention is just the opposite, and it is achieved: to isolate what happens from the realm in which it could affect the experience of the reader."[31] In this passage Benjamin explains the mechanism that enables the masses to forget promptly what they read in the news or see on television and proves their disaffected consumption of daily dosages of disaster in the media. Within the novel, however, the montage acts as an antidote to the nepenthe-induced complacency of the human community at large. The malaise of humankind, whose daily manifestation emanates a sense of its permanence, finds no moral resonance in the largely indifferent people who consume newspapers each day but do not incorporate the news in their own personal experience. The fusion of the news with Gesine's private life and the historical trends depicted in her family story brings readers to recognize and retain the tragedy that often makes up the daily news.

Thus, the montage acquires a pedagogical purpose in Johnson's narrative. By incorporating news reports in the personalized narrative of the protagonist, Johnson enables the news item to become the personal experience of Gesine in the act of narrating: "As soon as one begins to narrate it, it becomes her family experience."[32] Benjamin's distinction between experience and information becomes apparent in this dynamic connection.[33] Experience constitutes the affective absorption of an event that lays traces in the memory or creates an emotional stir in the reader. By incorporating the newspaper information into a personalized narrative, Johnson moves readers from objectified cognition to affective engagement of those events that are normally skimmed in the newspaper in a nonparticipatory manner. Johnson combines newspaper reports with his fiction to hinder the propensity of its consumers to read and forget. He arranges this radical processing of news reports (and other narratives of history) in such a way as to enable them to become part of readers' affective engagement with the novel. Here the newspaper's putative message, that something is wrong in the world, finally receives attention due to the emotive engagement that the novel can foster, as opposed to the deadening form of the daily newspaper. In other words, Johnson transforms information into experience, which by definition finds its most appropriate medium in a personal story. The montage enables the information to become experience because it disallows the objectification of the news items by fusing them with the subjective experience inherent to reading a novel. Yet from the opposite point of view, the montage does not permit the story entirely to consume the reader because it continually throws up barricades of newslike information that prohibit a comfort level that might otherwise permit readers to fictionalize the news—that is, allow it to appear unreal. News reports in the montage form remain objectified enough to reveal historical and societal circumstances, including those in which readers exist. Johnson demonstrates through the montage effect that connections among news events, recorded history, personal experience, and personal memory do exist and that these relationships can be efficaciously integrated in narrative fiction.

With his didactic gesture and his inclusion of events that point to the essence of history as violent and agonistic, Johnson subtly undermines readers' propensity to fall into a mode of intellectualizing history in which they compare events or seek causes and effects. Mecklenburg points out that Johnson does not use temporal connectors in "Versuch, einen Vater zu finden."[34] Such conjunctions are also lacking in *Anniversaries,* where Johnson creates no logical coupling of plot points or historical events. Equally important is the lack of comparative connectors such as *like, as if,* or *reminds one of* when events from the past and present stand juxtaposed. In fact, Marie and readers are forbidden to compare the past with the present, and vice versa (Jt 3:1048). Rather than a syntagmatically connected string of events whose causality and narrative logic is as subjective as any single point of view, Johnson offers history as paradigm, as events placed side by side with no grammatical connection or sequential causality. With a paradigmatic structure of history, the author does not control readers' views, as would be the case with events depicted in a syntagmatic structure. Johnson leaves history open for readers' interpretations and insights in connecting past and present events in a manner that collapses the disaffected relationship that they might otherwise maintain to both history texts and newspaper reports. Johnson's focus on the everydayness of history within greater, more sweeping events creates a history that is not so massive that it alienates readers or becomes distanced beyond the life experiences of individuals. The resemblances between past and present events are grasped intuitively, and therefore history is absorbed in a mode that traditional texts do not address. Although traditional historical narratives are explicative, they do not amplify interpretive possibilities; although they offer direct lines of cause-and-effect logic, they possess little experiential mass; although they portray writers' insights, they do not necessarily enable readers'. In entry after entry in *Anniversaries,* the dialogical property that Johnson imparts to history books and newspaper articles expands various historical narratives.

Johnson referred to his work as a "process of memory," and for a novel that features family history from the perspective of an individual family member, memory becomes an important thematic focus.[35] One of Gesine's and Johnson's most valuable sources or connections to the past is the memory as a storage area of images. As libraries, archives, letters, old books, family pictures, and films appear in the novel as a self-referential nod to the creative process, so memory receives its lines of explanation. The difficulty with memory is its abruptness, its unreliability, its unpredictability, and even its aloofness: "The cat called memory, as you say, [is] independent, incorruptible, intractable. And yet a comfortable companion, when it puts in an appearance, even if it stays out of reach" (A 1:436). Early in the novel, readers are alerted to the erratic results of research through memory by a description of its contrariness: "If only memory could contain the past in the receptacles we use to sort the elements of reality! But the multilayered sieve of earthly time and causality and chronology and logic that we use for thinking is not served by the brain, where it remembers the past" (A 1:47). Gesine desires to enter the past as if reentering a room, everything in the same place as it was when she left; this is where memory fails and frustrates Gesine's grasp on the past. The totality she seeks, the completeness of the past event, proves to be pure chimera: "At a nudge, prompted by even partial congruence, by the random and the absurd, it will volunteer facts, figures, foreign speech, unrelated gestures; . . . ask for the contents of the void that was once reality, life-awareness, action: it will refuse to supply them. The filter allows scraps, splinters, broken glass, shavings, to trickle through and scatter themselves without meaning over the plundered spaceless image, obliterating the traces of the sought-for scene" (A 1:47). Her intense desire for the reproduction or recollection of the past is the manifestation of her acute sense of loss where the past is concerned. Memory is, after all, her initial grasp on the past before she must turn to other sources to fill the frustratingly fragmentary rendition of the past that memory provides. The lacunae perceived between shards of remembered events, provided voluntarily or involuntarily to employ Marcel Proust's concept, are the fragments around which Gesine spins her tale:

"I never promised to tell the truth."
"Of course not. Only your truth." (A 1:436)

The object of the past released from memory must enter into a context that is perforce not its original place. But as an authentic remnant of the past, the object is preserved in Gesine's story in as close a proximity to the original experience as possible. It becomes a kernel of authenticity within the possibility of how the action of the past may have occurred. The totality of the lived moment is lost forever and "remains a secret, locked against Ali Baba's magic word, inimical, unapproachable, mute, and enticing like a great gray cat behind the windowpane" (A 1:47).

Johnson viewed history as stories about human choices, and he considered the novel a literary form uniquely appropriate to preserve the past. The record of Gesine's past and present is simultaneously a chronicle of Marie's present that will, in turn, become a journal of her past when her mother passes away (A 1:254). It will be useful for the day when Marie asks herself why her mother behaved as she did, why she made the choices she did, and how Marie herself thought and behaved in those days: "I have written this down for you so that you will understand, late though it will be, what I may begin this year—at the age of thirty-five, so help me—one last time. So that you won't have to guess, as I do" (A 1:448). Readers are not infrequently reminded that conversations are recorded or newspaper articles are clipped and saved, another self-referential element of the creative process behind *Anniversaries.* In the end Gesine hands over the 1,875 pages of the recorded year to her old friend and former English teacher, Dr. Kliefoth. Together with the memories that remain, these pages will serve as Marie's source for the past and are meant to function, in a pedagogical capacity, as guidelines for her life choices. Gesine hopes that Marie will avoid the mistakes of her mother and her relatives as well as live with an acute political and social awareness to avoid being caught in a web of guilt. Gesine is attempting to release her daughter from "becoming guilty," much as Lisbeth tried to do thirty years earlier. Lisbeth's method was the attempted elimination of her child, either by starvation or drowning; Gesine wishes to save Marie through conversations that provide the youngster with useful knowledge, prestructured memory, and information for future use. In this vein, knowledge about the past and present is a weapon against guilt, loss, groundlessness, and an uncertain future. The value of exploring the past is learning to avoid mistakes. In a similar fashion, *Anniversaries,* as a novel with a solid place in literary history, will help readers continue to resist forgetting as well as reveal the social context in which violence and injustice persist as permanent aspects of putatively humane communities. The fallen of the Vietnam War and of the Second World War as well as the victims of Nazi death camps, Soviet work camps, and racial prejudice are some of those casualties of history who have a literary monument to their plight in this novel.

## A Life of Loss, Guilt, and the Search for a Homeland

Johnson authenticates Gesine's propensity to seek out her family's history and explore how she fits into the historical events of Germany's past by providing her with experiences that psychologically explain her desire to know about the past. A definitive quality of Gesine's life is that it has been affected by emotionally and psychologically debilitating losses.[36] Gone from her life are her lover and the father of her child (Jakob Abs), her own father (Heinrich), her biological mother (Lisbeth), and her surrogate mother (Marie Abs). All died when Gesine could not be with them; she never properly mourned any of them, and, with the exception of her mother, she did not attend their funerals. Furthermore, she lost the village of her childhood, her property there (the house in which she grew up), the landscape of her beloved Mecklenburg, and her language, all of which exist, in 1967 and 1968, behind the infamous Iron Curtain: "That's one place I must not go back to" (A 1:320). She has also witnessed the defiling of her treasured socialist ideals by the GDR's dogmatic implementation of socialism. The narration of her life is a corrective gesture whose purpose is to fill the gaps in her consciousness left by these traumatic losses of family, community, and home in all their facets.

As in Johnson's other works, a motivating element of the narrative reveals itself at the novel's conclusion when Gesine reads the results of a psychologist's diagnosis concerning the voices that she hears in her thoughts (A 2:617–18). The psychologist, A. M., discusses the most prevalent symptom of loss's effect on Gesine, a feature represented by her uncanny capacity to speak with the dead, creating thereby an imagined family. She is accompanied wherever she goes by her deceased family and friends in the form of interjected voices, which Johnson distinguishes from the rest of the narrative by presenting them in italics. Gesine's almost shamanistic skill is the result of an intense desire to have those persons near, and it represents a level of denial that shapes her life. Her focus in life is to compensate for loss, make up for shortcomings in her past decisions, comprehend the evil elements of human nature, and obtain knowledge that will guide her to a better future. Having no temporal home, the voices of the dead typify the temporal dimensions in which Gesine's consciousness subsists. In the past they correct her story, defend and explain themselves, and remind her of conditions that influenced their decisions and how they conducted themselves in the face of specific, often forgotten, circumstances. They remind Gesine that she possesses the advantage of hindsight. In the New York present they act as Gesine's conscience, rebuking her for sending her child to a safe parochial school, criticizing her for not participating in demonstrations against the Vietnam War, and chastising her for not understanding better the plight of African Americans. For the future they exercise an almost prophetic function, warning her to drop her plans to go to Prague on her financial mission. They fill the role of the advising elders whom Gesine lost when she permanently left home in 1953 at the age of twenty.

An important and distinguishing theme in German literature of the 1960s, '70s, and '80s is the depiction of fictional main characters who attempt to come to terms with Germany's fascist past. Gesine fits into this important literary trend as she enters a process of *Bewältigung* in every sense of the word: she strives to cope with, overcome, and clear away the past so that she can approach the future with a greater awareness of who she is and without the onerous and burdensome feelings of guilt that preoccupy her. Her sense of loss is augmented by the sense of guilt that she feels as a German—that is, as a member of a nationality responsible for the murder of millions of people (Jt 1:232, 2:798). Guilt and national identity are closely related for this figure who measures her life in degrees of remorse. She feels the collective guilt she shares with the German and Austrian nations for the crimes of the Second World War. If she had grown up in Richmond, England, "I would not be German; I would talk about the Germans in an alien and remote plural. I would bear the guilt of a different nation" (A 1:224). In this respect she confuses the nation with the person, just as does her Czech acquaintance, Dmitri Weiszand: "For him I am Germany, the old one and the two present ones, for him I sometimes have no face at all but a national pigment instead, to him I am responsible for the West German state railways and for the West German Nazis" (A 1:104). She takes personal responsibility for an entire nation and feels accountable for the crimes of a government for which she did not vote and under which she existed in a state of ignorant bliss as a child. Gesine has yet to live in a society without the recurrent human infirmities of war, racial strife, religious persecution, mass murder, poverty, and political oppression. Her story is an individual's quest to locate what degree or kind of connection she has to such atrocities. She creates a fixation on the past and present that reveals the hidden network of guilt intrinsic to all societies in which some form of oppression, however subtle, is necessary for the maintenance of the status quo. She discovers in her explorations that guilt is not the concern of a single person but is something that crosses social classes, international boundaries, and historical periods. Guilt is part of the social fabric of any society whose members, in their smallest routines, perpetrate and perpetuate the injustices for which any moral being should feel guilty.

In demonstrating this actuality of human existence, Johnson utilizes the montage structure with great efficacy where Marie presents her "trouble" with Francine (A 1:147), a poor girl from Harlem and an "alibi-black" in Marie's school. Because Marie has been chosen to help Francine with her adjustment to the private school, Marie alienates her white friends. Francine and Marie's friends mistakenly believe that Marie does her task out of affection. The dialogue in which Marie presents her "trouble" Gesine intersperses excerpts from the 25 October 1967 *New York Times* that take Marie's apparently insignificant feelings and show their manifestation on a larger societal scale. American pupils in a Washington, D.C., area junior high school beat up fellow students from Eastern Europe, presumably because they were from communist countries, while black playwright LeRoi Jones was led away in handcuffs after denouncing his white prosecutors as "oppressors" (A 1:147–48). Readers realize that the difference between Marie's "trouble" and these incidents is only a question of degree along a wide scale of racism and nationalistic intolerance. The negative emotions that begin with a ten-year-old girl wanting to keep her white friends could logically end in hate-driven genocide; Johnson shows that the mass oppression of a race and mass murder begin small, in feelings and circumstances that average people, if they ever notice them, never take seriously. The systematic destruction of one race by another derives from a chauvinistic view of nationality, political beliefs, and race born out of a blind self-righteousness, sense of superiority, and sense of entitlement. These are, after all, the basic sentiments that guide fascist policy. Johnson illustrates that the great movements of history begin with individuals and that any ultimate change in the distopic condition of the world must also begin there. Gesine's realization that guilt is part of living in a Western society creates in her life a functional difficulty that affects her socially and psychologically. She avoids certain consumer behaviors for fear that they will increase the measure of guilt she feels as she attempts to remain on the margins of American society (A 1:251). Avoiding participation in society any more than absolutely necessary is her strategy for avoiding guilt by association. Avoiding guilt is, however, simultaneously incompatible with being at home.

In this novel Johnson deals with elements that connect all human beings, the most basic of which is the relationship to homeland in its broadest definition. Johnson's New York days were fitting times in which to think about homeland, not only because he felt at home there but also because he encountered there so many who had lost their homes as a result of German aggression. In *Anniversaries* Johnson outlines the evils of fascism and Stalinism in a historically conscious fashion, demonstrating how they, as political systems, upset the natural homeostasis intrinsic to community life. His direct encounter in New York with people who suffered under such governments, especially German fascism, occupied him for the rest of his literary career. Later, one of his English acquaintances would say that Johnson "felt a little bit guilty about being German,"[37] a classic British understatement given the evidence of the guilt-ridden German and the level of German self-hatred in *Anniversaries.*

When Johnson was asked what *home* meant to him, he replied, "Something lost. Whoever has abandoned it can never go back."[38] Every loss has a compensatory counterpart in Gesine's world. As discussed earlier, she compensates for the loss of her family with the voices in her thoughts. The loss of home in Mecklenburg could find its utopian counterpart in the emerging social democracy in Czechoslovakia or merely by accepting New York City as home. However, an undisturbed sense of home in the present is only feasible by denying the guilt that is an inevitable part of any place one might call home.[39] Gesine feels most comfortable in her position on the outside because it means that she does not need to feel responsible for the guilt of the United States: "It's got nothing to do with us, we're guests here, we're not to blame. We're not to blame yet" (A 1:66). She exists in a perplexing position of obfuscating her sense of home even as she seeks out home's positive impulses occurring around her. This double bind that Gesine experiences involves maintaining a safe distance from the aspects of American society that speak to her sense of home, including the cultural diversity that surrounds her in her Upper West Side community, with its at least superficial harmony. She also appreciates the communal spirit she senses with the people who sell her the *New York Times,* her morning coffee, her groceries, her solidarity with the people who ride the subway every day and aspects of New York that demonstrate similarities to her former home in northwestern Mecklenburg—the South Ferry, the sandy landscape of Long Island, and the close proximity of the ocean: "It is an illusion, and feels like home" (A 1:95). If she becomes too attached to these items, she runs the risk of becoming comfortable in a place that possesses an abundance of sources for guilt. She is therefore consistent about locating those elements of American society that help her maintain the distance that she views as protection from an even greater sense of guilt than she already possesses.

Gesine's sense of home is chimerical because her homeland is a vision from her childhood that disappeared with the past and will become realizable again only in the future, if at all. The ideals that she acquired in school in the emerging socialist society of the Soviet occupation zone (later the German Democratic Republic) she observes through the *New York Times* as a possibility in Dubcek's Czechoslovakia. Thus, her mission to Prague has both personal and professional dimensions. As someone who has lived under Hitler's fascism, Stalin's and Walter Ulbricht's brand of socialism, Konrad Adenauer's social market economy, and Lyndon Johnson's capitalist democracy, she has come to realize that power structures remain the same regardless of society's economic and political makeup. Gesine's basic stance is that governments rule by deception and that lying is a fundamental and frequently utilized political tool: "The *New York Times* is not of the opinion that President Johnson does his job worse than the cartoon figure Bugs Bunny, who is forever concocting inventions, ostensibly for the good of mankind but in fact to their disadvantage and detriment" (A 1:210). Here Gesine captures the essence of ideology as a belief system that is detrimental to the community at large but advantageous to the particular ruling power. Living under these systems also requires the participation of the individual in the lie, as Marie says: "You'd've been out of a job and I'd've been out of school long ago if we didn't lie like three American presidents in a row" (A 1:324). Thence comes the reason for Gesine's often-quoted lament, "Where is the moral Switzerland to which we might emigrate?" (A 1:251). It is no coincidence, then, that the women from whom Gesine and Marie take over the apartment on Riverside Drive are from Denmark and Switzerland. Besides being the home of one of Johnson's favorite authors and best friends, Max Frisch, Switzerland represents for Gesine a peaceful, multicultural society with little unemployment, an excellent social system, government policy decided through plebiscite, and a guarded policy of neutrality in world affairs. Denmark has a complete social welfare system and a capitalist economy that coexist to make one of the kindest societies on earth. Denmark is also the final leg of Gesine's journey to Prague, encoding the sense of hope that the Czechoslovakian project holds for her. She is prepared to take a chance on Dubcek's socialist democracy, where she hopes exploitation and societal alienation will cease to exist and individual freedom will be promoted. She sees in the correct implementation of socialist ideals a society in which self-interest, greed, and competition are no longer the motivators for existence, thus creating a community without societal losers, outsiders, alienated persons, or material want. Her daily toil for a bank— that is, for the quintessential capitalist establishment—appears directly to contradict her personal desires for the future. But Gesine reconciles the dissonance between her socialist convictions and the rationalistic approach to profits that motivates the bank's vice president by viewing her everyday professional activities as efforts to create a new opportunity for a democratic socialism.

Ironically, if Gesine did not live with an enervating guilt, she could not be such an idealist in search of a place where her guilt might be eradicated. As counterpart to her search in the past for the causes of guilt, she also seeks out ways to make up for it. That compensation could take the form of a homeland as she sees it in her childhood. The location of a new homeland represents a positive goal in Gesine's struggle against the debilitating effects of loss and guilt. Though apparently antithetical, guilt and homeland are elements interdependent to her anticipatory hope for the future. Although New York City was once such a possibility, Gesine's hope for a homeland is spurred on now by her aspirations for the political changes in Prague. Alleviation of the burden of guilt from the past and the desired security in, connectedness to, and reconciliation with the larger human community could be possible in the emerging Czechoslovakian democratic socialism. When she notes information in the newspaper like the quote from a Swedish sociologist saying that "the United States must spend 'trillions of dollars and at least one generation' in a realistic, nonracial attack on the country's poverty" (A 1:101), she realizes that there is little that one individual can do to change social conditions in the United States. She is reminded of her powerlessness to transform society in her present surroundings, which only frustrates her intense desire for an amelioration of the human condition. Beyond living with an awareness of what occurs around her, she can undertake nothing on her own to change the status quo: "It's what I've been left with: to find out about things. At least to live with my eyes open" (A 1:142). Her mission to Prague thus gains its significance as a way to turn back the infirmities of humankind and locate a homeland in whose creation she can participate.

Gesine's latent search for a homeland in *Anniversaries* reflects interesting parallels to the description of homeland in the final passage of Bloch's *The Principle of Hope*:[40]

> *True genesis is not at the beginning but at the end,* and it starts to begin only when society and existence become radical, i.e. grasp their roots. But the root of history is the working, creating human being who reshapes and overhauls the given facts. Once he has grasped himself and established what is his, without expropriation and alienation, in real democracy, there arises in the world something which shines into the childhood of all and in which no one has yet been: homeland.[41]

Gesine's activities and aspirations find resonance in this short but significant quotation. Bloch maintains that the root of all history is the working and creating human being. For Bloch, this is the agent who moves history, the historical subject, who, in *Anniversaries,* is organizing a loan for a reformist socialist government. De Rosny, then, might be considered just such an agent, but Bloch speaks of an agent who is neither self-serving nor serving a particular ideology. Historical agents understand themselves—that is, to bring about that homeland, free of social and ideological alienation, they must truly know that for which they strive. Gesine attempts to reach this stage of awareness through her detailed and candid explorations of her life's history and her understanding of democracy. The establishment of a "real democracy" completely free of alienation and disenfranchisement of those who live in it appears as childhood homes do, like Gesine's blissful years in Jerichow. Childhood was a time when home meant something because there was harmony with the environment, free of any false consciousness that socialization in ideologies and other dogmas creates. Since the dominant political, financial, and religious institutions of a given society need individuals to perpetuate them, the young are immediately indoctrinated into social contexts that legitimize the existence of these institutions. Herein lies the importance of school experiences for the narrative, in which Marie's and Gesine's educations are depicted in their definitive ideological orientations. Thus, no one has ever truly been home because no individuals have really existed for their own desires, which ideally exist as societal norms as well as individual guidelines for living. In Johnson's work, initial manifestations of this real democracy evidence themselves in the politeness with which his main characters approach others, especially in *Ingrid Babendererde* and *Speculations,* which, like *Anniversaries,* contain an implicit message that socialism could be better. "Real democracy" will evolve when government occurs by extant humanistic norms that will in turn be recognizable in the chosen governmental system. Although she has a healthy portion of guarded optimism, Gesine is working toward this utopian state where she detects signs of it in the emerging socialist democracy in Czechoslovakia.

## Collecting Utopian Moments

Johnson does not set before his readers a programmatic scheme of the ideal society or advance a notion of how to correct social problems. The utopia of *Anniversaries* manifests itself in the consistent impulses that Gesine gleans from her past and from her surroundings in New York City as well as from the events brought under her gaze in the *New York Times.* It may initially seem an interpretive stretch to say that *Anniversaries* contains a sense of utopia. So many of the entries concentrate on the negative occurrences in Gesine's past and in her present surroundings. But the utopian atmosphere is uniquely Blochian in the sense that it is not a totality in itself but manifests concretely in small ways. With every positive trend or action that Gesine notes, she observes a partial reversal of the apparent permanence of humankind's moral and spiritual destitution. She exists then in constant flux between fear and hope, thus evidencing two possible outcomes to her mission to Prague: disaster or homeland, apocalypse or utopia. Dread and celebration characterize, then, her stance toward the future as each calendric entry brings her closer to the execution of her impending mission. This double focus lies at the root of her divided self, in which one side appreciates human tradition in the pessimistic expectation that it will always reveal itself as flawed and incapable of amelioration. The other side sees the possibility for genuine positive change that would bring the human community closer to the ideal principles it sets for itself in the constitutions and moral codes that putatively guide its societies. However fragmented they might be, Gesine sees possibilities that tend to the positive in observable and conceivable manifestations.

Nonetheless, Gesine's quest to make sense of the world is impossible without the hopeful signs of existing utopian impulses that she gleans from her past and observes in the present. The systematic search in the past reveals impulses of a humanistic and democratic socialism of that time, experiments in which she was involved as a child in Jerichow and as a worker on Johnny Schlegel's farm commune. She remembers her childhood wishes (Jt 2:990) manifested in the small-scale social contexts in which all were propertyless, all were hungry, and all approached the harvest with equal interest. The nobility had fled, the local capitalists were powerless, the Nazis were defeated, and the harvest was ready to be reaped. Reviewing past encounters with these emerging experiments in socialism is part of her effort to put the present into perspective as it pertains to the future. The past is not a deadened, closed-off space in this respect, but rather it is alive with vestiges of hope that help her understand the reforms taking place in Prague. The past represents an initial contact with the innovation of democratic socialism motivated by hope and anticipation for an evolving humanistic community. Here she views Heinrich Cresspahl's and Johnny Schlegel's socialism as small-scale precursor to the new socialism evolving under Dubcek in Czechoslovakia. They are models of a disinterested, unselfish concern for the material and spiritual well-being of everyone in the collective. Due to their inclusive stance, they represent societies without willing or unwilling outsiders—that is, societies free of alienation, or Bloch's "homeland."

In the immediacy of Gesine's New York surroundings, utopian impulses also represent fragments of possible amelioration in an otherwise infirm society. One example in particular is a true sign of a hopeful but incomplete future manifest in the church of St. John the Divine, which will remain unfinished "until the anguish of the unadvantaged citizens in the surrounding slums has been relieved" (A 1:157). Gesine and Marie's residence on Manhattan's Upper West Side evidences in its descriptions a comfort level that one might call homey though "imaginary" (A 1:118) all the same. Gesine praises the New York subway for its convenience, for the courtesy shown on it, and for the riders' respect for each other's space (Jt 1:367–74). Gesine perceives a genuine sense of solidarity with the people who ride the subway when she includes herself in the "foreign army" that rides beneath the city (Jt 3:1229). The solidarity that she feels and the courteousness that she observes on the subway are radical responses to the malaise she reads about in the newspaper as she rides: "And then in the subway I saw a Negro boy of about eight or ten, holding an unwieldy shoe-cleaning box between his legs. He had fallen asleep right there in the crowded train and let his head droop trustingly against his neighbor's arm. So she moved her shoulder forward a little, to give him support" (A 1:276). Politeness on the subway, or anywhere, counteracts in small but concrete ways the ruthless, self-interested competition of big business, military forces, and national governments. Manifested in small ways, unmotivated politeness transforms the reality in which it occurs. Competition brings anxiety, while politeness instills the optimism that the brighter side of human nature will yet prevail. Gesine feeds her hope for the future with these gestures of politeness and in turn acts upon that hope with her work for a Czechoslovakian brand of socialism. The Prague Spring represents the greatest hope in Gesine's life for the opportunity to help a socialist cause to its fruition: "It might still be a new beginning. For that beginning I would work, of my own free will. I am sitting here alone . . . with an absurd confidence in this year" (A 1:448). Not only does Gesine take over the mission as her own but she approaches the coming departure with hopeful anticipation of what Dubcek's socialism will be (Jt 4:1415). The letter of "Two Thousand Words" (Jt 4:1438) galvanizes Gesine's hope for developments in Prague that proceed in textbook fashion (A 2:129).

As mentioned above, Gesine possesses a double focus concerning the future. The disastrous outcome of the Prague mission is a real possibility in Gesine's eyes. Just as there are positive utopian impulses that encode a successful arrival of a humanistic and democratic socialism, there is also evidence of its doom. Heinrich Cresspahl's effort to establish a socialist society in Jerichow met its end when Soviet authorities arrested him on false charges of fraud. He spent two years in a Soviet work camp at Fünfeichen, near the town of Neubrandenburg. Johnny Schlegel's successful commune came to an abrupt end when the East German authorities arrested him and confiscated his land because of a transaction he made in West Berlin. Both men worked toward the perfection of a collective society in their specific ways before their efforts were thwarted by a powerful military and political apparatus. Gesine, who possesses a highly sensitive understanding of her national identity and of the crimes her fatherland committed in the Second World War, is loathe to watch the East German state meddle in the affairs of a country that it had occupied and brutalized just twenty-five years earlier. The utopian impulses of the New York subway, the homey feeling of the Upper West Side, and the relatively harmonious multicultural society of New York City are counterbalanced by continual reminders of the civil strife that is also a reality of U.S. life. In *Anniversaries,* Gesine notes utopian and apocalyptic signals that create a deceptive and troublesome dialectic as one set of impulses appears to compete with the other for ultimate dominance. Johnson and his readers know that the experiment in Prague meets with disaster, yet he successfully maintains the ambivalence of Gesine's trepidation and hopeful anticipation throughout the calendar as the August date approaches when Gesine and Marie will board a plane to Prague.

Travel indubitably plays an important role in all of Johnson's works as a symbol of change. Such transitions, however, are always possibilities for both disaster and positive growth. In *Anniversaries,* the symbol of flight possesses a double significance where the utopian aspects of the novel are concerned. Possibilities for happiness with her friend and lover D. E. (Dietrich Erichson) end with his death in a plane crash on 4 August. Gesine's soul mate from school, Pius Pagenkopf, met his end when his prototype jet fighter crashed on a test flight in the Soviet Union. Death, loneliness, political stagnation, and the impossibility of a homeland are all symbolized by a distopic plunge from the skies. Humankind's infirmities force the high-flying possibilities violently back to earth. An anti-utopia of despair occurs in the dream where Gesine flies home on an aircraft called *Transall Ilyushin* (A 1:274), a name that renders the meaning "beyond all illusion." The illusion for dreamers is that they can safely go home, which is the implicit desire driving Gesine's activities for the Prague reform movement. Beyond this illusion, the dreamer learns from one of her fellow passengers, "You're just as condemned to crash as we are" (A 1:274). Even though this dream (a nightmare, really) appears relatively early in the novel, it foreshadows a closing leitmotif that begins on the day D. E. perishes in a plane crash: "We too are due to fly soon" (A 2:558). This is the first of several occurrences of this foreboding sentence. These words become a sign of fear, an emotion that, antithetical as it may appear, is intertwined with Gesine's sense of hope because the future she faces could be positive or negative in its realization.

Johnson weaves an intricate web of associations around the impending disaster of Gesine's mission to indicate that her quest is illusory and is something she undertakes in a dangerous state of denial. Nowhere does the anti-utopian end to Gesine's mission reveal itself more sinisterly than in Gesine's initial viewing of the film "The Fifth Horseman Is Fear." The movie confuses her as she attempts to decipher its message in relation to its strange title. Even though she sees in it "the prepared anticipation, the disappointed one" (Jt 3:1136), she fails to heed the warnings of the dead, who eventually must explain the film's meaning to her (Jt 3:1178–79). Despite the fact that she understands the movie linguistically, she does not comprehend its complexity as a work of art depicting a situation of historical significance, political gravity, and timeless relevance. The connection to Gesine's life becomes apparent when the director's name, Carlo Ponti, is reminiscent of the local commandant of the occupying Soviet forces, K. A. Pontij, whose name Johnson appropriated from the director of the apocalyptic film.[42] Pontij, as it turns out, not only ruins Cresspahl's form of democratic socialism by ordering his arrest but also takes away Gesine's father for two years. Pontij represents the unpredictability, arbitrariness, and ruthlessness of military, political, and economic power acting to protect its interests. He brings disaster to Gesine's life in the past wearing the same uniform, representing the same superpower, and acting on the same political convictions as the Soviet forces that will crush the reforms of the Dubcek regime.

Flying as a symbol of transformation thus acquires a double meaning in light of Gesine's dream trip home and Marie's childhood utopia, "Cydamonoe." Marie's childhood fantasy world in Cydamonoe has a house called Want and Will (Jt 4:1486) where all the children take as they need, but not from each other, and whatever they need, but there is always enough. It is a place where no child must be alone; a quiet whistle results in the immediate company of friends. All material and spiritual needs are instantly satisfied in this utopian society, which possesses many of the promises that Prague holds for Gesine. Both the negative and positive utopias can be reached only by flying, and yet one is the only country in which it is worthwhile to live (Jt 4:1485) while the other promises only death and destruction. Thus, the Czech airline O.K. is to Cydamonoe what *Transall Ilyushin* is to the apocalyptic end of Gesine's mission, which remains forever incomplete. In fact, four years later, Gesine is apparently in prison somewhere in Eastern Europe, as Marie intimates in an impromptu interview when a reporter recognizes her in Richmond, England.[43] Marie is completely on her own. As the interviewer and Marie make their way to central London, Marie speaks candidly about New York and the failed mission to Prague. She is a bit wiser, but she is homeless, and with only seventeen British pennies to her name, she disappears into Victoria Station to take a train to an undisclosed destination. It turns out that both Cresspahls have experienced the illusory quest for a homeland and the perfect society.

# Notes

## Chapter 1: Misunderstanding Uwe Johnson

1. Wilhelm Johannes Schwarz, *Der Erzähler Uwe Johnson* (Bern: Francke Verlag, 1970), 95.

2. Martin Meyer and Wolfgang Strehlow, "'Das sagt mir auch mein Friseur': Film- und Fernsehäußerungen von Uwe Johnson," *Sprache im technischen Zeitalter* 95 (1985): 179.

3. Information for this chapter comes from two main sources. They are Johnson's own *Begleitumstände* (Frankfurt am Main: Suhrkamp, 1980) (hereafter cited in the text as BU) and Bernd Neumann's biography, *Uwe Johnson* (Hamburg: Europäische Verlagsanstalt, 1994).

4. Reinhard Baumgart, "Uwe Johnson im Gespräch," in *"Ich überlege mir die Geschichte . . .": Uwe Johnson im Gespräch,* ed. Eberhard Fahlke (Frankfurt am Main: Suhrkamp, 1988), 225–26.

5. Jakob Hausmann, "'Das gesellschaftliche Klima in der westdeutschen Republik," in *"Ich überlege mir die Geschichte . . . ,"* ed. Fahlke, 120.

6. Horst Bienek, "Uwe Johnson," in *Werkstattgespräche mit Schriftstellern* (Munich: Carl Hanser, 1962), 88.

7. Uwe Johnson, *Der 5. Kanal* (Frankfurt am Main: Suhrkamp, 1987), 7.

8. Uwe Johnson, "Zur Auslassung von Satzzeichen," in *"Ich überlege mir die Geschichte . . . ,"* ed. Fahlke, 158.

9. Bernd Neumann, *Uwe Johnson,* 350–57.

10. Schwarz, *Der Erzähler Uwe Johnson,* 98.

11. Ibid., 92.

12. Uwe Johnson, "Concerning an Attitude of Protesting," in *Berliner Sachen* (Frankfurt am Main: Suhrkamp, 1975), 97.

13. Bernd Neumann, *Uwe Johnson,* 704–6.

14. Ibid., 706.

15. Schwarz, *Der Erzähler Uwe Johnson,* 101.

16. Thomas Mann, "Tonio Kröger," in *Stories of Three Decades,* trans. H. T. Lowe-Porter (New York: Alfred A. Knopf, 1936), 104.

17. Ibid., 108.

## Chapter 2: Approach to Narrative and Storytelling: Essays and Interviews

1. Uwe Johnson, "Berliner Stadtbahn (*veraltet*)," in *Berliner Sachen,* 7–21. Hereafter cited in the text as BSv. Johnson considers the essay "outdated" not because of its poetic message but because of the example he uses to elucidate his message. He takes into consideration a man crossing the border between East and West Berlin, which was no longer possible after August 13, 1961. The essay originally appeared in *Merkur* 15 (1961). Ursule Molinaro published a translation of the essay in *Evergreen Review* 5 (1961): 18–34. I will cite from the essay as published in *Berliner Sachen,* since it is more readily available, using my own translation. See also Uwe Johnson, "Vorschläge zur Prüfung eines Romans," in *Romantheorie: Dokumentation ihrer Geschichte in Deutschland seit 1880,* ed. Eberhard Lämmert et al. (Cologne: Kiepenheuer and Witsch, 1975), 398–403. I cite from a reprinting of the essay in the more accessible Rainer Gerlach and Matthias Richter, eds., *Uwe Johnson* (Frankfurt am Main: Suhrkamp, 1984), 30–36. This version is hereafter cited in the text as VPR. See Beatrice Schulz, "Die Aufgabe des Lesers: Zu Uwe Johnsons 'Vorschlägen zur Prüfung eines Romans,'" in *Internationales Uwe-Johnson-Forum: Beiträge zum Werkverständnis und Materialien zur Rezeptionsgeschichte,* ed. Carsten Gansel, Bernd Neumann, and Nicolai Riedel (Frankfurt am Main: Peter Lang, 1993), 3:139.

2. A. Leslie Willson, "An Interview with Uwe Johnson: 'An Unacknowledged Humorist,'" *Dimension* 15 (1982): 407.

3. Bernd Neumann, *Uwe Johnson,* 304.

4. Arnhelm Neusüß, "Über die Schwierigkeiten beim Schreiben der Wahrheit," in *Uwe Johnson,* ed. Gerlach and Richter, 39.

5. Gertrud Simmerding and Christof Schmid, eds., *Literarische Werkstatt* (Munich: R. Oldenbourg Verlag, 1972), 68.

6. Willson, "Interview," 402.

7. Bienek, "Uwe Johnson," in *Werkstattgespräche mit Schriftstellern,* 89.

8. Manfred Durzak, "Dieser langsame Weg zu einer größeren Genauigkeit: Gespräch mit Uwe Johnson," in *Gespräche über den Roman: Formbestimmungen und Analysen* (Frankfurt am Main: Suhrkamp, 1976), 435.

9. Ibid., 436.

10. Uwe Johnson, "Wenn Sie mich fragen . . . ," in *"Ich überlege mir die Geschichte . . . ,"* ed. Fahlke, 62–63.

11. Uwe Johnson, "Auskünfte und Abreden zu *Zwei Ansichten,*" in *Uwe Johnson,* ed. Gerlach and Richter, 221.

12. Schwarz, *Der Erzähler Uwe Johnson,* 96.

13. Jürgen Becker, Rolf Michaelis, and Heinrich Vormweg, "Gespräch mit Uwe Johnson," in *"Ich überlege mir die Geschichte . . . ,"* ed. Fahlke, 302.

14. Ibid., 301.

15. Rolf Michaelis, *Kleines Adreßbuch für Jerichow und New York: Ein Register zu Uwe Johnsons Roman* Jahrestage (Frankfurt am Main: Suhrkamp, 1983).

16. Virginia Woolf, "Mr. Bennett and Mrs. Brown," in *The Captain's Death Bed and Other Essays* (London: Hogarth, 1950), 92–93.

17. Ibid., 98.

18. Simmerding and Schmid, eds., *Literarische Werkstatt,* 65–66.

19. Ree Post-Adams, "Antworten von Uwe Johnson," in *"Ich überlege mir die Geschichte . . . ,"* ed. Fahlke, 278.

20. Simmerding and Schmid, eds., *Literarische Werkstatt,* 67.

21. Werner Bruck, "'Ein Bauer weiß, daß es ein Jahr nach dem andern gibt': Interview mit Uwe Johnson," in *"Ich überlege mir die Geschichte . . . ,"* ed. Fahlke, 272.

22. Simmerding and Schmid, eds., *Literarische Werkstatt,* 68.

23. Uwe Johnson, preface to *Das neue Fenster: Selections from Contemporary German Literature,* ed. Johnson (New York: Harcourt, Brace, and World, 1967), viii.

24. Meyer and Strehlow, "'Das sagt mir auch mein Friseur,'" 181.

25. Alois Rummel, "Gespräch mit Uwe Johnson," in *"Ich überlege mir die Geschichte . . . ,"* ed. Fahlke, 211.

26. Adalbert Wiemers, "Keine Mutmaßungen über Johnson mehr," in ibid., 218.

27. Simmerding and Schmid, eds., *Literarische Werkstatt,* 67.

## Chapter 3: *Ingrid Babendererde:* Political Maturation

1. Schwarz, *Der Erzähler Uwe Johnson,* 8.

2. Uwe Johnson, "Ein Briefwechsel mit dem Aufbau-Verlag," in *Über Uwe Johnson,* ed. Raimund Fellinger (Frankfurt am Main: Suhrkamp, 1992), 11.

3. Uwe Johnson, *Ingrid Babendererde: Reifeprüfung 1953* (Frankfurt am Main: Suhrkamp, 1985), 19. Hereafter cited in the text as IB.

4. Colin Riordan, "Reifeprüfung 1961: Uwe Johnson and the Cold War," in *German Writers and the Cold War, 1945–1961,* ed. Rhys W. Williams, Stephen Parker, and Colin Riordan (Manchester: Manchester University Press, 1992), 206.

5. "Autor braucht Gehirnwäsche," *Der Spiegel,* 6 January 1992, 132.

6. Siegfried Unseld, "Die Prüfung der Reife 1953," in *Ingrid Babendererde,* by Johnson, 258.

7. Ibid., 258–59.

8. Uwe Johnson, "'Schicksalhaft' war es nicht," in *Porträts und Erinnerungen,* ed. Eberhard Fahlke (Frankfurt am Main: Suhrkamp, 1988), 7.

9. Riordan, "Reifeprüfung 1961," 210.

10. Baumgart, "Uwe Johnson Im Gespräch," 226.

11. Norbert Mecklenburg, "Zeitroman oder Heimatroman? Uwe Johnsons 'Ingrid Babendererde,'" in *Literatur und Provinz: Das Konzept "Heimat" in der neueren Literatur,* ed. Hans-Georg Pott (Paderborn: Schöningh, 1986), 52.

12. Bernd Neumann, "Ingrid Babendererde als Ingeborg Holm: Über Uwe Johnsons ersten Roman," *Germanisch-Romanische Monatshefte* 37 (1987): 220.

13. Walter Benjamin, "ANKLEBEN VERBOTEN! Die Technik des Schriftstellers in dreizehn Thesen," in *Schriften,* ed. Theodor W. Adorno and Gretel Adorno (Frankfurt am Main: Suhrkamp, 1955), 1:538.

14. Neusüß, "Über die Schwierigkeiten beim Schreiben der Wahrheit," in *Uwe Johnson,* ed. Gerlach and Richter, 47.

15. Unseld, "Die Prüfung der Reife 1953," in *Ingrid Babendererde,* by Johnson, 298.

16. Mecklenburg, "Zeitroman oder Heimatroman?" 45.

17. Uwe Johnson, "Versuch, eine Mentalität zu erklären," in *Ich bin Bürger der DDR und lebe in der Bundesrepublik,* ed. Barbara Grunert-Bronnen (Munich: Piper, 1970), 121.

18. Baumgart, "Uwe Johnson im Gespräch," 222.

19. Willson, "Interview," 403.

20. Riordan, "Reifeprüfung 1961," 209–10.

21. Mecklenburg, "Zeitroman oder Heimatroman?" 46.

22. Walter Schmitz, "Die Entstehung der 'immanenten Poetik' Uwe Johnsons: Ein Fassungsvergleich zu *Ingrid Babendererde: Reifeprüfung 1953,*" in *Johnson. Ansichten. Einsichten. Aussichten,* ed. Manfred Jurgensen (Bern: Francke, 1989), 154.

23. Volker Bohn, "'In der anständigsten Art, die sich dafür denken läßt': Uwe Johnsons Erstlingsroman *Ingrid Babendererde,*" in *Über Uwe Johnson,* ed. Fellinger, 29.

24. Mecklenburg, "Zeitroman oder Heimatroman?" 43.

25. Günter Gaus, *Wo Deutschland liegt: Eine Ortsbestimmung,* (Munich: Deutscher Taschenbuch Verlag, 1986), 115.

26. Bertolt Brecht, "Über Schillers Gedicht 'Die Bürgschaft,'" in *Gedichte* (Frankfurt am Main: Suhrkamp, 1961), 4:166.

## Chapter 4: Deadly Choices: *Speculations about Jakob*

1. Uwe Johnson, *Speculations about Jakob,* trans. Ursule Molinaro (New York: Grove Press, 1963). Hereafter cited in the text as SAJ.

2. Günter Blöcker, "Roman der beiden Deutschland," in *Über Uwe Johnson,* ed. Reinhard Baumgart (Frankfurt am Main: Suhrkamp, 1970), 13.

3. Reinhard Baumgart, "Hoffnungsvoll und Hoffnungslos: Utopisch," in *Über Uwe Johnson,* ed. Baumgart, 18.

4. Neusüß, "Über die Schwierigkeiten beim Schreiben der Wahrheit," in *Uwe Johnson,* ed. Gerlach and Richter, 40.

5. Bienek, "Uwe Johnson," in *Werkstattgespräche mit Schriftstellern,* 88.

6. Eberhard Fahlke, *Die "Wirklichkeit" der Mutmassungen: Eine politische Lesart der* Mutmassungen über Jakob *von Uwe Johnson* (Frankfurt am Main: Peter Lang, 1982).

7. Hermann Weber, *Geschichte der DDR* (Munich: Deutscher Taschenbuch Verlag, 1985), 287–91.

8. Peter Brooks, *Reading for the Plot: Design and Intention in Narrative* (New York: Vintage Books, 1984), 12–13.

9. Hansjürgen Popp, *Einführung in Uwe Johnsons Roman* Mutmassungen über Jakob (Stuttgart: Ernst Klett, 1967), 8.

10. Alain Robbe-Grillet, "The Use of Theory," in *For a New Novel: Essays on Fiction,* trans. Richard Howard (New York: Grove Press, 1965), 12.

11. Bienek, "Uwe Johnson," in *Werkstattgespräche mit Schriftstellern,* 89.

12. Walter Schmitz, *Uwe Johnson* (Munich: C. H. Beck, 1984), 29.

13. Theodor W. Adorno, "Parataxis," in *Noten zur Literatur* (1974; Frankfurt am Main: Suhrkamp, 1981), 471.

14. Wolfgang Emmerich, *Kleine Literaturgeschichte der DDR,* 2d ed. (Frankfurt am Main: Luchterhand, 1989), 100–101.

15. Neusüß, "Über die Schwierigkeiten beim Schreiben der Wahrheit," in *Uwe Johnson,* ed. Gerlach and Richter, 40.

16. Ibid.

17. Bernd Neumann, "Utopie und Mythos: Über Uwe Johnson: *Mutmaßungen über Jakob,*" in *Uwe Johnson,* ed. Gerlach and Richter, 108.

18. Bernd Neumann, *Utopie und Mimesis: Zum Verhältnis von Ästhetik, Gesellschaftsphilosophie und Politik in den Romanen Uwe Johnsons* (Kronberg: Athenäum Verlag, 1978), 27.

19. Popp, *Einführung in Uwe Johnsons Roman* Mutmassungen über Jakob, 89–90.

20. Neusüß, "Über die Schwierigkeiten beim Schreiben der Wahrheit," in *Uwe Johnson,* ed. Gerlach and Richter, 41.

21. Emmerich, *Kleine Literaturgeschichte der DDR,* 102

22. Schmitz, *Uwe Johnson,* 31.

23. Fahlke, *Die "Wirklichkeit" der Mutmassungen,* 189.

24. Uwe Johnson, "Jonas zum Beispiel," in *Karsch und andere Prosa* (Frankfurt am Main: Suhrkamp, 1964), 84.

25. Schmitz, *Uwe Johnson,* 111.

26. Neusüß, "Über die Schwierigkeiten beim Schreiben der Wahrheit," in *Uwe Johnson,* ed. Gerlach and Richter, 47.

27. Schmitz, *Uwe Johnson,* 30.

## Chapter 5: The Frustrated Biographer: *The Third Book about Achim*

1. Uwe Johnson, *The Third Book about Achim* (New York: Harcourt, Brace, and World, 1967), 11. Hereafter cited in the text as TBA.

2. Marcel Reich-Ranicki, "Registrator Johnson," in *Über Uwe Johnson,* ed. Fellinger, 107.

3. Holger Helbig, *Beschreibung einer Beschreibung: Untersuchungen zu Uwe Johnsons Roman* Das dritte Buch über Achim (Göttingen: Vandenhoeck and Ruprecht, 1996), 172.

4. Arnulf Baring, *Uprising in East Germany: June 17, 1953,* trans. Gerald Onn (Ithaca: Cornell University Press, 1972). I obtained Information for this section from Baring's excellent book.

5. Schmitz, *Uwe Johnson,* 52.

6. Karl Migner, *Uwe Johnson, Das dritte Buch über Achim: Interpretationen zum Deutschunterricht* (Munich: R. Oldenbourg Verlag, 1966), 60–61.

7. Helbig, *Beschreibung einer Beschreibung,* 166–67.

8. Ibid., 153.

9. Karl Pestalozzi, "Achim alias Täve Schur: Uwe Johnsons zweiter Roman und seine Vorlage," in *Uwe Johnson,* ed. Gerlach and Richter, 152.

10. Bernd Neumann, *Utopie und Mimesis,* 125.

11. Migner, *Uwe Johnson,* 37.

12. Reich-Ranicki, "Registrator Johnson," in *Über Uwe Johnson,* ed. Fellinger, 113.

13. Gisela Ullrich, "'Das dritte Buch über Achim,'" in ibid., 117.

14. Mark Boulby, *Uwe Johnson* (New York: Frederick Ungar, 1974), 52.

15. Bienek, *Werkstattgespräche mit Schriftstellern,* 89.

16. Pestalozzi, "Achim alias Täve Schur," in *Uwe Johnson,* ed. Gerlach and Richter, 162.

17. Bernd Neumann, *Utopie und Mimesis,* 159; Boulby, *Uwe Johnson,* 53.

18. Emmerich, *Kleine Literaturgeschichte der DDR,* 129.

19. Ibid., 127.

20. Helbig, *Beschreibung einer Beschreibung,* 141.

21. Bernd Neumann, *Utopie und Mimesis,* 195.

22. Boulby, *Uwe Johnson,* 43.

23. Uwe Johnson, *An Absence,* trans. Richard and Clara Winston (London: Jonathan Cape, 1969). Hereafter cited in the text as AA.

24. Günter Blöcker, "Uwe Johnsons anderes Deutschland," in *Uwe Johnson,* ed. Gerlach and Richter, 204.

25. Norbert Mecklenburg, "Vorschläge für Johnson-Leser der neunziger Jahre," in *Über Uwe Johnson,* ed. Fellinger, 148

## Chapter 6: Of Sports Cars and Private Spaces: *Two Views*

1. Neusüß, "Über die Schwierigkeiten beim Schreiben der Wahrheit," in *Uwe Johnson,* ed. Gerlach and Richter, 39.

2. Baumgart, "Uwe Johnson im Gespräch," 227.

3. Johnson, "Auskünfte und Abreden zu *Zwei Ansichten,*" in *Uwe Johnson,* ed. Gerlach and Richter, 219.

4. Bernd Neumann, *Uwe Johnson,* 529. Information in this paragraph comes from Neumann's biography.

5. Uwe Johnson, *Two Views,* trans. Richard and Clara Winston (New York: Harcourt, Brace, and World, 1966), 130. Hereafter cited in the text as TV.

6. Weber, *Geschichte der DDR,* 325.

7. Bernd Neumann, *Utopie und Mimesis,* 283.

8. Kurt Fickert, *Dialogue with the Reader: The Narrative Stance in Uwe Johnson's Fiction* (Columbia, S.C.: Camden House, 1996), 73.

9. Horst Krüger, "Das verletzte Rechtsbewusstsein," in *Über Uwe Johnson,* ed. Baumgart, 148–49.

10. Bernd Neumann, *Utopie und Mimesis,* 234.

11. Johnson, "Auskünfte und Abreden zu *Zwei Ansichten,*" in *Uwe Johnson,* ed. Gerlach and Richter, 220.

12. Bernd Neumann, *Utopie und Mimesis,* 241.

13. Uwe Johnson, "Einführung in die *Jahrestage,*" in *Johnsons* Jahrestage, ed. Michael Bengel (Frankfurt am Main: Suhrkamp, 1985), 16–17.

14. Uwe Johnson, "Eine Kneipe geht verloren," in *Berliner Sachen,* 74. This story was originally published in June 1965 in *Kursbuch.*

15. Manfred Durzak, *Der deutsche Roman der Gegenwart* (Stuttgart: W. Kohlhammer, 1971), 227.

16. Patrick O'Neill, "The System in Question: Story and Discourse in Uwe Johnson's *Zwei Ansichten,*" *German Quarterly* 64 (1991): 539.

17. Johnson, "Auskünfte und Abreden zu *Zwei Ansichten,*" in *Uwe Johnson,* ed. Gerlach and Richter, 222.

18. Johnson, "Eine Kneipe geht verloren," in *Berliner Sachen,* 94.

## Chapter 7: The Poetizations of History: *Anniversaries: From the Life of Gesine Cresspahl*

1. Uwe Johnson, *Anniversaries: From the Life of Gesine Cresspahl,* trans. Leila Vennewitz (New York: Harcourt Brace Jovanovich, 1975), and Uwe Johnson, *Anniversaries II: From the Life of Gesine Cresspahl,* trans. Leila Vennewitz and Walter Arndt (New York: Harcourt Brace Jovanovich, 1987). This translation of *Anniversaries* would be nothing less than scandalous if not for Johnson's participation and support of the project. In the only authoritative study of the translation, Peter Ensberg writes, "The significance of the past for the present, the function of memory, the treatment of political events, the connection of private and societal living conditions are among the great themes of *Anniversaries* that are neglected in the English translation" ("Die englische Version von Uwe Johnsons 'Jahrestage,'" in *Uwe Johnson zwischen Vormoderne und Postmoderne,* ed. Carsten Gansel and Nicolai Riedel [Berlin: Walter de Gruyter, 1995], 126). Ensberg explains that of the 367 chapters, only 130 are completely retained, and 64 were cut out entirely. In his estimation, at least 30 percent of the novel is missing (115). Based on this information, I will quote the English version (A) with volume and page number where possible. Otherwise, I will cite the German *Jahrestage* (Jt) with volume and page number and create my own translations as necessary. Hereafter, all citations to both versions of *Anniversaries* will appear in the text.

2. This chapter represents an enhancement and continuation of my previous research. See Gary Lee Baker, "The Outsider Experience and Narrative Strategy in Uwe Johnson's *Jahrestage,*" *Colloquia Germanica* 24 (1991): 83–120; Baker, "(Anti-) Utopian Elements in Uwe Johnson's *Jahrestage: Traces of Ernst Bloch,*" *Germanic Review* 68 (1993): 32–45; Baker, "The Influence of Walter Benjamin's Notion of Allegory on Uwe Johnson's *Jahrestage:* Form and Approach to History," *German Quarterly* 66 (1993): 318–29; Baker, "Auntie 'Times' and Elvira's Tears: The Montage Effect in Uwe Johnson's *Jahrestage* and Christa Wolf's *Kindheitsmuster,*" in

*Internationales Uwe-Johnson-Forum,* ed. Gansel, Neumann, and Riedel, 3:121–38; Baker, "Die Poetisierung der Geschichte in Uwe Johnsons *Jahrestage,*" in *Uwe Johnson zwischen Vormoderne und Postmoderne,* ed. Gansel and Riedel, 143–51.

3. Dieter E. Zimmer, "Eine Bewußtseinsinventur: Das Gespräch mit dem Autor: Uwe Johnson," in *Johnsons* Jahrestage, ed. Bengel, 102.

4. Johnson, "Einführung in die *Jahrestage,*" in *Johnsons Jahrestage,* ed. Bengel, 25.

5. Durzak, *Der deutsche Roman der Gegenwart,* 255.

6. Information on the Prague Spring comes from the various October 1967–August 1968 *New York Times* articles that Johnson collected.

7. Bernd Neumann, *Uwe Johnson,* 837.

8. Bernd Neumann, "Wiederholte Spiegelungen, Metamorphosen, Correspondances: Zuordnungsprinzipien im Werk Uwe Johnson," in *Uwe Johnson zwischen Vormoderne und Postmoderne,* ed. Gansel and Riedel, 24.

9. Rolf Michaelis, "Eines langen Jahres Reise in den Tag: Rede zur Verleihung des Literaturpreises der Stadt Köln an Uwe Johnson," in *Johnsons* Jahrestage, ed. Bengel, 225.

10. Ulrich Fries, *Uwe Johnsons* Jahrestage: *Erzählstruktur und politische Subjektivität* (Göttingen: Vandenhoeck and Ruprecht, 1990), 63.

11. Eberhard Fahlke, "Das Handwerk des Schreibens: Das Uwe-Johnson-Archiv an der J. W. Goethe-Universität," *Forschung Frankfurt* 1 (1985): 2–8. Also see Fahlke's "Erinnerung umgesetzt in Wissen," in *Uwe Johnson: Für wenn ich tot bin,* by Siegfried Unseld and Eberhard Fahlke (Frankfurt am Main: Suhrkamp, 1991), 73–144.

12. Johnson, "Einführung in die *Jahrestage,*" in *Johnsons Jahrestage,* ed. Bengel, 25.

13. Schwarz, *Der Erzähler Uwe Johnson,* 99.

14. Durzak, "Dieser langsame Weg zu einer größeren Genauigkeit," 438.

15. Peter Pokay, "Vergangenheit und Gegenwart In Uwe Johnsons *Jahrestage*" (Ph.D. diss., University of Salzburg, 1983), 102.

16. Martin Polzin, *Kapp-Putsch in Mecklenburg: Junkertum und Landproletariat in der revolutionären Krise nach dem 1. Weltkrieg* (Rostock: Hinstorff, 1966), 191. The original German reads as follows:

Als Kapp schon dem Willen der Arbeiterklasse weichen mußte, ließ Baron le Fort am 18. März die Stadt Waren mit einer Kanone beschießen. . . .

Dieser Junkerkrieg kostete fünf Warener Einwohnern das Leben, elf weitere erlitten zum Teil schwere Verletzungen.

Als die Landarbeiter von den Untaten des verhaßten Mordbarons hörten, bewaffneten sich etwa 60 Mann mit Jagdflinten, Sensen und Forken und versammelten sich im Wald von Schmachthagen. Sie wollten den Arbeitern in Waren zu Hilfe eilen. Dem Gutsbesitzer von Groß Dratow (993 ha) und Bocksee (939 ha), Georg Lemcke, nahmen sie seine Gewehre ab.

17. Johnson actually found the information about the baron himself in Polzin, *Kapp-Putsch in Mecklenburg,* 188.

18. Ibid., 194–95.

19. One specific image involving Robert as the quintessential fascist is a leitmotif of the novel and one of Johnson's allegorical images of the twentieth century:

I couldn't see him take his revolver out of his pocket. He said: "Give me that horse, or I'll shoot."
"Go ahead, shoot."
I ducked, in fun. (A 1:43)

Compare this scene with later executions and assassinations that display resemblances in *Jahrestage:* 1:235, 1:163, 1:433, 2:672–73, 2:723–24, 3:957–60, 3:1298–1302, 4:1844

20. Zimmer, "Eine Bewußtseinsinventur," in *Johnsons* Jahrestage, ed. Bengel, 101.

21. Ibid.

22. Norbert Mecklenburg, "Ein Junge aus dem 'Dreikaiserjahr': Uwe Johnson's 'Versuch, einen Vater zu finden,'" in *Literature on the Threshold: The German Novel in the 1980s,* ed. Arthur Williams, Stuart Parkes, and Roland Smith (New York: Berg, 1990), 44; see also 41, 43.

23. Mikhail Bakhtin, *Problems of Dostoevsky's Poetics,* trans. R. W. Rotsel (Ann Arbor, Mich.: Ardis, 1973), 56.

24. Zimmer, "Eine Bewußtseinsinventur," in *Johnsons* Jahrestage, ed. Bengel, 99. "The book began as an attempt to portray the consciousness of Gesine Cresspahl—what it all contains from the past and present. Through the relationship with the daughter came the possibility to divide it up into conversations here and there. In the second volume there is certain information, concerning the present, that is given to the child as a precaution, so that it does not have to break its head in ten years about the decisions of her mother in the year 1968. Basically, however, it is such that the author has received the license and contract to portray the records of her consciousness."

25. Durzak, "Dieser langsame Weg zu einer größeren Genauigkeit," 438.

26. Bernd Neumann, *Utopie und Mimesis,* 302, and Neumann, "Wiederholte Spiegelungen," 17–29.

27. Theodor W. Adorno, "Über Tradition," in *Ohne Leitbild* (Frankfurt am Main: Suhrkamp, 1967), 36.

28. Walter Benjamin, *Das Passagenwerk,* ed. Rolf Tiedemann (Frankfurt am Main: Suhrkamp, 1982), 1:578. See Fries, *Uwe Johnsons* Jahrestage, 130.

29. Ludwig Wittgenstein, *Philosophical Investigations,* ed. G. E. M. Anscombe and R. Rhees, trans. G. E. M. Anscombe (Oxford: Basil Blackwell, 1953), 1:32.

30. Ernst Bloch, *Spuren, Werkausgabe* (Frankfurt am Main: Suhrkamp, 1985), 167.

31. Walter Benjamin, "On Some Motifs in Baudelaire," in *Illuminations,* ed. Hannah Arendt, trans. Harry Zohn (New York: Harcourt, Brace, and World, 1968), 160.

32. Durzak, "Dieser langsame Weg zu einer größeren Genauigkeit," 438.

33. Benjamin, "On Some Motifs," in *Illuminations,* ed. Arendt, 161.

34. Mecklenburg, "Ein Junge aus dem 'Dreikaiserjahr,'" 43

35. "Günter Grass—Peter Bichsel—Gabriele Wohmann—Uwe Johnson: Wie ein Roman entsteht," in *Literarische Werkstatt,* ed. Simmerding and Schmid, 65.

36. Bernd Neumann, "'Heimweh ist eine schlimme Tugend,'" in *Johnsons Jahrestage,* ed. Bengel, 269–70.

37. Tilman Jens, *Unterwegs an den Ort wo die Toten sind: Auf der Suche nach Uwe Johnson in Sheerness* (Munich: Piper, 1984), 36.

38. Hans Daiber, "Die Cooperation mit Gesine: Interview mit Uwe Johnson," in *Johnsons* Jahrestage, ed. Bengel, 131.

39. Schmitz, *Uwe Johnson,* 93.

40. Bernd Neumann, *Utopie und Mimesis,* 58. See also Norbert Mecklenburg, "Leseerfahrungen mit Johnsons *Jahrestagen,*" in *Uwe Johnson,* ed. Gerlach and Richter, 314.

41. Ernst Bloch, *The Principle of Hope,* trans. Neville Plaice, Stephen Plaice, and Paul Knight (Cambridge: MIT Press, 1986), 3:1375–76.

42. Michaelis, *Kleines Adreßbuch für Jerichow und New York,* 211. See also BU 421.

43. Uwe Johnson, "MARIE H. CRESSPAHL, 2.–3. Januar 1972," in *"Ich überlege mir die Geschichte . . . ,"* ed. Fahlke, 107.

# Bibliography

## Works by Uwe Johnson in order of publication

*Mutassungen über Jakob.* Frankfurt am Main: Suhrkamp, 1959. Translated by Ursule Molinaro as *Speculations about Jakob.* New York: Grove Press, 1963.

*Das dritte Buch über Achim.* Frankfurt am Main: Suhrkamp, 1961. Translated as *The Third Book about Achim.* New York: Harcourt, Brace, and World, 1967.

*Karsch, und andere Prose.* Frankfurt am Main: Suhrkamp, 1964. The main story of this collection, "Eine Reise weg wohin, 1960," is translated by Richard and Clara Winston as *An Absence.* London: Jonathan Cape, 1969.

*Zwei Ansichten.* Frankfurt am Main: Suhrkamp, 1965. Translated by Richard and Clara Winston as *Two Views.* New York: Harcourt, Brace, and World, 1966.

*Das neue Fenster: Selections from Contemporary German Literature.* New York: Harcourt, Brace, and World, 1967.

"Versuch, eine Mentalität zu erklären." In *Ich bin Bürger der DDR und lebe in der Bundesrepublik,* ed. Barbara Grunert-Bronnen, 119–29. Serie Piper 3. Munich: Piper, 1970.

*Jahrestage: Aus dem Leben von Gesine Cresspahl.* 4 vols. Frankfurt am Main: Suhrkamp, 1970–83. Translated by Leila Vennewitz as *Anniversaries: From the Life of Gesine Cresspahl.* New York: Harcourt Brace Jovanovich, 1975. The second volume is *Anniversaries II: From the Life of Gesine Cresspahl.* Translated by Leila Vennewitz and Walter Arndt. New York: Harcourt Brace Jovanovich, 1987. Vol. 1 of the translation covers the first six months of *Jahrestage,* and vol. 2 finishes the year.

*Eine Reise nach Klagenfurt.* Frankfurt am Main: Suhrkamp, 1974. In this volume Johnson recounts his visit to the hometown and grave of his friend and colleague, Austrian writer Ingeborg Bachmann.

*Berliner Sachen.* Frankfurt am Main: Suhrkamp, 1975. Johnson published several essays in this volume with political, literary, and sociological commentary. The short story "Eine Kneipe geht verloren" is included in this collection.

*Begleitumstände.* Frankfurt am Main: Suhrkamp, 1980. A series of autobiographical essays on Johnson's development as a writer.

*Skizze eines Verunglückten.* Bibliothek Suhrkamp 785. Frankfurt am Main: Suhrkamp, 1984. This piece originally appeared in *Begegnungen: Eine Festschrift für Max Frisch zum siebzigsten Geburtstag.* Frankfurt am Main: Suhrkamp, 1981. Many critics believe that this text represents Johnson's coming to terms with his marital problems.

*Ingrid Babendererde: Reifeprüfung 1953.* Afterword by Siegfried Unseld. Frankfurt am Main: Suhrkamp, 1985.

*Der 5. Kanal.* Frankfurt am Main: Suhrkamp, 1987. Contains Johnson's reviews of East

German television programs written for *Tagesspiegel*'s television supplement in the latter part of 1964.

*Porträts und Erinnerungen.* Ed. Eberhard Fahlke. Frankfurt am Main: Suhrkamp, 1988. This volume contains letters and speeches about Johnson's friends and colleagues.

*Versuch, einen Vater zu finden* and *Marthas Ferien.* Ed. Norbert Mecklenburg. Frankfurt am Main: Suhrkamp, 1988. Mecklenburg provides explanatory notes and an afterword to enhance readers' understanding of these rather cryptic stories. "Versuch, einen Vater zu finden" is related to Gesine Cresspahl's world in *Jahrestage,* while "Marthas Ferien" focuses on the Niebuhr family from both *Ingrid Babendererde* and *Jahrestage.* These stories were found among Johnson's papers after his death. The volume comes with a cassette recording of Johnson reading the stories.

*Uwe Johnson: "Entwöhnung von einem Arbeitsplatz" Klausuren und frühe Prosatexte mit einem philologisch-biographischen Essay.* Ed. Bernd Neumann. Schriften des Uwe Johnson-Archivs 3. Frankfurt am Main: Suhrkamp, 1992.

*Uwe Johnson: "Wo ist der Erzähler auffindbar?" Gutachten für Verlage 1956–1958.* Ed. Bernd Neumann. Schriften des Uwe Johnson-Archivs 4. Frankfurt am Main: Suhrkamp, 1992. Neumann edited texts from Johnson's work as an independent professional, writing opinions about proposed literary projects sent to publishers in the GDR.

*Vergebliche Verabredung: Ausgewählte Prosa.* Ed. Jürgen Grambow. Leipzig: Reclam, 1992. This collection contains items from Johnson's works that have interest for East German readers. It includes portions of the fourth volume of *Jahrestage,* texts that deal with divided Berlin, and "Eine Reise wegwohin, 1960." It also contains a conversation between the editor and East German writer Stephan Hermlin as well as an afterword by East German writer Fritz Rudolf Fries.

*Uwe Johnson: Inselgeschichten.* Ed. Eberhard Fahlke. Schriften des Uwe Johnson-Archivs 5. Frankfurt am Main: Suhrkamp, 1995. These stories have as their main focus Johnson's home in Sheerness, England.

*Heute Neunzig Jahr.* Ed. Norbert Mecklenburg. Frankfurt am Main: Suhrkamp, 1996. According to Mecklenburg, this fragment was part of Johnson's next project, which was to be a history of the Cresspahl family. Johnson had only finished 120 pages before he died.

# Critical Works on Uwe Johnson

## Biographical Works

Fahlke, Eberhard. "Das Handwerk des Schreibens: Das Uwe Johnson-Archiv an der J. W. Goethe-Universität." *Forschung Frankfurt* 1 (1985): 2–8.

———, ed. *"Die Katze Erinnerung" Uwe Johnson: Eine Chronik in Briefen und Bildern.* Frankfurt am Main: Suhrkamp, 1994.

Gotzmann, Werner. *Uwe Johnsons Testamente oder wie der Suhrkamp Verlag Erbe wird.* Afterword by Elisabeth Johnson. Berlin: Edition Lit.europe, 1996. This volume documents the history of the court battles involving Johnson's estate.

Jens, Tilman. "Auf den Spuren des toten Dichters Uwe Johnson." *Stern,* 25 May 1984, 126–35. A report on Johnson's lifestyle in Sheerness, England, that outraged his friends and family. Jens focuses on Johnson's problems with his wife, alcoholism, and relationships with people in the town of Sheerness.

———. *Unterwegs an den Ort wo die Toten sind: Auf der Suche nach Uwe Johnson in Sheerness.* Munich: Piper, 1984. Published soon after Johnson's death, this book created a scandal when it was revealed that Jens broke into Johnson's apartment to obtain information. In this book and in the article above, Jens went into details about Johnson's married life that led to court cases against Jens. This short work contains helpful information about Johnson's method of working and his daily routines.

Neumann, Bernd. *Uwe Johnson.* Hamburg: Europäische Verlagsanstalt, 1994. A well-written and informative piece of work, this book is the most exhaustive biography on Johnson. The author went to great lengths to interview people who knew Johnson and was granted permission to look at Johnson's unpublished notebooks for information about the author's life. Neumann also provides interpretations of individual works.

Unseld, Siegfried, and Eberhard Fahlke. *Uwe Johnson: Für wenn ich tot bin.* Schriften des Uwe Johnson-Archivs 1. Frankfurt am Main: Suhrkamp, 1991. This volume contains an essay by each of the authors. As Johnson's close friend and publisher, Unseld describes Johnson's difficult life and last days in Sheerness, discussing Johnson's difficulties in finishing *Jahrestage,* which were in no small part due to his failed marriage. Unseld also writes about going to Sheerness after hearing of Johnson's death and the arrangements to have Johnson's possessions transported to Frankfurt. Fahlke describes the process of setting up the archive in Frankfurt and details its more interesting contents. The volume has many photographs of Johnson, his friends and house in Sheerness, as well as holdings of the archive.

## Monographs

Boulby, Mark. *Uwe Johnson.* New York: Frederick Ungar, 1974. This book discusses Johnson's work up to the first two volumes of *Jahrestage.* In this respect it is somewhat limited but is nonetheless an accessible introduction to a difficult author.

Golisch, Stefanie. *Uwe Johnson zur Einführung.* Hamburg: Junius, 1994. Golisch provides a solid piece of interpretive and critical work that includes a bibliography. She discusses Johnson's major works.

Hanuschek, Sven. *Uwe Johnson.* Köpfe des 20. Jahrhunderts 124. Berlin: Morgenbuch, 1994.

Neumann, Bernd, ed. *Erläuterungen und Dokumente: Uwe Johnson* Mutmassungen über Jakob. Stuttgart: Reclam, 1989. This volume provides a line-by-line explanation of Johnson's first published novel. It also contains a history of the work's origins, discussions of its narrative structure, and a bibliography of secondary literature on Johnson's early works.

Nöldechen, Peter. *Bilderbuch von Johnsons Jerichow und Umgebung: Spurensuche im Mecklenburg der Cresspahls.* Schriften des Uwe Johnson-Archivs 2. Frankfurt am Main: Suhrkamp, 1991. The area in which fictitious Jerichow is located is a small corner of northwestern Mecklenburg. The author of this volume takes the reader on a tour through the area, including Klütz, the village after which many believe Jerichow is modeled.

Popp, Hansjürgen. *Einführung in Uwe Johnsons Roman* Mutmassungen über Jakob. Stuttgart: Ernst Klett, 1967. Popp provides the most thorough discussion to date of this difficult novel. Any student or scholar beginning research on *Speculations about Jakob* will want to read this book. Evidence in the Uwe Johnson Archive shows that Popp consulted with Johnson in preparing this introduction.

Riordan, Colin. *The Ethics of Narration: Uwe Johnson's Novels from* Ingrid Babendererde *to* Jahrestage. Bithell Series of Dissertations 14. London: Modern Humanities Research Association, 1989. Riordan's book is well written and well researched and offers a useful discussion of *Jahrestage* in its latter half.

Schmitz, Walter. *Uwe Johnson.* Autorenbücher 43. Munich: C. H. Beck, 1984. This introduction to Johnson's work discusses interpretations of Johnson's major novels and situates Johnson in the broader context of postwar German fiction, both East and West.

Schwarz, Wilhelm Johannes. *Der Erzähler Uwe Johnson.* Bern: Francke Verlag, 1970. This monograph is an interesting study of Johnson's work up to the appearance of *Jahrestage.* The most informative part of this book is the author's interview with Johnson, who appears to have been in an uncharacteristically talkative mood. This is the first text that offers insights into the first of Johnson's novels, *Ingrid Babendererde.*

Wünderich, Erich. *Uwe Johnson.* Köpfe des 20. Jahrhunderts 73. Berlin: Colloquium Verlag Otto H. Hess, 1973.

## Books

Adorno, Theodor W. *Noten zur Literatur.* 1974; Frankfurt am Main: Suhrkamp, 1981.

Adorno, Theodor W. *Ohne Leitbild.* Frankfurt am Main: Suhrkamp, 1967.

Bakhtin, Mikhail. *Problems of Dostoevsky's Poetics.* Trans. R. W. Rotsel. Ann Arbor, Mich.: Ardis, 1973.

Baring, Arnulf. *Uprising in East Germany: June 17, 1953.* Trans. Gerald Onn. Ithaca: Cornell University Press, 1972.

Benjamin, Walter. *Das Passagenwerk.* Ed. Rolf Tiedemann. Frankfurt am Main: Suhrkamp, 1982.

Bloch, Ernst. *The Principle of Hope.* Trans. Neville Plaice, Stephen Plaice, and Paul Knight. Cambridge: MIT Press, 1986.

————. *Spuren, Werkausgabe.* Frankfurt am Main: Suhrkamp, 1985.

Bond, D. G. *German History and German Identity: Uwe Johnson's* Jahrestage. Amsterdamer Publikationen zur Sprache und Literatur 104. Amsterdam: Rodopi, 1993. Bond's book is less theoretical than the title would suggest in these times of posthistoricism and identitarian theories. Nonetheless, it is a well-written and accessible account of how Johnson incorporates history into *Jahrestage.* Bond also devotes several pages to the interpretation of *Skizze eines Verunglückten,* which most critics read autobiographically.

Brecht, Bertolt. *Gedichte.* Frankfurt am Main: Suhrkamp, 1961.

Brooks, Peter. *Reading for the Plot: Design and Intention in Narrative.* New York: Vintage Books, 1984.

Burkhard, Jürg. *Uwe Johnsons Bild der DDR-Gesellschaft:* Das dritte Buch über Achim *Romaninterpretation.* Studien zur Germanistik, Anglistik und Komparatistik 117. Bonn: Bouvier, 1988. Burkhard concentrates his study on the East German characters of the novel, especially the Achim figure.

Emmerich, Wolfgang. *Kleine Literaturgeschichte der DDR.* 2d ed. Frankfurt am Main: Luchterhand, 1989.

Fahlke, Eberhard. *Die "Wirklichkeit" der Mutmaßungen: Eine politische Lesart der* Mutmaßungen über Jakob *von Uwe Johnson.* Frankfurt am Main: Peter Lang, 1982. This book covers the historical background of the events described in Johnson's first published book. Fahlke's research is so thorough that this book could be used as a reliable history of the autumn of 1956 in the former Eastern bloc.

Fickert, Kurt. *Dialogue with the Reader: The Narrative Stance in Uwe Johnson's Fiction.* Columbia, S.C.: Camden House, 1996. This book offers a survey of Johnson's major works plus a discussion of his short prose piece "Jonas zum Beispiel." Fickert also discusses Johnson's affinity for American and British literature.

————. *Neither Left nor Right: The Politics of Individualism in Uwe Johnson's Work.* Germanic Languages and Literature 59. New York: Peter Lang, 1987.

Fries, Ulrich. *Uwe Johnsons* Jahrestage: *Erzählstruktur und politische Subjektivität.* Palaestra Band 290. Göttingen: Vandenhoeck and Ruprecht, 1990. In terms of its theoretical nature, this book requires patience to read, but it is useful in understanding the significance of the beginning of *Jahrestage.*

Forster, E. M. *Aspects of the Novel.* New York: Harcourt, Brace and World, Inc., 1927.

Gaus, Günter. *Wo Deutschland liegt: Eine Ortsbestimmung.* Munich: Deutscher Taschenbuch Verlag, 1986.

Gerlach, Ingeborg. *Auf der Suche nach der verlorenen Identität: Studien zu Uwe Johnsons* Jahrestagen. Monographien Literaturwissenschaft 47. Königstein/Ts.: Scriptor, 1980. This book focuses on Gesine Cresspahl and her difficulties in relating to her immediate surroundings, her past, and her uncertain future.

Helbig, Holger. *Beschreibung einer Beschreibung: Untersuchungen zu Uwe Johnsons Roman* Das dritte Buch über Achim. Johnson-Studien 1. Göttingen: Vandenhoeck and Ruprecht, 1996. Helbig contextualizes the novel in question in the historical circumstances of its time. The research is excellent and provides a solid understanding of the Achim novel.

Hye, Roberta T. *Uwe Johnsons* Jahrestage: *Die Gegenwart als variierende Wiederholung der Vergangenheit.* Europäische Hochschulschriften Deutsche Literatur und Germanistik 225. Bern: Peter Lang, 1978.

Lämmert, Eberhard, Hartmut Eggert, Karl-Heinz Hartmann, Gerhard Hinzmann, Dietrich Scheunemann, Fritz Wahrenburg, eds. *Romantheorie: Dokumentation ihrer Geschichte in Deutschland seit 1880.* Cologne: Kiepenheuer and Witsch, 1975. "Vorschläge zur Prüfung einer Romons" appears on pp. 398–403.

Michaelis, Rolf. *Kleines Adreßbuch für Jerichow und New York: Ein Register zu Uwe Johnsons Roman* Jahrestage. Frankfurt am Main: Suhrkamp, 1983.

Migner, Karl. *Uwe Johnson,* Das dritte Buch über Achim: *Interpretationen zum Deutschunterricht.* Munich: R. Oldenbourg Verlag, 1966. Migner provides basic interpretations of the novel for use in a German Gymnasium class. The book is methodical and systematic in its approach to narrative structure, genre classification, and the close reading of the text.

Neumann, Bernd. *Utopie und Mimesis: Zum Verhältnis von Ästhetik, Gesellschaftsphilosophie und Politik in den Romanen Uwe Johnsons.* Kronberg: Athenäum Verlag, 1978. This book has become a standard in Johnson research. It was the first study that utilized sociological and political as well as psychological methods of interpreting Johnson's work. The chapter on *Jahrestage,* however, is short and fails to recognize the significance of the novel for Johnson's career.

Neumann, Uwe. *Uwe Johnson und der "Nouveau Roman": Komparatistische Untersuchungen zur Stellung von Uwe Johnsons Erzählwerk zur Theorie und Praxis des "Nouveau Roman."* Beiträge zur Literatur und Literaturwissenschaft des 20. Jahrhunderts 10. Frankfurt am Main: Peter Lang, 1992. At the end of this exhaustive work, Neumann concludes that Johnson, though he may possess similarities to the new novelists of France, is no new novelist himself.

Paulsen, Wolfgang. *Uwe Johnson: Undine geht: Die Hintergründe seines Romanwerks.* Bern: Peter Lang, 1993. Paulsen's book concentrates mainly on *Jahrestage,* discussing the problems of *Heimat* and memory as well as the structure of the novel. The author includes biographical elements to explicate Johnson's literary production.

Polzin, Martin. *Kapp-Putsch in Mecklenburg: Junktertum und Landproletariat in der revolutionären Krise nach dem 1. Weltkrieg.* Rostock: Hinstorff, 1966.

Post-Adams, Ree. *Uwe Johnson: Darstellungsproblematik als Romanthema in* Mut-massungen über Jakob *und* Das dritte Buch über Achim. Studien zur Germanistik, Anglistik und Komparatistik 64. Bonn: Bouvier, 1977. This study deals primarily with the narratological problems of Johnson's first two published novels.

Riedel, Ingrid. *Wahrheitsfindung als epische Technik: Analytische Studien zu Uwe Johnsons Texten.* Munich: Uni-Druck, 1971. This book contains a discussion of Johnson's works utilizing the theory of cubism.

Riedel, Nicolai. *Uwe Johnson: Bibliographie 1959–1980.* Abhandlungen zur Kunst-, Musik-, und Literaturwissenschaft 200. Bonn: Bouvier, 1981. This is the most comprehensive bibliography of primary and secondary literature concerning Johnson. Riedel is currently working on a new comprehensive bibliography.

Robbe-Grillet, Alain. *For a New Novel: Essays on Fiction.* Trans. Richard Howard. New York: Grove Press, 1965.

Schulz, Beatrice. *Lektüren von Jahrestagen: Studien zu einer Poetik der* Jahrestage *von Uwe Johnson.* Tübingen: Max Niemeyer, 1995. This work contains discussions of specific entries in *Jahrestage* bracketed in the broader concepts of Johnson's poetic stance.

Simmerding, Gertrud, and Christof Schmid, eds. *Literarische Werkstatt.* Munich: R. Oldenbourg Verlag, 1972.

Storz-Sahl, Sigrun. *Erinnerung und Erfahrung: Geschichtsphilosophie und ästhetische Erfahrung in Uwe Johnsons* Jahrestagen. Deutsche Sprache und Literatur 1094. Frankfurt am Main: Peter Lang, 1988. This important and highly theoretical book explores the relationship of Walter Benjamin's work to Johnson's.

Weber, Hermann. *Geschichte der DDR.* Munich: Deutscher Taschenbuch Verlag, 1985.

Wittgenstein, Ludwig. *Philosophical Investigations.* Ed. G. E. M. Anscombe and R. Rhees. Trans. G. E. M. Anscombe. Oxford: Basil Blackwell, 1953.

Zetzsche, Jürgen. *Die Erfindung photographischer Bilder im zeitgenössischen Erzählen: Zum Werk von Uwe Johnson und Jürgen Becker.* Frankfurter Beiträge zur Germanistik 27. Heidelberg: C. Winter, 1994.

## Collections of Articles, Interviews, Conference Proceedings, and Yearbooks

Most of the important articles and treatises on Johnson's works are contained in the volumes listed here.

Arnold, Heinz Ludwig, ed. *Uwe Johnson: Text + kritik Sonderband.* Munich: Edition text + kritik, 1980. The most important critics of Johnson's work are represented here. Norbert Mecklenburg's fictional piece written as a dialogue between two frustrated readers of *Jahrestage* is a revealing discussion of the novel's reception.

Baumgart, Reinhard, ed. *Über Uwe Johnson.* Frankfurt am Main: Suhrkamp, 1970. The first collection of secondary literature on Uwe Johnson, this volume includes reviews and articles on Johnson's first four publications. There is also a short vita and afterword by Baumgart.

Bengel, Michael, ed. *Johnsons* Jahrestage. Frankfurt am Main: Suhrkamp, 1985. Bengel has provided the most comprehensive compilation of articles, reviews, and interviews available on Johnson's most ambitious novel, including some original pieces by Johnson about his *Jahrestage* project.

Berbig, Roland, and Erdmut Wizisla, eds. *"Wo ich her bin . . .": Uwe Johnson in der D.D.R..* Berlin: editionKONTEXT, 1993. Many of Johnson's colleagues contributed to this volume. There are also interviews and letters published here for the first time. The third part of the volume contains interpretations of Johnson's works. Nicolai Riedel published a bibliography here that focuses on Johnson's reception in the GDR.

Fahlke, Eberhard, ed. *"Ich überlege mir die Geschichte . . .": Uwe Johnson im Gespräch.* Frankfurt am Main: Suhrkamp, 1988. This volume contains all the important interviews with Johnson as well as speeches and many of Johnson's witty answers to questionnaires. There is also an important section by Jeremy Gaines on Johnson's correspondence with Leila Vennewitz, the translator of *Jahrestage.*

Fellinger, Raimund, ed. *Über Uwe Johnson.* Frankfurt am Main: Suhrkamp, 1992. The advantage of the Fellinger collection over other Suhrkamp products on Johnson is that it includes items from the archive and deals with Johnson's entire opus. *Ingrid Babendererde* is included here, along with some East German views of Johnson.

Fries, Ulrich, and Holger Helbig, eds. *Johnson-Jahrbuch.* 1–3. Göttingen: Vandenhoeck and Ruprecht, 1994–96. The *Johnson-Jahrbuch* includes specialized articles on Johnson that address both biographical and literary topics. Many young scholars find a vehicle for their research in these volumes.

Gansel, Carsten, and Jürgen Grambow, eds. *Biographie ist unwiderruflich . . . Zu Uwe Johnson: Materialien des Kolloquiums zum Werk Uwe Johnsons im Dez. 1990 in Neubrandenburg.* Frankfurt am Main: Peter Lang, 1992. These are published papers from the first public discussion of Johnson's life and works in the former GDR.

Gansel, Carsten, Bernd Neumann, and Nicolai Riedel, eds. *Internationales Uwe-Johnson-Forum: Beiträge zum Werkverständnis und Materialien zur Rezeptionsgeschichte.* 1–6. Frankfurt am Main: Peter Lang, 1989–96. Many young scholars publish their work in these volumes, and as a result the articles are new research and are often specialized. Articles in these volumes have biographical, comparativistic, or interdisciplinary approaches to Johnson material. Riedel includes a bibliography of new works on, translations of, and newly published material by Johnson in every volume.

Gansel, Carsten, and Nicolai Riedel, eds. *Uwe Johnson zwischen Vormoderne und Postmoderne.* Berlin: Walter de Gruyter, 1995. Papers given at the "Internationales Uwe Johnson Symposium" in September 1994 were revised, expanded, and selected for inclusion in this volume. Most of the articles discuss *Jahrestage.* Kurt Drawert's talk, "Die Abschaffung der Wirklichkeit," is also published here.

Gerlach, Rainer, and Matthias Richter, eds. *Uwe Johnson.* Frankfurt am Main: Suhrkamp, 1984. All of Johnson's major works are addressed in this volume that contains reviews, articles, interviews, and Johnson's treatise "Vorschläge zur Prüfung eines Romans."

Jurgensen, Manfred, ed. *Johnson. Ansichten. Einsichten. Aussichten.* Bern: Francke, 1989. This volume addresses many of Johnson's works and contains two important articles on *Ingrid Babendererde.*

Riedel, Nicolai, ed. *Uwe Johnsons Frühwerk im Spiegel der deutschsprachigen Literaturkritik: Dokumente zur publizistischen Rezeption der Romane* Mutmaßungen über Jakob, Das dritte Buch über Achim, *und* Ingrid Babendererde. Abhandlungen zur Kunst-, Musik-, und Literaturwissenschaft 371. Bonn: Bouvier, 1987. This volume includes early impressions of Johnson narrated by leading literary critics of the late 1950s and early 1960s in West Germany.

## Selected Articles and Chapters in Books

Baker, Gary Lee. "(Anti-) Utopian Elements in Uwe Johnson's *Jahrestage:* Traces of Ernst Bloch." *Germanic Review* 68 (1993): 32–45.

———. "The Influence of Walter Benjamin's Notion of Allegory on Uwe Johnson's *Jahrestage:* Form and Approach to History." *German Quarterly* 66 (1993): 318–29.

———. "The Outsider Experience and Narrative Strategy in Uwe Johnson's *Jahrestage.*" *Colloquia Germanica* 24 (1991): 83–120.

Bauschinger, Sigrid. "Mythos Manhattan: Die Fazination einer Stadt." In *Amerika in der deutschen Literatur: Neue Welt—Nordamerika—USA,* ed. Sigrid Bauschinger, 382–97. Stuttgart: Reclam, 1975.

Benjamin, Walter. "ANKLEBEN VERBOTEN! Die Technik des Schriftstellers in dreizehn Thesen." In *Schriften,* ed. Theodor W. Adorno and Gretel Adorno, 1:536–38. Frankfurt am Main: Suhrkamp, 1955.

———. "On Some Motifs in Baudelaire." In *Illuminations,* ed. Hannah Arendt, trans. Harry Zohn, 155–200. New York: Harcourt, Brace, and World, 1968.

Berbig, Roland. "'Als sei er süchtig, im Zustand einer Folter zu verharren!' Leid und Leiden: Schreibmotive Uwe Johnsons." *Wirkendes Wort* 42 (1992): 283–94.

Bienek, Horst. "Uwe Johnson." In *Werkstattgespräche mit Schriftstellern,* 85–98. Munich: Carl Hanser, 1962.

Bond, D. G., and Julian Preece. "'Cap Arcona' 3 May 1945: History and Allegory in Novels by Uwe Johnson and Günter Grass." *Oxford German Studies* 20–21 (1991–92): 147–63.

Bond, D. G. "The Dialogic Form of Uwe Johnson's *Mutmaßungen über Jakob.*" *Modern Language Review* 84 (1989): 874–84.

———. "Two Ships: Correspondences between Uwe Johnson and Johann Peter Hebel." *German Quarterly* 64 (1991): 313–24.

Boulby, Mark. "Surmises on Love and Family Life in the Work of Uwe Johnson." *Seminar* 10 (1974): 131–41.

Bürger, Christa. "Uwe Johnson: der Erzähler." In *Prosa der Moderne,* ed. Peter Bürger, 353–82. Frankfurt am Main: Suhrkamp, 1988.

Durzak, Manfred. "Dieser langsame Weg zu einer größeren Genauigkeit: Gespräch mit Uwe Johnson," and "Mimesis und Wahrheitsfindung. Probleme des realistischen Romans: Uwe Johnsons *Jahrestage.*" In *Gespräche über den Roman: Formbestimmungen und Analysen,* 428–60 and 461–81. Frankfurt am Main: Suhrkamp, 1976.

———. "Wirklichkeitserkundung und Utopie. Die Romane Uwe Johnsons." *Der deutsche Roman der Gegenwart.* Sprache und Literatur 70. Stuttgart: W. Kohl-hammer, 1971. 174–249.

Fahlke, Eberhard. "'Gute Nacht, New York—Gute Nacht, Berlin': Anmerkungen zu einer Figur des Protestierens anhand der *Jahrestage* von Uwe Johnson." In *Literatur und Studentenbewegung,* 186–218. Lesen 6. Opladen: Westdeutscher Verlag, 1977.

Fickert, Kurt. "Biblical Symbolism in *Mutmassungen über Jakob.*" *German Quarterly* 54 (1981): 59–62.

———. "The Reunification Theme in Johnson's *Das dritte Buch über Achim.*" *German Studies Review* 16 (1993): 225–33.

Gaines, Jeremy. "Richmond in Literature: On Three Themes in Uwe Johnson's *Jahrestage.*" *German Life and Letters* 56 (1992): 74–93.

Geisthardt, Hans-Jürgen. "Das Thema der Nation und zwei Literaturen. Nachweis an: Christa Wolf—Uwe Johnson." *Neue Deutsche Literatur* 14 (1966): 48–69. A rare East German discussion of Johnson and his work.

Gerlach, Ingeborg. "Über die politische Verbindlichkeit von Literatur: Die Kontroverse zwischen Weiss, Enzensberger und Johnson, und was daraus wurde." *Diskussion Deutsch* 15 (1984): 511–17. Gerlach describes these authors' varying notions of political engagement.

Grambow, Jürgen. "Heimat im Vergangenen." *Sinn und Form* 38 (1986): 134–57. This article was the first positive public acknowledgment of Johnson's work in the former GDR.

Hatfield, Henry. "A World Divided: Uwe Johnson's *Two Views.*" In *Crisis and Continuity in Modern German Fiction,* 150–65. Ithaca: Cornell University Press, 1969.

Hoesterey, Ingeborg. "Die Erzählsituation als Roman: Uwe Johnsons *Jahrestage.*" *Colloquia Germanica* 16 (1983): 13–26.

Krätzer, Anita. "To Want the Unthinkable: Uwe Johnson's *Anniversaries.*" In *Amerika! New Images in German Literature,* ed. Heinz D. Osterle, 149–73. German Life and Civilization 2. New York: Peter Lang, 1989.

Lennox, Sara. "Die *New York Times* in Johnsons *Jahrestagen.*" In *Die USA und Deutschland. Wechselseitige Spiegelungen in der Literatur der Gegenwart,* ed. Wolfgang Paulsen, 103–9. Munich: Francke, 1976.

———. "From Yoknapatawpha to Jerichow: Uwe Johnson's Appropriation of William Faulkner." *Arcadia* 14 (1979): 160–76.

———. "History in Uwe Johnson's *Jahrestage.*" *Germanic Review* 64 (1989): 31–41.

Mecklenburg, Norbert. Afterword to "Versuch einen Vater zu finden," by Uwe Johnson, 71–96. Frankfurt am Main: Suhrkamp, 1988.

———. "Ein Junge aus dem 'Dreikaiserjahr': Uwe Johnson's 'Versuch einen Vater zu finden.'" In *Literature on the Threshold: The German Novel in the 1980s,* ed. Arthur Williams, Stuart Parkes, and Roland Smith, 29–47. New York: Berg, 1990.

———. "Grossstadtmontage und Provinzchronik: Die epische 'Aufhebung' des regionalen Romans in Uwe Johnsons *Jahrestage.*" In *Erzählte Provinz: Regionalismus und Moderne im Roman,* 180–224. Königstein/Ts.: Athenäum, 1982.

———. "Zeitroman oder Heimatroman? Uwe Johnson's 'Ingrid Babendererde.'" In *Literatur und Provinz: Das Konzept "Heimat" in der neueren Literatur,* ed. Hans-Georg Pott, 39–59. Paderborn: Schöningh, 1986.

Meyer, Martin, and Wolfgang Strehlow. "'Das sagt mir auch mein Friseur': Film- und Fernsehäußerungen von Uwe Johnson." *Sprache im technischen Zeitalter* 95 (1985): 170–83. Meyer and Strehlow have compiled some of Johnson's difficult-to-access utterances and categorized them under headings such as "writing as an occupation," "writing a diary," and other literary topics.

Neumann, Bernd. "Ingrid Babendererde als Ingeborg Holm: Über Uwe Johnsons ersten Roman." *Germanisch-Romanische Monatshefte* 37 (1987): 218–26.

O'Neill, Patrick. "The System in Question: Story and Discourse in Uwe Johnson's *Zwei Ansichten.*" *German Quarterly* 64 (1991): 531–43.

Pestalozzi, Karl. "Achim alias Täve Schur: Uwe Johnsons zweiter Roman und seine Vorlage." *Sprache im technischen Zeitalter* 6 (1963): 479–86. Johnson takes this article to task in *Begleitumstände.* Pestalozzi locates Johnson's Achim figure close to the historical person of Gustav Adolf Schur.

Pokay, Peter. "Utopische Heimat: Uwe Johnsons *Jahrestage.*" *Studia Germanica Posnaniensia* 10 (1982): 51–76.

————. "Vergangenheit und Gegenwart in Uwe Johnsons *Jahrestage.*" Ph.D. diss., University of Salzburg, 1983.

Reich-Ranicki, Marcel. "Registrator Johnson." In *Deutsche Literatur in West und Ost: Prosa seit 1945,* 231–46. Munich: Piper, 1966.

Riordin, Colin. "Reifeprüfung 1961: Uwe Johnson and the Cold War." In *German Writers and the Cold War, 1945–1961,* ed. Rhys W. Williams, Stephen Parker, and Colin Riordin, 203–20. Manchester: Manchester University Press, 1992.

Stewart, Mary E. "A Dialogic Reality: Uwe Johnson, *Mutmaßungen über Jakob.*" In *The German Novel in the Twentieth Century: Beyond Realism,* ed. David Midgley, 164–78. New York: St. Martin's Press, 1993.

Willson, A. Leslie. "An Interview with Uwe Johnson: 'An Unacknowledged Humorist.'" *Dimension* 15 (1982): 401–13.

# Index